Hellenistic Philosophy

D1559320

Hellenistic
Philosophy

John Sellars

OXFORD
UNIVERSITY PRESS

OXFORD
UNIVERSITY PRESS

Great Clarendon Street, Oxford, OX2 6DP,
United Kingdom

Oxford University Press is a department of the University of Oxford.
It furthers the University's objective of excellence in research, scholarship,
and education by publishing worldwide. Oxford is a registered trade mark of
Oxford University Press in the UK and in certain other countries

Published in the United States of America by Oxford University Press
198 Madison Avenue, New York, NY 10016, United States of America

British Library Cataloguing in Publication Data
Data available

Library of Congress Control Number: 2017963784

ISBN 978-0-19-967411-4 (hbk.)
ISBN 978-0-19-967412-1 (pbk.)

Printed and bound by
CPI Group (UK) Ltd, Croydon, CR0 4YY

Contents

Detailed Contents

Preface

This book is intended to serve as an introduction to Hellenistic philosophy for those new to the subject. My aim is to introduce some of the central philosophical preoccupations of Hellenistic philosophers, inevitably with an eye towards topics that remain of interest to philosophers today. Consequently this is not intended to be a complete history of Hellenistic philosophy or to offer encyclopaedic coverage of the wide range of philosophers active in the period. Instead it offers a thematic introduction to the subject.

Inevitably not all of the topics discussed in the period can be covered here and not all of the philosophers who were active during the period will be mentioned, let alone discussed in the detail they deserve. Even so, I hope that along the way I shall have the opportunity at least to note all the major ideas and figures of the period and to point readers in the direction of further discussion elsewhere.

Although the book intends to be fairly self-contained, readers will benefit from having access to the central ancient texts. There currently exist two very helpful collections of Hellenistic philosophical texts in translation, by Inwood and Gerson (IG) and Long and Sedley (LS). Throughout this book, readers will find cross-references to these two volumes, which give by far the most convenient access in English to the wide range of ancient texts that are relevant to Hellenistic philosophy, although I have not relied on or limited myself to their selections of texts. For the sake of completeness, cross-references to some of the standard scholarly editions of fragments for the various schools and philosophers are also included, even though most of these volumes do not include translations into English. I have tried not to presuppose any knowledge of Greek or Latin, although we shall encounter a variety of terms, most of which are discussed when they first appear. In the main text, all titles of ancient works are given in English, while in the notes they are referred to by their standard Latin abbreviations. The notes and the Bibliography point readers new to the subject to further discussions. Neither pretends to offer a comprehensive guide to the literature. I also include a brief Guide to Further Reading.

I thank Peter Momtchiloff for suggesting that I write this book and for guiding it through to publication. I have to thank three anonymous reviewers who made some helpful suggestions and saved me from some errors. I should also thank an audience at the Humboldt-Universität zu Berlin for their helpful comments on parts of the final chapter.

List of Abbreviations

For the titles of ancient texts I generally follow the abbreviations listed in the fourth edition of *The Oxford Classical Dictionary* (*OCD*) or, where it does not list one, Liddell and Scott's *Greek–English Lexicon*. Where no title is given, it means the author only has one work (e.g. Lucretius). I have added cross-references (printed in bold) to the two most useful anthologies of texts in English:

IG Inwood, B., and Gerson, L. P., *Hellenistic Philosophy: Introductory Readings*, Second Edition (Indianapolis, IN: Hackett, 1997).

LS Long, A. A., and Sedley, D. N., *The Hellenistic Philosophers*, 2 vols (Cambridge: Cambridge University Press, 1987).

I also supply references to some of the standard scholarly collections of fragments for the various Hellenistic philosophers and schools, although not all of these include English translations:

Ar. Arrighetti, G., *Epicuro, Opere*, Second Edition (Turin: Giulio Einaudi Editore, 1973).

DC Decleva Caizzi, F., *Pirrone Testimonianze* (Naples: Bibliopolis, 1981).

EK Edelstein, L., and Kidd, I. G., *Posidonius I: The Fragments* (Cambridge: Cambridge University Press, 1972); translated in Kidd, I. G., *Posidonius III: The Translation of the Fragments* (Cambridge: Cambridge University Press, 1999).

FHSG Fortenbaugh, W. W., Huby, P. M., Sharples, R. W., and Gutas, D., *Theophrastus of Eresus: Sources for his Life, Writings, Thought, and Influence*, 2 vols (Leiden: Brill, 1992).

SVF Arnim, H. von, *Stoicorum Veterum Fragmenta*, 4 vols (Leipzig: Teubner, 1903–24).

Us. Usener, H., *Epicurea* (Leipzig: Teubner, 1887); facs. repr. with facing Italian translation by I. Ramelli (Milan: Bompiani, 2002).

Other abbreviations used, mainly standard, include:

DK Diels, H., and Kranz, W., *Die Fragmente der Vorsokratiker*, 3 vols (Berlin: Weidmann, 1952).

DPhA *Dictionnaire des Philosophes Antiques*, ed. R. Goulet, 7 vols and
      supplement (Paris: CNRS, 1989–2018).
LCL   Loeb Classical Library (Cambridge, MA: Harvard University Press).
SSR   *Socratis et Socraticorum Reliquiae*, ed. G. Giannantoni, 4 vols
      (Naples: Bibliopolis, 1990).

Introduction

There is a traditional view, dating back to around the time of Hegel, which claims that the philosophy of the Hellenistic period is second rate when compared with the work of Plato and Aristotle. Fewer people hold that view today, but many philosophy programmes in the English-speaking world still limit themselves to teaching the works of Plato and Aristotle, while passing over their Hellenistic successors more or less in silence. Some specialists in ancient philosophy perpetuate a habit of stressing the debts of the Hellenistic schools to their two great predecessors, looking for Platonic or Aristotelian influences on Hellenistic ideas. For many today, the highpoint in ancient philosophy came before the Hellenistic period, and so Hellenistic philosophy continues, if only implicitly, to be seen as marked by derivation and decline, in the shadows of giants rather than on their shoulders.

All of this would have seemed absurd to the generations immediately preceding Hegel. In the seventeenth and eighteenth centuries, the Hellenistic schools of Epicureanism and Stoicism were key points of reference alongside Hellenistic brands of scepticism. Via the widely accessible Latin works of Cicero and Lucretius, alongside works by Seneca, Sextus Empiricus, Plutarch, and others, philosophers such as Descartes, Gassendi, Grotius, Leibniz, Shaftesbury, Hume, Kant, Diderot, Voltaire, and La Mettrie all drew on or explicitly discussed the philosophy of the Hellenistic period. Key themes that we now readily associate with early modern and Enlightenment philosophy, such as empiricism, materialism, natural law, and religious scepticism, can all be found in Hellenistic philosophy. Indeed, because of this some aspects of Hellenistic philosophy can often appear surprisingly modern, well ahead of their time. It is sometimes difficult to believe that Lucretius's *On the Nature of Things*, with its thoroughgoing materialism, polemics against religious superstition, and history of the development of human civilization, is in fact the product of the first century BC and not, as its contents might lead us to suppose, the eighteenth-century Enlightenment. That Lucretius was probably relying on an even earlier source written in the third century BC (Epicurus's *On Nature*) is all the more unsettling. How could such works have been written so long ago? Much of our modern way of looking at the world, we are often told, has its origins in the Enlightenment, yet the Enlightenment was itself marked by a sustained and productive assimilation of Hellenistic ideas. If we go back a bit earlier, to the sixteenth century, we find Montaigne, whom we are told inaugurated a distinctively modern sceptical attitude and laid the foundations for modern ways of thinking about the self. Yet these too would be unthinkable without the wide range of Hellenistic philosophical ideas that Montaigne took up from writers such as Plutarch, Seneca, and Sextus Empiricus, all of whom were for him (as they are for us) key sources for Hellenistic philosophy.

For many early modern philosophers, then, the key ancient points of reference were Hellenistic; Plato and Aristotle were somewhat on the margins. Our present tendency to prioritize Plato and Aristotle over the philosophers of the Hellenistic period dates back only to the nineteenth century, although it is all too easy to see this as an almost inevitable consequence of the fact that their writings have survived in significant quantity, while those of the Hellenistic philosophers have not. Plato and Aristotle can appear to tower over, say, Epicurus and Chrysippus simply because of the contingent processes that have preserved some texts and let others perish. No doubt our judgements would look quite different if instead we had a thousand pages of Chrysippus and only the fragments of Aristotle's dialogues. It is noteworthy that in later antiquity it was commonplace to refer to the *four* schools of philosophy—Platonic, Aristotelian, Stoic, and Epicurean—all on a par with one another.

Not only did Hellenistic philosophy inform the development of many of our modern ways of thinking about the world, it was also intensely practical, with many of the key figures presenting philosophy as a therapeutic and life-changing activity. Readers have drawn inspiration from this side of Hellenistic philosophy ever since the Renaissance, and they continue to do so today. The central traditions of Hellenistic thought held that much of human suffering is due to errors in judgement, errors that with philosophical guidance we can fix. Within the context of this practical outlook there was also no shortage of highly technical work on topics in metaphysics and logic that pre-empts many of the concerns of professional philosophers today, such as vagueness and topics in modal logic.

In what follows I shall introduce some of the central ideas of Hellenistic philosophy, as well as giving some sense of the philosophical history of the period. In the opening chapter I shall try to delimit 'Hellenistic philosophy' and then give a historical overview that will introduce the key personalities along the way. The subsequent chapters discuss different philosophical topics, picking out what seem to me to be some of the more important and interesting ideas and debates from the period.

1

What, When, Where, and Who

What is 'Hellenistic philosophy'? This is a potentially complex question and a proper answer requires some reflection on the meaning of the word 'Hellenistic', which refers to a historical time period, and an attempt to specify the chronological limits of that period. Next, one might want to know who were the philosophers active during the period. This opening chapter tries to answer the question along these lines; most of it is devoted to introducing the principal figures and schools. Readers who are keen to get straight to discussion of the philosophical topics that preoccupied Hellenistic philosophers can go directly to the next chapter, perhaps returning here at a later stage. Readers in less of a hurry can stay here to consider how we might define 'Hellenistic philosophy' and to gain a sense of the variety of philosophical schools and thinkers that make up what is usually referred to under that name.

So, what is 'Hellenistic philosophy'? The adjective 'Hellenistic' (literally 'Greek-like') is primarily used to describe a historical period, a period running from the death of Alexander the Great in 323 BC to Octavian's defeat of Mark Anthony and Cleopatra at the Battle of Actium in 31 BC. After the death of Alexander, the vast territories he conquered were divided into a number of kingdoms by his generals; the death of Cleopatra marked the end of the last of these and the consolidation of Rome as the dominant political force in the ancient world. As such, the Hellenistic period was one of transition, sandwiched between the flowering of classical Greek culture in small city-states before and the political and cultural unification of the ancient world under the Roman Empire after.[1]

---

[1] The word 'Hellenistic' derives from the German 'Hellenismus', which was first coined by J. G. Droysen in his *Geschichte des Hellenismus*, the first volume of which was published

That tells us what 'Hellenistic' refers to, but what about 'Hellenistic philosophy'? Unsurprisingly, it is philosophy that took place in the Hellenistic period, between 323 and 31 BC. That gives us a fairly straightforward historical definition. We might wonder, however, how well this historical periodization maps onto the history of philosophy. We might also ask if there was anything distinctively 'Hellenistic' about Hellenistic philosophy. At the beginning of the period, Athens remained the predominant centre of philosophical activity, even if it had lost its political standing. After Alexander the ancient world became more politically and culturally cosmopolitan, and it is striking how many Hellenistic philosophers migrated to Athens from the east. Some have suggested that philosophy, like the rest of the ancient world in this period, became more cosmopolitan in outlook, with the new social context impacting on the development of at least some philosophical ideas.[2] By the end of the period, many of the central philosophical figures were Roman, or working in Rome, and some were writing philosophy in Latin. In this sense Hellenistic philosophy reflected the wider process of transition in which the cultural pre-eminence of Athens before was slowly overshadowed by the pervasive influence of Rome after.

We might be able to point to a few 'Hellenistic' characteristics of Hellenistic philosophy in this way, but it is unlikely to get us very far. The label 'Hellenistic philosophy' has proved to be useful because the start and end dates of the Hellenistic period roughly coincide with significant changes in the history of ancient philosophy, giving the period a distinctive philosophical character of its own. What were those events?

The beginning of the Hellenistic period saw the rise of two completely new philosophical schools—Epicureanism and Stoicism—and a significant transformation of an existing school—the Academy. The dates do not all line up exactly of course, but around 300 BC the philosophical landscape in Athens changed considerably.[3]

in 1836. For further discussion of the label and the history of the period see Shipley (2000) and, more concisely, Thonemann (2016).

[2] Hegel is famous for suggesting that philosophical ideas in part reflected wider historical changes, an idea taken up by Marx (himself a student of Epicureanism).

[3] Scholz (2004), 316–18, suggests 307 BC as a key turning point. Before that date philosophers in Athens had been forced into exile on a number of occasions; after 307 they were tolerated in Athenian society, which enabled new and existing schools to flourish.

The end of the period also saw some dramatic changes. Here there has been some debate as to precisely when the most significant change occurred. Some have argued for a date around 100 BC. Others have suggested 86 BC, the date of the siege of Athens by the Roman general Sulla, which quite literally brought an end to philosophical activity in the city, at least for a while: the Academy was destroyed, possibly the Lyceum and Epicurean Garden too, and the siege inevitably meant that Athens was no longer an attractive destination for prospective students.[4] After 86 BC we do see a number of significant changes, including an increase of philosophical activity in Italy and the rise of Latin as a medium for philosophy, most notably with Lucretius and Cicero. But *philosophically* speaking not much changed, and for much of the first century BC philosophy remained recognizably Hellenistic, with, for instance, philosophers such as Lucretius and Philodemus continuing the existing Epicurean tradition. Indeed, Cicero's philosophical works, all written in Latin and many in a single year (45–44 BC), stand as a summation of philosophy in the Hellenistic period, offering valuable accounts of Epicurean, Stoic, and Academic philosophy. Although for a long time Cicero has been seen as merely a source for the ideas of others, rather than a significant philosopher in his own right, it should not be forgotten that he studied with and knew personally a number of significant philosophers of the period. He was one of the last people who had direct contact with members of the living Athenian schools, and so did not have to rely for his knowledge of them on texts alone. Thus Cicero was not merely a source for earlier doctrines and arguments, he was also a first-hand chronicler of and contributor to Hellenistic philosophy.[5] Although some will continue to argue about the extent, if any, of Cicero's original contributions to philosophy, when we read his works we get the sense that we are reading Hellenistic philosophical texts. He is summarizing and engaging with the debates of the preceding three centuries, not turning away from them. So, for this reason among others, one might align the end of Hellenistic philosophy with the end of the historical Hellenistic period, around 31 BC or thereabouts.

---

[4] See especially Frede (1999b) and Sedley (2003). For Sulla's siege see Plutarch, *Sull.* 12.1–13.4 and Appian, *Mith.* 30–45.

[5] For a defence of Cicero's status as a philosopher see Powell (1995) and now Woolf (2015).

Towards the end of the first century BC we do see some significant changes. By this point the Academy had ended its sceptical phase, with hard-line sceptics departing and regrouping under the banner of Pyrrhonism, and we see the revival of 'dogmatic' Platonism and the beginnings of a commentary tradition on Plato. Cicero, writing at this time, reports some of these developments. We also see the rediscovery of the texts that we know as Aristotle's works and the beginnings of a commentary tradition on them. We also see the rise of indigenous philosophical schools in Rome, such as the school of Sextius, and the beginnings of people 'doing philosophy' in Latin. These changes really do mark the end of a distinctive Hellenistic period in the history of philosophy, and they lay the foundations for what will happen in late antiquity.

So, while imposing a historical periodization like 'Hellenistic' onto the history of philosophy runs the risk of creating arbitrary divisions, in this case there is a reasonably happy fit. 'Hellenistic philosophy' refers to a 300-year period dominated by Epicureanism, Stoicism, and a sceptically minded Academy. However, it would be a mistake to reduce Hellenistic philosophy to these three schools. Other things went on too. The end of the period saw the rise of another brand of scepticism in response to changes taking place in the Academy: Pyrrhonism. This new form of scepticism claimed inspiration from the philosopher Pyrrho who lived at the beginning of the period. And we ought not to forget Aristotle's school, the Lyceum, which continued throughout the period, often engaging in debate with other Hellenistic philosophers, especially the Stoics. Indeed it is worth noting that Aristotelianism in the Hellenistic period had a distinct characteristic of its own, not yet shaped by the rediscovery of the texts we now know as Aristotle's works. While Aristotelianism from the late first century BC onwards focused on the interpretation of Aristotelian texts, what we might call 'Hellenistic Aristotelianism' was more concerned with following the spirit rather than the letter of Aristotle's own philosophy. While traditionally the label 'Hellenistic philosophy' has been used as shorthand for 'Stoics, Epicureans, and Sceptics', a fuller account of Hellenistic philosophy might also pay attention to the distinctive brand of 'Hellenistic Aristotelianism' that flourished as well, not to mention other philosophers active in the period.

We now have one sort of answer to the question 'what is Hellenistic philosophy?'. It is the philosophy that took place during a particular historical period, predominantly in Athens, beginning around 300 BC and coming to an end during a long process of transition during the first century BC. But we might also ask whether there is anything *distinctive* about the philosophy of this period. Does Hellenistic philosophy differ in character from the philosophy in the periods before and after it? Is there any specific feature shared by all the philosophers of this period that marks them out as having a shared identity? Did, for instance, all Hellenistic philosophers embrace a single conception of philosophy and feel as if they were contributing to a common project? A number of commentators have indeed tried to point to a distinctively Hellenistic approach to philosophy, suggesting a therapeutic project whose practitioners were working towards a good, harmonious, and tranquil life. In the words of Martha Nussbaum:

There is in this period broad and deep agreement that the central motivation for philosophizing is the urgency of human suffering, and that the goal of philosophy is human flourishing.[6]

Other commentators have claimed that this sort of statement goes too far.[7] To what extent, if any, might Chrysippus's analysis of hypothetical syllogisms contribute to the cultivation of a good life? It may be that a case can be made along the lines of it being a contribution to the development of our rationality, which the Stoics claimed is central to a good life. One can certainly show that Epicurus's discussions of meteorology fed into a therapeutic project that included overcoming fear of the gods. But what about the epistemological scepticism of Plato's Academy under Carneades or the scientific researches in the Lyceum under Strato? Were these intellectual pursuits conceived as parts of therapeutic projects? The danger with insisting that all philosophers in the Hellenistic period shared a single therapeutic project is that one might start to twist the evidence to fit the generalization.

Having said that, there clearly was a therapeutic element in ancient philosophy, and this is especially striking in some of the schools that arose and flourished in the Hellenistic period. There is no doubt that Epicureanism saw itself as a therapeutic project, with the study of nature undertaken in part to free us from superstitions that inhibit our ability to

---

[6] Nussbaum (1994), 15.

[7] See especially Bernard Williams's review of Nussbaum, in Williams (1994), and his subsequent exchange with Richard Sorabji (Sorabji (1997b) and Williams (1997), both in Sorabji (1997a)).

live a tranquil life. Stoicism too had strong therapeutic ambitions among some of its later Roman proponents, although it is less clear how strongly this marked the earlier Stoics of the Hellenistic period. But we do know that the earlier Stoics were admirers of Socrates and the Cynics, even if their theoretical concerns led to a philosophical system much broader and richer than anything contemplated by those predecessors. The Pyrrhonism formulated by Aenesidemus towards the end of the period also had clear therapeutic aims. But it is also worth stressing that many things not explicitly therapeutic in intent also went on under the banner of philosophy during this period, especially in the Lyceum. Today we might classify some of this as science rather than philosophy, but that distinction was unknown to the practitioners: Theophrastus's researches into plants, for instance, were in their day part of philosophy. The clear-cut distinction that we are familiar with today between philosophy and science only comes much later.[8] Equally we might return to the example of Chrysippus's hypothetical syllogisms that, as part of logic, were for a Stoic explicitly part of philosophy.

At first glance, then, we might want to be cautious about insisting that all philosophy in the Hellenistic period was therapeutic in intent. But it would be equally misleading to ignore the therapeutic side of the principal Hellenistic schools of thought and to present them as merely bodies of theoretical doctrine that have no impact on the lives of their proponents. Indeed, one of the great virtues of the principal Hellenistic schools is that philosophy is presented as a life-changing pursuit, and this has itself led to a revival of interest in the therapeutic value that Stoicism or Epicureanism might have for people today. At the same time, it is also important to stress that Stoicism and Epicureanism were not merely sources of therapy for the soul but also—indeed, primarily— philosophies, committed to uncovering the way things really are. Both schools would agree that it is only by gaining a proper understanding of how we acquire knowledge, how our minds work, and how nature as a

---

[8] In antiquity much of what we now call 'science' would have fallen under either 'natural philosophy' (*phusikê*) or 'natural history' (*peri phuseôs historia*). These very crudely correspond to theoretical science (e.g. theoretical physics) and empirical science (e.g. botany) respectively. The former was firmly a part of philosophy, the latter not necessarily, although some philosophers engaged in this too. For a general introduction to Hellenistic science see Lloyd (1973) and Irby-Massie and Keyser (2002). On ancient natural history see French (1994).

whole works that we shall be able to attain the harmonious and tranquil frame of mind that is essential for a good life.[9] In short, the therapeutic goal can only be reached via a proper grasp of the seemingly 'theoretical' philosophy. We might put this by saying that they did not conceive philosophy as merely therapeutic but rather held that philosophy itself has some therapeutic value.

These preliminary remarks hopefully give us some idea of what to expect in what follows. We shall return to the therapeutic aspects of Hellenistic philosophy in the final chapter, after we have a better sense of the philosophy of the period. But before we go any further it might be helpful to say a bit more about the different schools of Hellenistic thought and to introduce some of the most important philosophers of the period.

Epicurus's Garden

The first of the new Hellenistic schools of philosophy to be founded was Epicurus's Garden.[10] The word 'school' is potentially misleading and ought to be understood in the sense of 'school of thought' rather than an organized centre of education, for Epicurus's Garden might best be described as an informal community of like-minded people, drawn together by a desire to live according to a shared set of ideas.[11] The Garden was indeed just that: a physical garden just outside the city walls of Athens and not far from Plato's Academy. Epicurus bought the plot of land around 306 BC and friends of his came from far and wide to live a simple life with him away from the distraction of the everyday concerns of city life.[12] Epicurus himself came to Athens from the island of Samos, where he had been born to Athenian parents in 341 BC. We are told that he was first inspired to study philosophy when, as a schoolboy, he read in Hesiod that everything was born out of Chaos; Epicurus asked, 'but out

---

[9] This may have been a feature of Hellenistic philosophy, but that does not necessarily make it a distinctively Hellenistic feature. Philosophers both before and after held this view too, leading some (e.g. Hadot (1995) and (2002)) to propose that *all* ancient philosophy was conceived in this way.

[10] The principal ancient source of information about Epicurus, the Garden, and his immediate successors is the life of Epicurus in Diog. Laert. 10.1–28 (part IG I-1). For a modern account see Clay (2009). There is an older but fuller account in DeWitt (1954).

[11] See further Dorandi (1999b), 56–7.

[12] See Diog. Laert. 10.10–11 (IG I-1).

of what was Chaos born?' and his schoolteacher was unable to give him an answer.[13] Later he taught in Mytilene and Lampsacus before moving to Athens, and it was in these places that he met and became friends with a number of people who would go on to become key members of his Athenian community. These included Hermarchus, Metrodorus, and Polyaenus.[14] Later Epicureans such as Philodemus (on whom more shortly) referred to these three alongside Epicurus as the elder men of the school, suggesting that in its early days the Garden was more a collaboration between friends than a guru with unthinking disciples.[15] After founding the Garden community Epicurus remained in Athens for the rest of his life, and died in 270 BC.

Epicurus was a prolific author: his *magnum opus*, called *On Nature*, extended to thirty-seven books and we also have a list of titles of numerous other works.[16] By the end of antiquity all of these were lost, although significant portions of *On Nature* have been recovered from the papyrus scrolls unearthed at Herculaneum. What did survive antiquity were a series of letters summarizing Epicurus's central ideas, along with a collection of sayings, all preserved by the later historian of philosophy Diogenes Laertius in Book 10 of his *Lives and Opinions of the Philosophers*.[17] His close friends also wrote works of philosophy and we have lists of titles for these too.[18] To those already mentioned we might add Colotes who, like Metrodorus and others, followed Epicurus from Lampsacus to Athens and wrote a series of works attacking Plato.[19] Subsequent members of the Garden continued to write numerous texts and the slightly later Apollodorus is said to have written over 400 books.[20] So, although the Garden might best be thought of as a community of friends

---

[13] See Diog. Laert. 10.2 (IG I-1) and, more fully, Sextus Empiricus, *Math.* 10.18–19.

[14] The ancient evidence for these three can be found in Longo Auricchio (1988), Körte (1890), and Guerra (1991) respectively.

[15] See e.g. Philodemus, *Rhet.* 1 (*PHerc* 1427, col. 7), translated in Chandler (2006), 22, with comment in Clay (2009), 17, and Sedley (2009), 37.

[16] See Diog. Laert. 10.26–8.

[17] These are the *Letter to Herodotus* (on physics), the *Letter to Pythocles* (on meteorology), the *Letter to Menoeceus* (on happiness), and the collection of *Key Doctrines*, all in Diog. Laert. 10.

[18] See e.g. the list of works by Metrodorus and Hermarchus in Diog. Laert. 10.24–5, with further evidence collected in Körte (1890) and Longo Auricchio (1988) respectively.

[19] On Colotes see *DPhA* II 448–50.

[20] Diog. Laert. 10.25.

rather than a formal organization devoted to teaching and research, it is clear that the Epicureans were nevertheless very intellectually active.[21]

After Epicurus died, Hermarchus took over as leader of the community and he was in turn succeeded by a series of heads of the Epicurean school. Statues of Epicurus were erected and a monthly feast day in his honour was instituted, all contributing to a certain cult status.[22] New members joined, the most famous of whom were Zeno of Sidon (c. 150–72 BC) and Demetrius of Laconia. The school was also notable for admitting female members; the resulting mixed-sex private community inevitably became a subject of gossip in its day.

Nothing remains of the Garden today, although there have been archaeological excavations of the site. It seems likely that it was destroyed during Sulla's siege of the city in 86 BC, although we do have names of heads of the Epicureans in Athens after that date, such as Phaedrus (head c. 75–c. 70) and Patro (head c. 70–late 50s), so it looks as if the community continued in some form for a while longer.[23] We might end the story of Hellenistic Epicureanism there, if we decide to follow those scholars who suggest that Hellenistic philosophy comes to an end early in the first century BC. However, if we continue the narrative until the end of the Hellenistic period proper, around 30 BC, then we have an opportunity to mention two of the most important Epicureans after Epicurus himself: Philodemus and Lucretius.

Philodemus was born in Gadara (in Syria) around 110 BC and like many philosophers of the Hellenistic period was drawn to Athens as the pre-eminent centre of philosophical activity.[24] There he joined the Epicureans under the guidance of Zeno of Sidon. At some point he relocated to Italy and appears to have been based in or near Naples. For centuries he was merely a footnote in the history of Epicureanism until in the eighteenth century a library of mainly philosophical texts was unearthed in a villa at Herculaneum, buried by the eruption of Vesuvius in 79 AD.

---

[21] For further discussion of the Epicureans and their textual activities see Snyder (2000), 45–65.

[22] On the canonization of Epicurus see Clay (2009), 25, and on the authority invested in the founders of the Hellenistic schools see Sedley (1989).

[23] See Dorandi (1999a), 45. In a letter from 51 BC Cicero records Patro's attempt to acquire the remains of Epicurus's private house (distinct from the Garden) in Athens; see Fam. 13.1 (63 Shackleton Bailey, LCL).

[24] There is a helpful short guide to his life and works in De Lacy and De Lacy (1978), 145–55. See also Gigante (1995) and Sider (1997), 3–24.

Many of the texts recovered from the villa were by Philodemus, and consequently it is widely assumed that he must have had a close connection with the place, perhaps working under the patronage of the villa's owner, who was likely to have been Lucius Calpurnius Piso, father-in-law to Julius Caesar.[25] We know of other Epicureans active in the same area, such as Siro in Naples. Cicero mentions Philodemus and Siro together in the same breath and both knew the poet Virgil, so although Philodemus was far away from Athens (which in any case was a shadow of its former self by this date), he was by no means intellectually isolated.[26]

His works reflect a wide range of philosophical interests: theological (*On Piety, On the Gods*), ethical (*On Anger, On Death*), and aesthetic (*On Poems, On Rhetoric, On Music*), among others.[27] That may suggest that Philodemus was less concerned with physical theory, but it is worth noting that the very same library that contained so many of his works also contained more than one copy of Epicurus's monumental *On Nature*. At least one of his works (*On Frank Criticism*) appears to be a report of Zeno of Sidon's lectures in Athens, so although Philodemus ended his career in a distinctively Roman context, his work can be seen as a continuation of the Hellenistic Athenian philosophical tradition that by this point was more or less at an end.[28]

The other major Epicurean of the first century BC was Titus Lucretius Carus (94–c. 55 BC). There is very little information about his life and all we have to go on is his single work, *On the Nature of Things*.[29] Unlike Philodemus, who migrated from Athens and wrote in Greek, Lucretius was a Roman writing in Latin. He was not the first home-grown Roman

---

[25] Philodemus mentions Piso in *Epigram* 27 (in Sider (1997), 152). See also Cicero, *Pis.* 68–72 for a polemical account of Piso's interest in Epicureanism.

[26] See Cicero, *Fin.* 2.119. Donatus, *Vit. Verg.* 79 reports that Virgil studied with Siro and he is mentioned in a poem previously attributed to Virgil (*Catalepton* 5, now in the Virgilian Appendix). On Virgil and Philodemus see Armstrong et al. (2004).

[27] Because of the fragmentary way in which discoveries from the papyri have been published and often re-edited in new editions, Philodemus's bibliography is especially complex. For a fairly full list, up to 1990, see Berkowitz and Squitier (1990), 308–14. However, the best editions, using modern technology to assist in deciphering the scrolls, have been published since then (e.g. Obbink (1996), Janko (2000) and (2011)). Many other discoveries have been published in articles in the journal *Cronache Ercolanesi*.

[28] See Sedley (2009), 36.

[29] Beyond the poem itself there are few contemporary references to Lucretius. He is mentioned in one of Cicero's letters to his brother Quintus (*QFr.* 2.10 (14 Shackleton Bailey, LCL)). According to Jerome, Cicero prepared Lucretius's poem for posthumous publication, although the veracity of this claim has been doubted (see Hardie (2007), 113).

Epicurean, however, and Cicero refers to earlier Roman Epicureans such as Amafinius, Rabirius, and Catius,[30] but Lucretius's poem is the earliest work of a Roman Epicurean to survive and indeed the earliest work of philosophy in Latin that we have. It seems to have been a more or less independent production, inspired in its form by the poetry of the Presocratic Empedocles, drawing on Epicurus's *On Nature* for its content,[31] but not really engaging with any other contemporary philosophers or displaying much sign of influence from members of the school after Epicurus, although some have argued that Lucretius was in fact a member of the Epicurean group surrounding Philodemus.[32] Either way, *On the Nature of Things* is a magnificent production and a vital source for our knowledge of Epicurean philosophy, preserving ideas not recorded elsewhere (such as the discussion of atomic movement in Book 2), as well as offering its own original elaborations on Epicurus's arguments (such as the discussion on death in Book 3).[33]

This brings us more or less to the end of the story for the Epicureans. I mentioned earlier Phaedrus, one of the last heads of the Epicurean school in Athens. Phaedrus also spent time in Rome during the first century where he taught both Cicero and his close friend Atticus, who became a committed Epicurean.[34] Both Cicero and Atticus also spent time in Athens, attending the lectures of Zeno of Sidon.[35] Cicero's first-hand knowledge of contemporary Epicureanism via Zeno and Phaedrus is worth noting given that his philosophical works include a number of important, albeit critical, accounts of Epicurean doctrine, produced right at the end of the Hellenistic period.

Zeno and the Painted Stoa

The other major new school of philosophy in the Hellenistic period arose around the same time as Epicurus was setting up his Garden community and was also driven by an incomer to Athens. Unlike Epicurus, Zeno of

---

[30] See e.g. Cicero, *Tusc.* 4.5–7, *Fam.* 15.16 (215 Shackleton Bailey, LCL).

[31] See Sedley (1998) for discussion of both the Empedoclean form (ch. 1) and Epicurean content (ch. 4) of Lucretius's poem.

[32] See e.g. Kleve (1997).

[33] For more on Lucretius see two collections of essays: Gale (2007) and Gillespie and Hardie (2007).

[34] See Cicero, *Fam.* 13.1 (63 Shackleton Bailey, LCL). For the life of Phaedrus see Raubitschek (1949). There is an ancient biography of Atticus by Cornelius Nepos.

[35] See Cicero, *Fin.* 1.16, *Tusc.* 3.38.

Citium (in Cyprus) did not already have Athenian citizenship and is unlikely to have arrived with enough money to buy plots of land. According to one ancient source, Zeno was travelling on a business trip for his merchant father when the boat he was on was shipwrecked. According to the story, Zeno was washed up on the coast near Athens and as he made his way into the city he stopped to browse at a bookstall. There he started reading Xenophon's *Memorabilia of Socrates* and was so impressed by the figure of Socrates that he asked the bookseller if men like him could still be found in Athens. At that moment the Cynic philosopher Crates walked by and the bookseller said 'follow that man'.[36] So began Zeno's introduction to philosophy.

The Cynic Crates and his own teacher Diogenes of Sinope did indeed try to emulate Socrates; Plato thought Diogenes was 'a Socrates gone mad'.[37] They followed Socrates in holding that all one needs for a good life is virtue; external goods and the trappings of a socially conventional life are not only unnecessary in order to live well but can often get in the way of seeing what is of most value. Consequently the Cynics rejected both material possessions and social customs, proposing instead a life in accordance with Nature.[38] This idea was to prove an important influence on Zeno and the development of Stoicism.[39] However, Zeno decided against becoming a Cynic himself and looked to other philosophers in Athens for further instruction.

Zeno next studied with Stilpo of Megara, perhaps for as long as ten years.[40] Stilpo was, like Zeno, inclined towards Cynic ethics but, as a member of the Megarian school, also had strong interests in logic, something that would later become an important part of Stoic philosophy. He also held that a good life is one free from emotions, pre-empting

---

[36] See Diog. Laert. 7.2–3 (**IG II-1**). Inevitably most modern scholars doubt the veracity of the story.

[37] Diog. Laert. 6.54.

[38] For a colourful account of Diogenes of Sinope see Diog. Laert. 6.20–81. For a recent introduction to the Cynics see Desmond (2008). Note also the excellent collection of essays in Branham and Goulet-Cazé (1996), especially Long (1996b), who discusses the Cynic influence on Hellenistic ethics. The older history in Dudley (1937) also remains useful.

[39] For a discussion of Cynic influences on Stoicism (in French) see Goulet-Cazé (2003).

[40] Diog. Laert. 7.2 (*SVF* 1.1; *SSR* II O 4, **IG II-1**), who says that Zeno studied with Stilpo and the Academic Xenocrates for ten years. He later says that he studied for a total of twenty years after leaving Crates (Diog. Laert. 7.4, **IG II-1**), so perhaps ten years with each.

and perhaps influencing the famous Stoic view.[41] The ancient biography of Stilpo records numerous arguments with Zeno's previous teacher Crates, and one passage describes Crates trying forcibly to remove Zeno from Stilpo in an attempt to return him to the Cynics.[42]

We are also told that Zeno spent time in the Academy, listening to the lectures of both Xenocrates and Polemo (on whom more later). It has been suggested that Zeno's own pantheistic conception of Nature was influenced by Polemo and in particular by his interpretation of Plato's *Timaeus*.[43] It was out of this mix of influences—Cynic ethics, Megarian logic, and Platonic physics—that Zeno slowly forged his own distinctive philosophical position.

When Zeno eventually struck out on his own after this lengthy philosophical apprenticeship, he chose to teach not in a secluded school but right in the centre of the city, following the model of the Cynics and, of course, Socrates. The marketplace in the heart of Athens, the Agora, was bordered by a number of buildings containing covered walkways offering some respite from the sun. On the northern edge stood the Painted Stoa, so named because it contained a series of paintings of important scenes in Athenian history.[44] It was here that Zeno started to share his philosophy with whomever would listen. In time he gained regular listeners who were first referred to as 'Zenonians' but later came to be known as 'Stoics' after the place where they met.[45]

On Zeno's death in 261 his follower Cleanthes of Assos (*c.* 330–*c.* 230 BC) became head of the Stoic school. As with the Epicureans, 'school' ought to be understood in the sense of 'school of thought' rather than a formally organized educational institution, although in both cases there seems to have been a defined post of head or leader ('scholarch'). Cleanthes remained head for some thirty years, before his death around

---

[41] See Seneca, *Ep.* 9.1–2 (*SSR* II O 33, part **IG** I-53). Seneca also reports that Epicurus attacked Stilpo on this point.
[42] The ancient biography is in Diog. Laert. 2.113–20. All the evidence for Stilpo is gathered together in *SSR* II O 1–38. The anecdote about Zeno's abduction is in Diog. Laert. 7.24 (*SVF* 1.278; *SSR* II O 4, **IG** II-1).
[43] See Sedley (2002a).
[44] On the Stoa and its paintings see Camp (1986), 66–72. For an ancient description of the paintings see Pausanias's *Description of Greece*, 1.15.1–4.
[45] See Diog. Laert. 7.5 (*SVF* 1.2, **IG** II-1), who seems to imply that 'Zenonian' was only used by his followers before he took up residence at the Painted Stoa.

230, when he was somewhere in the region of a hundred years old.[46] As with so many writers of the period, we have an extensive list of book titles for Cleanthes, although the works themselves are lost. Among other things, he is said to have written a four-volume commentary on the work of the Presocratic philosopher Heraclitus.[47] We know that Cleanthes had particular interests in theology and that he championed poetry as a medium for conveying philosophical truths.[48] Both of these come together in the one extended text that has come down to us under his name: the *Hymn to Zeus*.[49] Joining some of our preliminary dots, we might say that the *Hymn* takes up the Cynic idea of living according to Nature that Zeno learned from Crates and takes on board the pantheist physics Zeno developed under the influence of Polemo, combining them to present a concept of living in accordance with Nature that amounts to the same thing as living in accordance with God's divine will, which is itself identified with the universal reason permeating all of Nature.

Cleanthes was succeeded by the third head of the Stoa, Chrysippus of Soli, who was widely held to have been the most important member of the school in its early days, systematizing the ideas of his predecessors.[50] He was a prolific author and is said to have written some 705 books.[51] Sadly these are all lost save for various quotations preserved by (often hostile) later authors. The most substantial of these fragments come from his works *On the Soul* and *On the Passions*, in both cases preserved by the philosopher and doctor Galen.[52] However, a fairly full list of book titles survives which helps to give us an idea of his range of philosophical interests.[53] There have also been more recent discoveries, with parts of previously lost works turning up alongside the works of Epicurus and Philodemus among the papyri unearthed at Herculaneum. These include

[46] For a brief account of his life and dates see Thom (2005), 2–7. For the ancient biography see Diog. Laert. 7.168–76 (*SVF* 1.463, part IG II-1).

[47] See Diog. Laert. 7.174 (*SVF* 1.481).

[48] On both of these points see Thom (2005), 5–6. The latter is attested by Seneca, *Ep.* 108.10 (*SVF* 1.487).

[49] Preserved in Stobaeus 1,25,3–1,27,4, printed in *SVF* 1.537, IG II-21, LS 54I, and edited and discussed in Thom (2005). See Ch. 7 below for further discussion.

[50] For an older overview of his philosophy see Gould (1970).

[51] See Diog. Laert. 7.180 (IG II-1).

[52] Passages from both of these works can be found in *SVF* 3.879–910 and 456–90 respectively. For detailed discussions of the Galenic evidence see Tieleman (1996) and (2003).

[53] See Diog. Laert. 7.189–202 (*SVF* 2.13–17, parts LS 37B, 32I).

parts of his *On Providence* and fragments of *Logical Questions*, a work said to have occupied thirty-nine books and so as monumental as Epicurus's *On Nature*.[54]

After Chrysippus the headship of the Stoa passed to Zeno of Tarsus and then Diogenes of Babylon (*c.* 230–*c.* 145 BC).[55] Diogenes is remembered for being one of three Athenian philosophers sent on an embassy to Rome in 155 BC.[56] This trip is often considered to be a key moment in the introduction of Greek philosophy into the Roman world. Diogenes' most famous pupil was Panaetius of Rhodes (*c.* 185–*c.* 110 BC), who studied with both him and his successor as head of the Stoa, Antipater of Tarsus. As well as studying in Athens, Panaetius also spent time in Pergamum, famous for its library that for a while tried to rival the library in Alexandria, and well known as a centre of Stoic activity.[57] He later spent time in Rome, joining the circle of people around the famous Roman general Scipio Africanus. He succeeded Antipater to become head of the Stoa in 128 BC.

After the death of Panaetius, the headship of the Athenian Stoa passed jointly to Mnesarchus and Dardanus, about whom we know very little. Panaetius's most famous pupil, Posidonius of Apamea (*c.* 135–*c.* 51 BC), decided not to stay in Athens and instead moved to Rhodes, where he taught philosophy.[58] With Rhodes as his base, Posidonius made a number of trips around the Mediterranean making cultural and scientific observations. He was an impressive polymath, interested in and writing on almost every conceivable subject, from earthquakes to Homeric interpretation, as well as all of the central areas of philosophy.

Posidonius is probably the last Stoic of note active during the Hellenistic period. As with the Epicureans, it seems fitting to end the story of

---

[54] For the *Logical Questions* see Marrone (1997). For further discussion of Stoic papyri (in Italian), see Marrone (1987) and (1988).

[55] The fragments for Diogenes are gathered together in *SVF* 3. For an overview of Diogenes and his successors Panaetius and Posidonius see now Veillard (2015). On Panaetius, see also Tieleman (2007).

[56] For references to the embassy see e.g. Cicero, *De or.* 2.155 (Critolaus fr. 5 in Wehrli (1969d)); Aulus Gellius 6.14.8 (*SVF* Diog. 8, Critolaus fr. 9 Wehrli); Plutarch, *Cat. Mai.* 22 (*SVF* Diog. 7); Lactantius, *Div. inst.* 5.14.3–5 (**LS 68M**).

[57] See Pfeiffer (1968), 234–51, who mentions Crates of Mallos and Athenodorus of Tarsus as Stoics active in Pergamum. On the library at Pergamum see Casson (2001), 48–53.

[58] For an introduction to Posidonius see Kidd (1999), 3–28.

the Hellenistic Stoa by mentioning Cicero. As well as travelling to Athens to study philosophy, Cicero also made a trip to Rhodes in order to attend Posidonius's lectures.[59] He had already learned much about Stoicism at home from the Stoic Diodotus who lived with him for many years.[60] As with Epicureanism, Cicero's accounts of Stoicism drew on his own first-hand contact with some of the leading Stoics of the day.

The Academy Turns Sceptic

These two new schools of Epicurean and Stoic philosophy arrived on the scene not long after the beginning of the Hellenistic period, around 300 BC. By this time, around a hundred years after the trial and execution of Socrates, Athens was already a very well-established centre of philosophical activity. Of the already established schools, by far the most famous was the Academy, founded by Plato and continued after his death by his nephew Speusippus. Plato's immediate successors in the Academy (sometimes referred to as the 'Old Academy') developed what we would now call doctrinal Platonism, that is, a body of positive doctrines drawn from Plato's works (and presumably in part passed down orally as well).[61] This tradition continued under Xenocrates and Polemo, whom we met earlier as teachers of Zeno of Citium.

This doctrinal version of Plato's teaching seemed increasingly unsatisfactory to at least one member of the Academy, Arcesilaus (c. 318–242 BC), who became head around 268 BC.[62] He initiated a new period in the institution's history that is sometimes called the 'Middle Academy'.[63] The shift seems to have been prompted by looking afresh at Plato's dialogues and starting to read them in a new way. Socrates' disavowal of

---

[59] Cicero refers to Posidonius throughout his works as his teacher and friend; see *Fat.* 5–7; *Nat. D.* 1.6, 1.123, 2.88 (**LS 54L**); *Fin.* 1.6; *Tusc.* 2.61 (EK T30–4); note also Plutarch, *Cic.* 4.5 (EK T29).

[60] See Cicero, *Brut.* 309.

[61] For an accessible introduction see Dillon (2003).

[62] For an ancient biography see Diog. Laert. 4.28–45 (**IG III-1**, part **LS 68E, 3E**), which is discussed in Long (1986). For an introduction see Thorsrud (2010), 58–70. The ancient evidence is gathered together in Mette (1984), 44–74.

[63] Sextus Empiricus, *Pyr.* 1.220 (**IG III-27**), divides the history of the Academy into 'Old' (Plato), 'Middle' (Arcesilaus), and 'New' (Carneades), referring also to a 'fourth' (Philo) and 'fifth' (Antiochus). Compare this with the discussion in Cicero, *Acad.* 1.46 (**IG III-19, LS 68A**). See also Diog. Laert. 4.28 (**IG III-1, LS 68D**) for the label 'Middle Academy'.

knowledge is well known, most famously in Plato's *Apology* where he says that the only thing he knows above other people is how little he knows for sure. That thought is then played out by Plato in a number of the early dialogues, where Socrates submits an initially confident interlocutor to cross-examination until they come to realize that they do not possess the secure knowledge that up until that point they thought they did. In these dialogues Socrates himself offers no positive doctrine to replace the vacuum he has generated. In some of his subsequent works, such as the *Republic*, Plato does seem to offer more positive doctrines in response to the Socratic search for knowledge and definitions, but it is also noteworthy that in his later dialogues many of those positive doctrines are themselves subjected to much criticism. Plato's use of the dialogue form for his philosophy might lend further weight to the thought that his primary intention was to provoke inquiry into philosophical questions rather than to present a fully worked-out set of philosophical doctrines.

It looks as if this is how Arcesilaus approached Plato's works, and the fact that he secured the headship of the Academy suggests that he must have had support from its other members too. Proceeding very much in the spirit of Socrates, Arcesilaus would examine the claims to knowledge held by others, offer objections, and also draw out the (often unwelcome) consequences of those claims. He also offered arguments of his own for opposing views, all it seems aimed at undermining his interlocutors' claims to secure knowledge.[64] Thus, like Socrates, Arcesilaus argued dialectically. However, he is reported to have claimed that he went even further than Socrates, by denying even that he knew he knew nothing.[65] Just like his great Athenian role model, Arcesilaus left no written works.

This new sceptical approach held sway in the Academy for much of the Hellenistic period.[66] It may in part have been a response to Stoic claims that *they* were the true heirs to Socrates. Arcesilaus was followed

---

[64] For his approach (and its Socratic pedigree) see e.g. Cicero, *Fin.* 2.2 (**IG III-16, LS 68J**) and *Acad.* 1.45 (**IG III-19, LS 68A**); note also *Nat. D.* 1.11. For further discussion of the Socratic origins see Annas (1994) and Shields (1994).

[65] See Cicero, *Acad.* 1.45, although the view of Socrates as a negative dogmatist seems misleading and the earlier description of his position at *Acad.* 1.16 seems closer to the mark.

[66] For general introductions to ancient scepticism see Thorsrud (2009) and the studies in Bett (2010).

by a series of heads, culminating in his most famous successor, Carneades of Cyrene (213–128 BC).[67] In many respects Carneades continued in the same vein as Arcesilaus and, like him, wrote nothing. He was well known for arguing against the dogmatic claims of the Stoics. This was a potentially hazardous enterprise, with arguments against rational proofs for God's existence running the risk of being taken as arguments for atheism, or arguments against theories of virtue being taken as assaults on virtue itself.[68] He is famous for being part of the embassy of Athenian philosophers who went to Rome in 155 BC (with the Stoic Diogenes of Babylon whom we met earlier) and for defending a model of justice on one day and then refuting it the next, to the shock of his Roman audience, some of whom saw this as an attack on the very idea of justice.[69]

According to the later sceptic Sextus Empiricus, Carneades went beyond the suspension of judgement of Arcesilaus by asserting that the truth cannot be known, a position often referred to as 'negative dogmatism'. Thus Sextus suggests that Carneades initiated a new phase in the history of the Academy, which he calls the 'New Academy'.[70] However, some modern scholars have questioned Sextus's account.[71] Part of the difficulty is that, as we have already noted, Carneades himself wrote nothing. Another part is that his students, Clitomachus and Metrodorus, developed divergent views and it is difficult to know which, if either, was faithful to Carneades' own.[72] In the case of Clitomachus, who succeeded Carneades as head of the Academy, we find a position that stresses a refusal ever to give assent combined with the claim that even so it is reasonable to follow what seems plausible when it comes to action.[73] This latter claim was a response to the criticism from others (known as the

[67] Arcesilaus's immediate successor was Lacydes of Cyrene who was followed by a number of minor figures (see Dorandi (1999a), 32–3). For an introduction to Carneades see Thorsrud (2010), 70–8, with the ancient biography in Diog. Laert. 4.62–6 (IG III-3). The ancient evidence is gathered together in Mette (1985), 55–109.

[68] See e.g. Cicero, Nat. D. 3.44.

[69] See Lactantius, Div. inst. 5.14.3–5 (LS 68M). For an account of the negative reaction see Plutarch, Cat. Mai. 22.

[70] See Sextus Empiricus, Pyr. 1.220 (IG III-27), cited earlier. It is worth noting that Diog. Laert. 4.59 credits Lacydes as the founder of the 'New Academy'.

[71] See e.g. Thorsrud (2010), 71.

[72] See Cicero, Acad. 2.78 (IG III-10, LS 69H).

[73] On Clitomachus see the introduction in Lévy (2010), 82–5. There is a brief ancient life in Diog. Laert. 4.67 (IG III-5) and further references are collected in Mette (1985), 142–4.

'inactivity' (*apraxia*) objection) that it would be impossible to live according to the precepts of scepticism. If Carneades did introduce an innovation, it looks likely that it was not a version of negative dogmatism but rather this claim about following the plausible.

Another of Carneades' followers, Philo of Larissa (159–84 BC), developed this position further, arguing that although knowledge is ultimately beyond our grasp, it is still acceptable to hold reasonable beliefs.[74] Philo stands right at the end of the history of the Academy. He became head of the Academy in 110 BC and was still head in 86 BC during the siege of Athens that led to the physical destruction of the site of the Academy. Along with a number of other prominent Athenians he fled to Rome, where he was to become the most important of Cicero's teachers, shaping the latter's whole approach to philosophy.

Although we have mentioned him a number of times already, this might be the appropriate point formally to introduce Marcus Tullius Cicero (106–43 BC). As we have seen, Cicero studied with both Epicureans and Stoics, in particular Phaedrus and Diodotus. When Philo came to Rome Cicero spent time with him too and was initially very drawn to his brand of scepticism.[75] By this point Cicero was well versed in all three of the major traditions of Hellenistic thought. A few years after the siege of Athens was over, Cicero travelled there to attend lectures by another member of the Academy, Antiochus (on whom more shortly).[76] He also met up with his old friend Atticus who took him to hear the lectures of the Epicurean Zeno of Sidon. After a brief stay in Athens Cicero also visited Rhodes where he heard the lectures of the Stoic Posidonius.[77] By the end of this extended trip it looks as if Cicero was less convinced by Philo for a while, but towards the end of his life he reaffirmed his commitment to Philo's brand of moderate scepticism.[78] This approach can be seen in his own philosophical works, many of which were written in a single year (45–44 BC) towards the end of his life, which offer critical

---

[74] For a thorough introduction to Philo see Brittain (2001), which includes all of the ancient evidence along with translations, 345–70. Note also an earlier collection of ancient evidence in Mette (1986–7), 12–20.

[75] See Cicero, *Brut.* 306.

[76] See Cicero, *Brut.* 315 and note also *Fin.* 5.1–3.

[77] See n. 59.

[78] On Cicero's intellectual biography see Glucker (1988).

discussions of Epicurean and Stoic positions from a broadly sceptical point of view.

If Cicero turned away from Philo's scepticism and the 'New Academy' for a while, it was due to the impact of hearing the lectures of Antiochus of Ascalon (c. 130–68 BC) during his trip to Athens.[79] Antiochus had studied with Philo at the Academy in Athens for a number of years.[80] When Philo fled to Rome, Antiochus relocated to Alexandria, returning to Athens later. Although initially sympathetic to the scepticism that had dominated the Academy since Arcesilaus, over time Antiochus was increasingly inclined to view Plato as a doctrinal thinker, not a sceptic, and so sought to revive the 'Old Academy' of Plato's immediate successors. However, he also proposed something new, namely that Aristotle was in many ways an heir to Plato's philosophy and that the two were broadly in agreement with one another. He also brought the Stoics (with whom he also studied in Athens) into his syncretic philosophical position, seeing them as merely expounders and developers of ultimately Platonic ideas. Disputes between these various schools were seen to be more verbal than substantial, and the lively debate between sceptical Academics and Stoics was replaced by a conception of a single, unified philosophical tradition.[81] This model was to shape the history of philosophy from the first century BC until the end of antiquity, and so Antiochus decisively brings to an end one of the distinctive characteristics of philosophy in the Hellenistic period and ushers in a new era.[82]

The end of the Academy as an institution and Antiochus's move away from scepticism were not the complete end of ancient scepticism, however—far from it. One member of the Academy in its final years, Aenesidemus of Cnossos, was increasingly unhappy with the version of scepticism adopted by Philo and strongly opposed to the return to dogmatism initiated by Antiochus. In response he decided to break

---

[79] For an introduction to Antiochus see Sedley (2012), containing both a biography (Hatzimichali (2012)) and the ancient evidence with translations, 334–46. Note also the previous collection of ancient evidence in Mette (1986–7), 30–54. Previous studies include Dillon (1977), 52–113; Glucker (1978); Barnes (1989); Tarrant (2007).

[80] See Cicero, *Acad.* 2.69. On his relationship with the Academy see Polito (2012).

[81] See Cicero, *Acad.* 1.17, 2.15. The speech by Varro in *Acad.* 1.15–42 is an extended account of Antiochus's approach to the history of philosophy.

[82] See Karamanolis (2006) for a discussion of the attempt to harmonize Plato and Aristotle, from Antiochus onwards.

away and to set up on his own.[83] He wanted to return to a purer form of scepticism and in the process of doing so turned for inspiration to a much earlier and largely neglected philosopher active at the very beginning of the Hellenistic period, Pyrrho of Ellis (*c.* 360–*c.* 270 BC). How much Aenesidemus really knew about the philosophical thought of Pyrrho is hard to know, but even so he pledged his philosophical allegiance to him in his book *Pyrrhonist Discourses*, now lost.[84] One of his central concerns was to distinguish his version of Pyrrhonian Scepticism from Academic Scepticism. While some Academic Sceptics were prepared to deny the possibility of ever attaining secure knowledge, a genuine sceptic (literally an 'enquirer') will refuse to judge one way or another and so will simply suspend judgement. On this account, discussed in detail in the works of the later Pyrrhonian Sextus Empiricus, Academic Sceptics are not really sceptics at all and have more in common with those whom he called dogmatists. A dogmatist is someone who holds a firm view; someone who holds the view that knowledge is impossible is thus a dogmatist, albeit a negative dogmatist.[85] Whether this is a fair account of Academic Scepticism is another matter; it certainly doesn't seem to capture the cautious scepticism of Arcesilaus, but in the process of breaking away from the Academy it was perhaps inevitable that Aenesidemus would want to define his new position in opposition to Academic Scepticism.

We are reliant on the much later Sextus Empiricus for much of our knowledge of Pyrrhonian Scepticism and it is difficult to know for sure whether he significantly develops or merely reports Aenesidemus's position.[86] It is equally difficult to know whether Aenesidemus's Pyrrhonism was entirely his own invention or had some genuine foundation in the thought of the historical Pyrrho.

---

[83] For an introduction to Aenesidemus see Hankinson (2010). The ancient evidence is gathered together, translated, and discussed in Polito (2014). Whether he was ever a member of the Academy has been subject to debate, on which see Decleva Caizzi (1992) and Mansfeld (1995).

[84] Our information about this work comes from Photius, *Bibl.* 212, 169b18–170b3 (B1–4 in Polito (2014), **IG III-25, LS 71C**).

[85] See Sextus Empiricus, *Pyr.* 1.1–4 (**IG III-26**).

[86] Sextus was active *c.* 200 AD and so is not part of our story here, although we shall draw on him for information about the Pyrrhonist revival of the first century BC, which does fall within the Hellenistic period.

What, if anything, Pyrrho himself believed remains a matter of debate.[87] Like some of the other sceptics we have encountered, he wrote nothing, so we are dependent for information on the writings of his pupil Timon of Phlius (*c*. 320–*c*. 230 BC),[88] who appears to have been his only significant follower. Timon reports that Pyrrho held that all things are 'equally indifferent, unmeasurable, and inarbitrable', and so one ought to remain 'unopinionated, uncommitted, and unwavering'.[89] It may be that what Timon attributes to Pyrrho reflects Timon's own thought more than it does Pyrrho's own. According to one ancient writer on this question, it is almost meaningless to concern ourselves with what Pyrrho believed, given that he did not hold any positive views; instead we should reserve the label 'Pyrrhonian' to those who follow Pyrrho's way of life.[90]

What was Pyrrho's life like? The ancient biography suggests an unusual one that attracted critics in antiquity.[91] He is said to have travelled to India alongside Alexander the Great, where he encountered a number of ascetic Indian sages, the gymnosophists (naked wise men), and to have been influenced by their teaching.[92] Back in Greece, it is said that he acted with complete indifference to his own safety, only saved from numerous accidents by the intervention of friends. This looks more like another version of the 'inactivity' objection rather than a genuine account of his life and the same source reports that Aenesidemus rejected such claims.[93] More plausible is that he lived a largely solitary and tranquil life, unmoved by events around him, and for those reasons we are told that Epicurus admired him greatly.[94]

[87] The evidence for Pyrrho is gathered together in DC. It is now widely held that Pyrrho ought not to be seen as a sceptic at all; see e.g. Bett (2000). For more recent discussion see Svavarsson (2010).

[88] Ancient biography in Diog. Laert. 9.109–16 (IG III-23). The evidence for Timon is gathered together in Di Marco (1989). For a modern study see Clayman (2009).

[89] Timon's account was preserved by the Peripatetic Aristocles, whose account itself only survives as quoted by the Church Father Eusebius, *Praep. evang.* 14.18.2–3 (DC 53, IG III-24, LS 1F). The interpretation of this passage has been subject to debate, and complicated by the fact that the text itself has been disputed. We shall return to this when we discuss this passage in Ch. 2 below.

[90] See Diog. Laert. 9.70, citing Theodosius.

[91] The biography is in Diog. Laert. 9.61–108.

[92] See Diog. Laert. 9.61 (DC 1A, IG III-22, LS 1A), 9.63 (DC 10, IG III-22, LS 1B), with discussion in Flintoff (1980) and Bett (2000), 169–78, and some further comments in the Appendix below.

[93] See Diog. Laert. 9.62 (DC 7, IG III-22, LS 1A).

[94] See Diog. Laert. 9.64 (DC 28, IG III-22, LS 1B).

Aristotelians and Others

The Epicurean, Stoic, and Academic schools were the most prominent during the Hellenistic period, but they were not the only ones. The fourth major school of philosophy in Athens was Aristotle's Lyceum.[95] Aristotle died in 322 BC, a year after the death of his most famous pupil, Alexander. The control of the Lyceum passed to another of his pupils, Theophrastus of Eresus (c. 371–c. 287 BC). Although Theophrastus is not usually included among the Hellenistic philosophers, his headship of the Lyceum falls squarely within the period.[96] His philosophical works continue in the same vein as his teacher. They include a short treatise on metaphysics (or, more properly, 'first philosophy') and an extension of Aristotle's biological researches on animals into the world of plants.[97] He also shared his teacher's interest in the history of philosophy and did important work gathering information on the earlier Presocratic philosophers.[98]

After Theophrastus's death the headship of the Lyceum passed to Strato of Lampsacus (d. 269 BC).[99] A number of ancient sources describe Strato as a *phusikos*,[100] a naturalist or physicist, and the surviving evidence that we have for him suggests strong interests in physics, psychology, and zoology. Strato's own brand of Aristotelianism has sometimes been characterized as moving further in the direction of empiricism and materialism. If that is

[95] For overviews of the Hellenistic Lyceum see Lynch (1972), Sharples (1999), and now Baltussen (2017).

[96] On Theophrastus's impact on the Hellenistic schools see a number of the papers collected together in Ophuijsen and Raalte (1998).

[97] For Theophrastus's *Metaphysics* see Ross and Fobes (1929), Raalte (1993), and Gutas (2010), all containing translations. His biological works on plants, *Enquiry into Plants* and *On the Causes of Plants*, can be found in LCL. A number of other shorter works also survive; for a complete list see Sharples (1999), 173–5. The evidence for his many lost works is gathered together and translated in FHSG.

[98] According to the list of his works in Diog. Laert. 5.42–50 (FHSG 1), Theophrastus wrote books on Anaxagoras, Anaximenes, Democritus, Empedocles, and Xenocrates, as well as Plato and Aristotle. Famously, Hermann Diels argued that much of the later evidence for the Presocratics derived ultimately from Theophrastus's historical researches; see Diels (1879), 475–95. The surviving evidence is in FHSG 224–45.

[99] There is an ancient biography in Diog. Laert. 5.58–64 and the evidence is collected together in Wehrli (1969a), but now see the new collection of texts with facing translations in Sharples (2011), which is printed in Desclos and Fortenbaugh (2011) alongside a number of helpful essays by others.

[100] See e.g. Diog. Laert. 5.58 (fr. 1 in Sharples (2011)), with further examples in fr. 10, 11, 35, 45A, 45B, 54, 60, 61, 63B, 75.

right then it might suggest an influence from either the Epicureans or the Stoics, placing him firmly within wider intellectual trends of the day. But whether this counts as a move away from Aristotle depends in large part on how we characterize Aristotle's own philosophy.[101] There have also been other attempts to connect Strato to the other Hellenistic schools: his attempt to explain the soul with reference to *pneuma* rather than Aristotelian hylomorphism might suggest a Stoic influence, but equally it might simply reflect developments in contemporary medical theory by Erasistratus and others.[102]

The next heads of the Lyceum, Lyco of Troas and Aristo of Ceos, appear to have made little contribution to philosophy, at least on the basis of the evidence that has survived.[103] The next significant figure to appear was Critolaus of Phaselis (second century BC), who was one of the three Athenian philosophers who visited Rome in 155 BC, alongside the Stoic Diogenes and the Academic Carneades.[104] He is noteworthy for defending Aristotelian doctrines against Stoic criticisms.[105]

This suggests a certain amount of contact and interaction between the Lyceum and the other philosophical schools of the period. Unfortunately, our evidence for members of the Hellenistic Lyceum is fragmentary and limited, and it would soon be overshadowed when the Aristotelian tradition was completely transformed at the end of the period by the recovery of Aristotle's lecture notes, the texts we now know as Aristotle's works.

Beyond the Lyceum, Academy, Stoa, and Garden there were other philosophers active in the Hellenistic period too. Earlier we met the Cynic Crates, who taught Zeno of Citium, and he was followed by further Cynics during this period.[106] These included Bion of Borysthenes,

---

[101] See the helpful discussion in Sharples (1999), 149.

[102] See further Ch. 4 below.

[103] The meagre evidence is gathered together in Wehrli (1968b). For Lyco see Stork et al. (2004), a new collection of the evidence with a facing English translation, and, for Aristo, Stork et al. (2006). For an ancient assessment of the philosophical decline of the Lyceum see Cicero, *Fin.* 5.13–14.

[104] The ancient evidence for Critolaus is gathered together in Wehrli (1969d). On the embassy to Rome see Cicero, *De or.* 2.155 (fr. 5 in Wehrli (1969d)); Aulus Gellius 6.14.8 (fr. 9 Wehrli). For a discussion see Hahm (2007).

[105] For his criticisms of Stoic physics see Ch. 3 below.

[106] On Cynics in the Hellenistic period see Dudley (1937), chs 3–7.

Menippus, and Teles. A series of diatribes attributed to Teles survive, addressing stock Cynic themes such as self-sufficiency and poverty.[107]

At the very beginning of the period we should also note Diodorus Cronus, a gifted logician associated with the Megarian school of philosophy.[108] The founder of Stoicism, Zeno, is said to have studied with him, and he is thought to have influenced the development of Stoic propositional logic.[109] Diodorus is also remembered for propounding the so-called 'Master Argument' about the nature of possibility.[110] His discussion of the 'heap' (*sôritês*) paradox contributed to its notoriety. These concerns with both possibility and vagueness make Diodorus a precursor to some of the central themes in philosophy today.

* * *

At the beginning of this chapter I asked the question, 'what is Hellenistic philosophy?'. We now have a clearer sense of the chronological period, the central philosophical traditions, and the key figures. In the light of what we have seen thus far, can we point to any defining characteristics? One feature that I hope is beginning to come through is that this was a period of vibrant philosophical activity, with a number of competing schools all active in Athens and attracting students from all over the ancient Mediterranean world. As the period progressed, more and more of those students were Romans, and by the end philosophy had firmly arrived in Rome.

As I mentioned earlier, precisely when we think the period comes to an end is a matter of scholarly debate, and attempts to limit historical periods with precise dates will always be somewhat arbitrary. One thing that is clear, however, is that the first century BC was a period of transition and by the time we get to 30 BC the distinctively 'Hellenistic' period in the history of philosophy is well and truly over. By the end of the first century BC Athens is no longer the predominant centre of philosophical activity in the ancient world and Greek is no longer the exclusive language in which philosophy is written. There is a much

---

[107] Teles' diatribes are edited in Hense (1909) and reprinted with a translation in O'Neil (1977). There is a more recent translation in Dobbin (2012), 110–34.

[108] The ancient evidence is gathered together in *SSR* II F 1–33. For his influence on subsequent Hellenistic philosophy see Sedley (1977).

[109] See Diog. Laert. 7.25 (*SVF* 1.5; *SSR* II F 3, **IG II-1**).

[110] See further Ch. 6 below.

stronger attention to the study of texts, perhaps a direct consequence of the decentralization and dispersal of philosophical activity, and the rise of a tradition of writing commentaries on earlier texts, especially on the works of Plato and Aristotle.[111]

Having said that, the principal Hellenistic schools of philosophy do not vanish overnight and they continue under these new circumstances in various forms for another two centuries or so.[112] The Stoics in particular flourished in Rome, influencing the school of Sextius where Seneca studied, and later in the hands of Musonius Rufus and his pupil Epictetus, who went on to found his own school at Nicopolis in western Greece.[113] We also hear of Cynics in Rome, often in close connection with Stoics.[114] Epicureanism found a later representative in Diogenes of Oenoanda, and the Pyrrhonians found their champion in Sextus Empiricus. The Platonic tradition, revived by Antiochus, flourished, developing into what is often called 'Middle Platonism', and then ultimately 'Neoplatonism'.[115]

In late antiquity we hear very little about any of the Hellenistic schools of thought, with the Neoplatonic tradition dominating affairs. This was inspired by the philosophy of Plotinus, and systematized by his pupil Porphyry, who stands as an heir to Antiochus's desire to synthesize the Platonic and Aristotelian traditions into a single, unified pagan philosophy. This may have been in part prompted by a desire to offer the strongest possible opposition to the increasingly dominant 'philosophy' of Christianity.[116]

It was this Neoplatonic tradition that went on to shape much of medieval philosophy in both the Latin and Arabic traditions. Hellenistic ideas were not entirely forgotten during the Middle Ages, and Cicero's

---

[111] On the renewed attention to texts, especially those of Plato and Aristotle, see Hatzimichali (2013). For the claim that decentralization may have contributed to this, see Sedley (2003). For the beginnings of the commentary tradition see Griffin (2015).

[112] See the collection of studies in Sorabji and Sharples (2007). Some people have called this period 'Post-Hellenistic'; see e.g. Boys-Stones (2001).

[113] On Stoicism in the imperial period see Gill (2003).

[114] On Cynicism as it developed in the imperial period see Dudley (1937), chs 7–9, and Griffin (1996).

[115] These are modern scholarly labels and not terms with which any ancient philosopher would have identified.

[116] On this point see Baltussen (2008), 85, 207.

philosophical works remained in circulation, but it was only after the rediscovery of ancient texts during the Renaissance—especially the works of Lucretius, Diogenes Laertius, and Sextus Empiricus—that Hellenistic ideas came back to the fore, becoming important influences on the development of early modern philosophy.[117]

[117] The literature on this topic is ever growing: on the influence of scepticism see Popkin (2003), on Epicureanism Wilson (2008), and on Stoicism Sellars (2016). Note also the essays in Osler (1991) and Miller and Inwood (2003).

2

Knowledge

Epicurus famously said 'empty are the words of that philosopher who offers therapy for no human suffering'.[1] Zeno and the Stoics saw philosophy as an activity directed towards achieving a 'smooth flow of life'.[2] Sceptics such as Pyrrho, and perhaps also Arcesilaus, appear to have been motivated in their suspension of judgement by the thought that it is this that leads to tranquillity (*ataraxia*).[3] For the main philosophical schools in the Hellenistic period, then, philosophy was seen as something practical, existential, and life changing.[4] Yet at the same time they all remained deeply concerned with a wide range of abstract philosophical questions about the nature of existence, what sorts of things exist, and how we can know them. Writing at the end of the period, Lucretius was quite explicit that these two things in fact go hand in hand.[5] For an Epicurean like him, human suffering is primarily the product of confused or superstitious beliefs about the nature of the world and what exists. If we want to overcome that suffering, we must first attend to our beliefs about what exists and what we do and do not know. Thus questions about knowledge and about what exists are by no means tangential to the very practical philosophies of the Hellenistic period; on the contrary, they are foundational. It would be a mistake, then, to think that the therapeutic goals of Epicureanism and Stoicism might lead them to be less concerned about what one believes. Neither school thought that one could believe anything one liked, so long as it has the

---

[1] Porphyry, *Marc.* 31 (Us. 221, Ar. 247, **IG I-124, LS 25C**).

[2] Diog. Laert. 7.88 (**IG II-94, LS 63C**).

[3] See e.g. Sextus Empiricus, *Pyr.* 1.232 (**IG III-27, LS 68I**). On Arcesilaus's position see Ch. 9 below.

[4] See further Long (2003).

[5] See e.g. Lucretius 1.146–8, and repeated at 2.59–61 (**LS 21W**), 3.91–3, 6.39–41.

right therapeutic effect. In fact, both schools held that the foundation of their therapeutic projects was the rejection of false beliefs.

In this chapter we shall focus our attention on knowledge. Where to begin when thinking about knowledge? Our most obvious source of knowledge is the senses. We know about the world around us through sight, hearing, and touch, along with taste and smell. Yet sometimes our senses can mislead us. So how can we know if any particular sensation is reliable? By extension, how can we know if *any* of our sensations are reliable, given that sometimes they can and do deceive us? These central questions in philosophy were intensively debated in the Hellenistic period.

In addressing these questions the Epicureans and Stoics were in some respects close to one another, both holding that knowledge was readily obtainable and that the way we obtain it is via the senses. We shall need to qualify this very broad judgement in a number of ways and to examine the quite different routes by which these two schools reached their positions. Even so, there was a clear contrast between their empiricism and the attitude of the sceptical Academy under Arcesilaus and Carneades. As we shall see, there was much debate during the Hellenistic period about whether knowledge of any kind was possible, especially between the Academics and the Stoics. Towards the end of the period there was also much debate within the Academy about what, if anything, a sceptic might acknowledge as a reasonable belief. This debate ultimately led to the end of the Academy's sceptical phase, with Philo, Antiochus, and Aenesidemus all going in different directions. In this chapter we shall try to get a sense of the positions put forward by each school, the reasons that led to those positions, and the objections that others raised against them.

Epicurean Epistemology

The Hellenistic debates about knowledge open with Epicurus. He was keen to defend the common-sense view that we do indeed get our knowledge of the world via the senses.[6] Yet he also defended the

---

[6] Diog. Laert. 10.31 (**IG** I-7, **LS** 17A). For literature on Epicurean epistemology see Striker (1977), Taylor (1980), Everson (1990b), Asmis (1999), and Asmis (2009). For those new to the subject the last of these may be the best place to begin.

seemingly paradoxical claim that *all* of our sensations (*aisthêseis*) are true and, as such, cannot be refuted.[7] Given that we might be more inclined to think that at least some of our sensations are from time to time false—sensations such as dreams or hallucinations, for instance—we shall want to know how Epicurus reached this view. Fortunately we have an extended passage that offers a number of arguments for the claim:

i) For a perception from one sense cannot refute another of the same type, because they are of equal strength; ii) nor can a perception from one sense refute one from a different sense, because they do not judge the same objects. iii) Nor indeed can reasoning [refute them]; for all reasoning depends on sense-perceptions. iv) Nor can one sense-perception refute another, since we attend to them all. And the fact of our awareness of sense-perceptions confirms the truth of the sense-perceptions. And it is just as much a fact that we see and hear as that we feel pain.[8]

Here Epicurus makes four distinct points. i) We have no reason to trust one visual image we receive any more than any other; they all carry the same weight. If we are going accept some sensations that we get through sight then we ought to accept them all. ii) Sensations that we get through one sense cannot undermine the truth of sensations we get from another. If, for instance, we hear a loud noise nearby but see nothing that could have caused it, that is no reason to deny the fact that we did indeed hear a loud noise. iii) We should be wary of developing arguments against the reliability of our sensations given that all of our reasoning is ultimately dependent in one way or another on information we get via the senses. Such arguments will ultimately collapse by undermining their own foundations. iv) Our sensations of the world via our senses are like our experiences of pain. It is simply a fact that we have sensations, just as it is a fact that we experience pleasure and pain. Epicurus says that 'the fact of our awareness of sense-perceptions confirms the truth (*alêtheia*) of the sense-perceptions'. This might seem as if he is simply saying that our sense-perceptions are phenomenologically real for us. They are, but the Epicurean claim is stronger than simply saying that our sense-perceptions exist; it is more importantly a claim

---

[7] Diog. Laert. 10.31–2 (IG I-7, LS 16B).

[8] Diog. Laert. 10.32 (IG I-7, LS 16B), trans. IG, who take this to be part of an extended quotation from Epicurus himself. The numbers added are mine. Compare with Lucretius 4.483–9 (IG I-27, LS16A).

about the content of our sense-perceptions, and in particular the claim that their content is unassailable. However, that content will be of images that are produced by objects (as we shall see, films of atoms that objects emit) rather than the objects themselves. Sextus Empiricus, discussing Epicurean epistemology, gives an example that brings out the distinction:

Orestes, when he seemed to see the Furies, his sensation, being moved by the images, was true, in that the images objectively existed; but his mind, in thinking that the Furies were solid bodies, held a false opinion.[9]

So, the Epicurean claim that all sensations are true refers to the truth of the images we receive. These images are not merely subjective experiences disconnected from the external world, but rather give knowledge of something physical with which the perceiver is in direct contact (films of atoms).[10] We might compare these images with a photograph, which will accurately record the light entering the camera at the moment that it is taken, but does not necessarily accurately represent the object whose picture is being taken.[11] Even if the photograph gives us a distorted view of the object in question, it nevertheless remains a true account of the image that reached the camera at that instant. The camera never lies, although that does not mean that it cannot sometimes mislead.

Indeed, we can be, and often are, mistaken about things that we perceive, so if Epicurus's position is to be convincing it is going to have to be able to take this into account. He does this by drawing a distinction between our sensations or perceptions (aisthêseis) and the judgements we make about them. While all of our sensations are true, the opinions that we form on the basis of them can be true or false.[12] Our opinions (as one report puts it) are judgements that we make on the basis of our sensations and if they add or subtract anything from those sensations then they run the risk of becoming mistaken.[13] So, all of our sensations are true, but the opinions we form about them can be either true or false.

---

[9] Sextus Empiricus, *Math.* 8.63 (Us. 253, IG I-70, LS 16F), trans. LS.
[10] One might draw a contrast here between the Epicurean position and that held by the Cyrenaics, who proposed that all experiences (pathê) are true, but denied that it was possible to infer from them anything about the physical world (Sextus Empiricus, *Math.* 7.191 (SSR IV A 213)). On the difference between the Epicurean and Cyrenaic positions see Tsouna (1998), 115–23.
[11] I owe this analogy to Long and Sedley (1987), 85.
[12] Diog. Laert. 10.34 (IG I-7, LS 18B); Sextus Empiricus, *Math.* 7.211 (IG I-68, LS 18A).
[13] See Sextus Empiricus, *Math.* 7.210 (IG I-68, LS 16E).

Why would Epicurus want to make this seemingly paradoxical claim in the first place? It was most likely his way of responding to previous philosophers who had been sceptical about the reliability of the senses. One common line of sceptical argument is to say that if you can doubt any of your sense-perceptions then there is no good reason not to doubt all of them. If one perception can be misleading, so can the rest.

Epicurus also responded to a different kind of objection to empiricism made famous by Plato. In the *Meno* Plato presents an argument for the claim that it is impossible to look for something unless you already know what you are looking for.[14] If Socrates goes looking for virtuous people in order to find out what virtue is, he must already have at least some idea of what virtue is in order to know which people will count as relevant to his search. If he already has some idea, then the search becomes redundant. It seems, then, as if we must *already* have knowledge of general concepts before we open our eyes, so to speak (i.e. *a priori*). If that is so then empiricism (the claim that all our knowledge is *a posteriori*) cannot be true.

The Epicurean response to this involves what Epicurus calls precon-ceptions (*prolêpseis*).[15] These are general concepts—virtue, human being, horse, cow, and so on—that enable us to recognize things as instances of a particular type of thing. Here Epicurus is in harmony with Plato. Where he differs from Plato is in his account of where these come from. Epicurus suggests that these preconceptions are themselves derived from experience, formed by repeatedly seeing the same object again and again. If someone sees a dog and recognizes it as a dog, it is only because they have seen dogs many times before, have come to form a concept of dog based on those repeated experiences, and then associ-ated that concept with a name, 'dog'. Plato was right to argue that any kind of search requires prior knowledge of what is being searched for, but Epicurus argues that this does not automatically refute empiricism. It is possible, he claims, to offer an empiricist account of concept formation that solves the problem.

Later Epicureans continued to respond to sceptical challenges to their empiricism, no doubt prompted in part by the rise of the sceptical Academy. We can see this in the work of Lucretius who, in Book 4 of

---

[14] See Plato, *Meno*, esp. 80d.   [15] See Diog. Laert. 10.33 (IG I-7, LS 17E).

his *On the Nature of Things*, responds to a whole series of sceptical points during the course of a discussion of sensation.[16]

The person who claims to know nothing, Lucretius argues, is unable to know that nothing can be known. So, the claim that knowledge is impossible falls into self-contradiction.[17] This on its own is enough to undermine the claims of that sort of sceptic, but nevertheless Lucretius offers further arguments against scepticism. If the sceptic claims that knowledge is impossible, and so has never encountered anything true, then where does his notion of truth come from? The sceptic cannot claim to have gained his conceptions of truth and falsehood via sensation, if he denies that we can ever know for sure that any of our sensations are true, so how did he acquire them? Lucretius follows Epicurus in holding that our notions and conceptions ultimately derive from our sensations, so he cannot see any other plausible source for them. Of course, one might respond by saying that some of these notions (including 'true' and 'false') are innate, but that solution is unlikely to be attractive to a sceptic, who would presumably be equally keen to reject claims to innate knowledge. Lucretius also repeats an argument that we often find in the Hellenistic period, the 'inactivity' (*apraxia*) objection, which argues that scepticism makes everyday life impossible, and so the sceptic cannot live his scepticism.[18] It would be impossible to function in daily life if one actually rejected all beliefs, and all our beliefs are founded on what we experience with the senses. Scepticism is thus either unworkable as a philosophy according to which one might actually live or it is merely empty theoretical posturing. (That this was considered an important philosophical objection underlines the way which philosophy was widely held to be a practical way of life.)

---

[16] See Lucretius 4.469–521 (part IG I-27, LS 16A).

[17] If Lucretius is thinking of the sceptical Academy here, then his account would support the claim made later by Sextus Empiricus that the Academics were indeed negative dogmatists. Leonard and Smith (1942), 565, suggest that Lucretius is thinking of Metrodorus of Chios, a partial follower of Democritus, on whom see Cicero, *Acad.* 2.73 (DK 70B1). However, the view that Cicero ascribes to Metrodorus does not accord with the position Lucretius is arguing against (but whether Cicero accurately represents Metrodorus's position has itself been subject to debate).

[18] See Lucretius 4.505–10 (LS 16A). This argument was earlier made by Epicurus's follower Colotes in a book titled *On the Point that Living in Conformity to the Views of the Other Philosophers Actually Makes it Impossible to Live*; see Plutarch, *Adv. Col.* 1120d. Plutarch reports that, among others, Colotes' argument was directed against Arcesilaus.

In sum, then, the Epicureans offer three responses to scepticism: i) the dogmatic sceptic is inconsistent; ii) the sceptic makes use of concepts derived from sensations; and iii) the sceptic cannot live in accordance with their principles.

Having responded to doubts about the reliability of the senses and argued that wholesale scepticism undermines itself, the Epicureans went on to offer a causal account of how our sense-perceptions come about. As we shall see in the next chapter, the Epicureans were atomists, holding the view that all of the objects in the physical world are composed of atoms, which move around in a void. The surface of each object emits fine films (*tupoi*, also called 'images', *eidôla*) of atoms that travel in all directions.[19] Our sense-perceptions are generated when the film from an object reaches one of our sense organs, such as the eyes or ears. Lucretius, who discusses this part of Epicurean theory at length, gives a number of reasons why he thinks this is a plausible theory. He suggests that it explains a wide variety of phenomena with which we are all familiar. To take just one example: when we see a reflection in a mirror, the most plausible explanation of how the image of an object is transmitted from the object to the mirror and then to us is that something leaves the surface of the object, travels to the mirror, and is bounced off it towards us.[20] It can even explain why the images are reversed.[21]

All of our sense-perceptions, then, are the product of interactions between films of atoms that reach us and our sense organs. If a sense-perception does not accurately represent its object, that simply reflects the fact that the film of atoms will have been altered in some way on its journey from the object to our sense organs. Sometimes the film will be altered only minimally; other times it might be hopelessly corrupted. Either way, it seems inevitable that some atoms in the film will have got lost or mixed up along the way. Lucretius gives the example of a square city tower seen from some distance:

> And when we see the square towers of a city
> From far away, they often appear to be round.
> This is because every angle when seen at a distance
> Is blurred, or rather is not seen at all.
> Its flow is lost, it does not strike our eyes,

---

[19] Epicurus, *Ep. Hdt.* 46–8 (IG I-2, LS 15A); Lucretius 4.29–32; 4.225–9.
[20] See Lucretius 4.269–91.   [21] See Lucretius 4.292–323.

> And the air, while the images (*simulacra*) travel so far through it,
> Inflicts many blows upon them and blunts them.[22]

This atomist account of perception thus not only offers an explanation of how our sense-perceptions come about, it also tries to explain how it is that they can sometimes seem misleading. However, the Epicureans nevertheless insist that all of our sense-perceptions are reliable and that any mistaken beliefs we hold are the product of our judgements about sensations rather than the sensations themselves. As Lucretius himself puts it a little later on:

> And many marvels in this way we see
> Which seek as it were to break the credit of our senses,
> But all in vain, since the most part of them
> Deceive because of notions of the mind
> Which we ourselves bring to them, so that things
> Seem so be seen which senses have not seen.
> For nothing is more difficult than to distinguish
> And separate plain things from doubtful things
> Which all at once are added by the mind.[23]

Knowledge, for an Epicurean, is in principle easy to come by. Our confusions are our own making.

Stoic Logic and Epistemology

The Stoics were, like the Epicureans, empiricists, taking perception to be the ultimate foundation for human knowledge.[24] On this foundation they developed a complex system of logical reasoning, on a par with Aristotle's.[25] Unlike Aristotle, who presented logic as simply a tool to be used while working through philosophical problems, the Stoics took logic to be an integral part of philosophy, alongside physics and ethics.[26]

[22] Lucretius 4.353–9 (LS 16G), trans. Melville. Lucretius uses the Latin *simulacra* to translate the Greek *eidôla*.

[23] Lucretius 4.462–8, trans. Melville.

[24] For introductions to Stoic epistemology see Annas (1990), Frede (1999a), and Hankinson (2003).

[25] For overviews of Stoic logic, see Bobzien (2003) and, in greater detail, Bobzien (1999b). Older studies in English include Bocheński (1951), 77–102; Mates (1961); Kneale and Kneale (1962), 113–76.

[26] See e.g. Diog. Laert. 7.39 (IG II-2, LS 26B). Some commentators have noted that the division Diogenes Laertius reports is of philosophical discourse, not philosophy itself.

By 'logic' they meant something broader than merely formal logic, encompassing not just formal reasoning but also rhetoric and the study of language, including grammar.[27] All these, they suggested, were parts of philosophy proper and the Stoics made significant contributions to many of these fields, including the study of grammar and formal logic.[28] Chrysippus was famed as a logician in antiquity (and parodied by the satirist Lucian for his logic-chopping);[29] today he is widely held to be second only to Aristotle in antiquity in his contribution to the subject. Aristotle's syllogistic logic is what we might call a logic of terms, with letters replacing terms such as 'human' or 'animal'.[30] Thus when Aristotle writes 'All As are Bs, all Bs are Cs, therefore all As are Cs',[31] he is recording the logical structure of arguments such as 'All humans are animals, all animals are mortal, therefore all humans are mortal'. Stoic logic, by contrast, is concerned with propositions. An example of a Stoic syllogism would be: 'If it is daytime, it is light; it is daytime; therefore it is light'.[32] This they formalized to: 'If p, q; p; therefore q', with 'p' and 'q' standing for the propositions 'it is daytime' and 'it is light' respectively. The propositions out of which Stoic syllogisms are constructed were called 'assertibles' (axiômata).[33] These can be either true or false ('it is daytime' is either true or false) and their truth-value can change over time ('it is daytime' will not be true in the middle of the night). They can also be simple (like 'it is daytime' or 'it is light') or they can be complex, containing more than one simple assertible (such as 'if it is daytime, then it is light').[34]

Chrysippus identified five basic types of indemonstrable syllogism that he took to be self-evidently valid.[35] Diogenes Laertius reports that these were:[36]

> If the first, then the second; the first; therefore the second.
> If the first, then the second; not the first; therefore not the second.
> Not the first and the second; the first; therefore not the second.
> Either the first or the second; not the first; therefore the second.
> Either the first or the second; not the second; therefore the first.

[27] See Diog. Laert. 7.41–4 (IG II-3, LS 31A).
[28] On Stoic contributions to grammar see e.g. Blank and Atherton (2003); note also Atherton (1993) and Janko (1995).
[29] See e.g. Lucian, Vit. auct. 21–5 (part LS 37L).   [30] See Aristotle, An. pr. 1.1.
[31] See e.g. Aristotle, An. pr. 1.4, 25b40–26a2.
[32] See Diog. Laert. 7.77 (IG II-3, LS 36A).   [33] See Diog. Laert. 7.65–6 (IG II-3).
[34] See Diog. Laert. 7.68–9 (IG II-3).   [35] See Diog. Laert. 7.79 (IG II-3, LS 36A).
[36] See Diog. Laert. 7.80–1 (IG II-3, LS 36A); compare with Sextus Empiricus, Math. 8.227.

These indemonstrable syllogisms form the foundation on which more complex arguments can be built. At the same time, more complex arguments that are not self-evidently valid can be reduced to these indemonstrables, in order to confirm their validity, and the Stoics proposed a series of rules (*themata*) for this.[37]

There are a number of things one might note about these indemonstrable syllogisms. The first is that they share a common structure: the first premise is a complex assertible, the second premise is a simple assertible, and the conclusion is a simple assertible. The second is that they use only a handful of key terms—'if' (conditional), 'or' (disjunction), 'and' (conjunction), and 'not' (negation)—and these are different to those used in Aristotelian syllogisms ('all', 'some', 'is', 'is not'). The Stoics were also interested in modal logic, drawing on the work of earlier Hellenistic logicians Philo and Diodorus Cronus.[38] They are said to have divided propositions into the modalities of the possible, the impossible, the necessary, and the non-necessary.[39]

For the Stoics, formal logic was a vital tool in the development of knowledge (*epistêmê, scientia*). By 'knowledge' they meant something quite substantial: a systematically organized body of knowledge that, they claimed, only a sage would attain.[40] However, this complex body of knowledge is ultimately built upon true simple assertibles or propositions, such as 'it is daytime'. The Stoics claimed that the impressions we receive via the senses are presented to the mind in the form of such propositions, which we either assent to or reject.[41] That claim was first made by Zeno, who illustrated both the role of assent and the difference between knowledge (*epistêmê*) and *katalêpsis* (which we might translate as 'cognition') in a striking simile:

He [Zeno] would spread out the fingers of one hand and display its open palm, saying 'an impression is like this'. Next he clenched his fingers a little and said, 'assent is like this'. Then, pressing his fingers quite together, he made a fist, and

---

[37] On these *themata* see Bobzien (2003), 111–20.

[38] On Philo and Diodorus (sometimes referred to as Megarians, although recent scholarship has questioned the legitimacy of this label) see Bobzien (1999a); note also Kneale and Kneale (1962), 113–28.

[39] See Diog. Laert. 7.75 (*SVF* 2.201, **IG II-3, LS 38D**). We shall discuss this further in Ch. 6 below.

[40] See Cicero, *Acad.* 2.145 (*SVF* 1.66, **IG II-6, LS 41A**).

[41] This is so for rational adults, who have rational impressions presented to the mind in propositional form; non-rational animals (including children) do not. See Diog. Laert. 7.51 (**IG II-3, LS 39A**), with the discussion in Frede (1983).

said that this was cognition. . . . Then he brought his left hand against his right fist and gripped it tightly and forcefully, and said that knowledge was like this and possessed by none except the sage.[42]

Zeno's account of how humans gain knowledge via the senses was taken up and refined by Chrysippus and Diogenes of Babylon in the light of criticisms from the Academic Arcesilaus. The refined version attracted further criticisms from the Academic Carneades, to which later Stoics such as Antipater responded. This lively debate between Stoics and Academics continued right down to the first century BC when Cicero defended a version of the Academic view against Antiochus's restatement of the Stoic position.[43] Cicero's book the *Academica* (in fact the remnants of two distinct versions of the work) offers a valuable account of both that debate and the preceding arguments between Stoics and Academics stretching all the way back to Zeno.[44] In what follows, then, we shall follow the outline of Cicero's report of the debate.

Zeno's account of knowledge is complex and some in antiquity thought it to be the most original part of his philosophy.[45] He suggested that our perceptions are made up of two distinct elements: an impression produced by the impact of something external and our assent to that impression.[46] Assenting to an impression generates a belief; assenting to an impression that does not accurately reflect what it appears to show will generate a false belief, and the problem, of course, is knowing which impressions deserve our assent and which do not. Zeno claimed that some impressions both accurately present what they purport to show

---

[42] Cicero, *Acad.* 2.145 (*SVF* 1.66, IG II-6, LS 41A), trans. LS modified. In this passage 'impression' translates *visum* (i.e. *phantasia*), 'assent' translates *adsensio* (i.e. *sunkatathesis*), 'cognition' translates *comprehensio* (i.e. *katalêpsis*), and 'knowledge' translates *scientia* (i.e. *epistêmê*).

[43] This happened in literary form, if not actually: the first edition of Cicero's *Academica* presents (the character) Lucullus representing Antiochus's Stoic position in debate with (the character) Cicero defending the Academics.

[44] The book we now have called the *Academica* is in fact the fragmentary remains of two distinct editions: *Acad.* 1 is Book 1 (out of 4) from the second edition of the work, while *Acad.* 2 (sometimes referred to as *Lucullus*) is Book 2 (out of 2) from the earlier first edition. For the Latin text see Plasberg (1922); for a recent translation with helpful annotation see Brittain (2006). There are a number of valuable studies in Inwood and Mansfeld (1997).

[45] This was the view of Antiochus, as reported by the character Varro in Cicero, *Acad.* 1.40 (*SVF* 1.55, IG II-4, LS 40B). For a similar modern assessment see Sedley (2002b), 135.

[46] See Cicero, *Acad.* 1.40 (*SVF* 1.55, 1.61, IG II-4, LS 40B). Here 'perception' translates *aisthêsis* (in Cicero's Latin *sensus*), 'impression' translates *phantasia* (in Latin *visum*), and 'assent' translates *sunkatathesis* (in Latin *adsensio*).

and do so in a way that makes them self-evidently true. These impressions we can assent to confident in their reliability without having to refer to anything else. Indeed, in so far as they present themselves as self-evidently true, we might say that we cannot but assent to them, and when we do, we do so confident that we are generating a true belief. A later Stoic put it like this: when out in the midday sun, with the heat upon us and sweat on our faces, it is simply not possible to reject the proposition 'it is daytime'. The impression that 'it is daytime' is so self-evident that it simply demands our assent.[47] This sort of impression Zeno called *kataleptikê*, a word he coined himself and which is particularly difficult to translate into English.[48] An assent to this kind of kataleptic impression he called a *katalêpsis*, a grasp or apprehension (in Cicero's Latin, *comprehensio*), and this for Zeno counted as an instance of cognition. Any claims to substantial scientific or philosophical knowledge (*epistêmê*) ultimately rest upon foundations built out of these assents to kataleptic impressions.

This account immediately raises the question of whether there are in fact any impressions that are both self-evidently true and always distinguishable from other, potentially misleading impressions. The theory appears to rely on the claim that there are some cases where it is impossible to make a mistake. Central, then, to Zeno's account is this notion of a kataleptic impression, and a number of sources record his definition, which specifies its essential features.[49] Zeno is reported to have said that:

A kataleptic impression is i) one which arises from what is and ii) is stamped and impressed exactly in accordance with what is, iii) of such a kind as could not arise from what is not.[50]

We might gloss the first two parts of this definition by saying that such an impression is produced by something that exists and accurately represents that existing thing. Thus some have argued that we can

---

[47] See Epictetus, *Diss.* 1.28.2–3.

[48] See Cicero, *Acad.* 1.41 (*SVF* 1.60, **IG II-4, LS 40B**). In what follows I simply Anglicize it as 'kataleptic'.

[49] See e.g. Cicero, *Acad.* 2.18, 2.77 (**IG III-10, LS 40D**); Sextus Empiricus, *Math.* 7.248 (**LS 40E**), all in *SVF* 1.59; note also Diog. Laert. 7.46 (**IG II-3, LS 40C**).

[50] Sextus Empiricus, *Math.* 7.248 (*SVF* 1.59, **LS 40E**), trans. LS modified, with numbering added.

determine which impressions are kataleptic and which not with reference to their causal history.[51] Only impressions produced under normal
conditions, without interference, can be kataleptic. The third part is
harder to pin down. These impressions represent a thing to us in a way
that means we cannot doubt their veracity.[52] As one source puts it:

> This [kataleptic] impression being self-evident and striking, all but seizes us by
> the hair, they say, and pulls us to assent, needing nothing else to achieve this
> effect or to establish its difference from other impressions.[53]

There is something about their inherent power or richness that means
these impressions are their own guarantee of their truthfulness. They
simply cannot be false. By contrast, non-kataleptic impressions may or
may not be given assent, and may or may not be true. Assent to one of
these generates an opinion (*doxa*). The Stoics claimed that a sage will not
hold opinions, which is to say they will not assent to non-kataleptic
impressions.[54] The imperfect non-sage, by contrast, will hold both opinions and cognitions, but will never reach comprehensive and systematic
knowledge.

The motivation here is to try to give an empirical foundation for all of
our knowledge that does not need to refer to anything outside of itself.
For a thoroughgoing empiricist, knowledge via the senses must be its
own foundation.

The Academic Response

This Stoic view attracted a number of criticisms from members of the
sceptical Academy, starting with Arcesilaus, and Cicero reports the main
objections.[55] The first objection claimed that people do sometimes
experience impressions of things that do not exist that are quite

---

[51]   See in particular Frede (1983).

[52]   Sextus Empiricus, *Math.* 7.253–6 (**LS 40K**) reports that some later Stoics qualified this
and admitted that it is possible to deny a kataleptic impression, such as when someone sees
something they cannot believe to be true, but the implication remains that after further
scrutiny its veracity will become obvious.

[53]   Sextus Empiricus, *Math.* 7.257 (**LS 40K**), trans. LS.

[54]   See Sextus Empiricus, *Math.* 7.151–2 (**IG III-18, LS 41C**).

[55]   In Cicero's account in *Acad.* 2 the character Lucullus follows the views of Antiochus
who, though not a Stoic, broadly follows the Stoics in epistemology, and the account of the
academic objections is presented from his pro-Stoic perspective.

convincing, such as mirages or hallucinations, brought on by abnormal states of mind.[56] They also sometimes have especially vivid dreams. The Academics claimed that these sorts of impressions can sometimes be so convincing that one might assent to them believing them to be true. If that is so then it shows that it is impossible always to distinguish between true and false impressions.

A second objection claimed that some objects are identical, or at least appear identical to us, and so it is possible to confuse one with the other and so assent to a false impression.[57] One might think of identical twins or objects with few unique characteristics, such as a pair of eggs. If we were presented with a pair of eggs and then later shown just one of them, we might find it impossible to judge which of the two it was. The false impression that it is 'egg A' is indistinguishable from the true impression that it is in fact 'egg B'. If that is so then it shows that false impressions can be mistaken for true ones. In such a situation there is no kataleptic impression that is *self-evidently* true.

Both of these objections make the point that it is possible to have a false impression that is phenomenologically indistinguishable from a true one. If that is so, then the foundation for all Stoic claims to knowledge is no longer secure. For them, a kataleptic impression *must* in some way be phenomenologically distinctive, even if its distinctiveness is not immediately apparent to the non-sage.

The Stoics responded to these objections in a number of ways.[58] They responded to the first by simply denying that hallucinations or dreams are ever convincing enough to be confused with genuine kataleptic impressions. The reliability of an impression is assessed in relation to other impressions and not in isolation, and so although one might for a moment be convinced by an especially vivid dream, as soon as one wakes up and can compare it to impressions of the real world there is no doubt about its fictitiousness.[59] They responded to the second objection by denying that two objects could ever in fact be absolutely identical (the doctrine of the identity of indiscernibles, made famous later by

[56] See Cicero, *Acad.* 2.47–54.
[57] See Cicero, *Acad.* 2.54–8 (part **LS 40I**).
[58] These responses are Lucullus's account of Antiochus's replies to Academic objections on behalf of the Stoa, presumably deriving from the Stoic school.
[59] See Cicero, *Acad.* 2.51.

Leibniz).[60] But of course impressions of non-identical objects might still *appear* to be identical. To that concern they address their second response, which was to say that although some impressions might appear to be identical to a novice, an expert will always be able to distinguish between them and, by extension, be able to distinguish between true and false impressions. The mother of identical twins can easily tell them apart, even if others might get confused. An expert in eggs, with skill built up after years of experience, may well be able to distinguish between two seemingly identical eggs.[61] Just because the non-expert cannot distinguish between the two does not mean that there are no distinguishing features in either the eggs or the impressions of them. The prudent thing for the non-expert, then, would simply be to withhold assent in such cases. Suspension of judgement in these situations is entirely consistent with the view that, with more experience and expertise, it would be possible to judge correctly.[62]

The Stoics also responded in another way, this time attacking the consistency of the alternative view outlined by the Academics rather than defending their own.[63] They argued that to live a life at all requires assent to impressions, because action requires beliefs, and beliefs are the product of assents. Thus the alternative view made life impossible and was ultimately disingenuous.[64] We saw this 'inactivity' (*apraxia*) objection earlier in Lucretius, and it was a common line of attack against epistemological scepticism. Both the Stoics and Epicureans directed it against the Academic Arcesilaus. His response was to say that even if it is necessary to suspend judgement about the truthfulness of one's impressions, one can still function as an agent in the world by following what seems to be most reasonable (*eulogos*).[65] A Stoic might respond to this by dismissing it as a mere playing with words ('true' and 'false' have simply been re-labelled 'reasonable' and 'unreasonable'). A sceptic might equally respond by saying that the Stoic account presupposes a theory

---

[60] For the Stoic claim that everything is 'peculiarly qualified' (*idiôs poion*) see Cicero, *Acad.* 2.84 (LS 40J), with further texts in LS 28. On the similarities with and differences from Leibniz, see Forman (2016), 226–7.

[61] See Cicero, *Acad.* 2.57 (LS 40I).

[62] See Cicero, *Acad.* 2.56, 2.58.

[63] We might ask whether this alternative view was sincerely held by the Academics or merely proposed by them as part of the dialectical debate.

[64] See esp. Cicero, *Acad.* 2.61–2.

[65] See Sextus Empiricus, *Math.* 7.158 (IG III-18, LS 69B).

about how we form beliefs for which we have no firm evidence. On the one hand, then, the Stoics and Academics were locked in an intractable dispute. However, on the other, there were in fact some points of common ground: the Stoics agreed that one should suspend judgement when matters are unclear; they also agreed that the vast majority of people lacked the ability to consistently judge impressions correctly. As we shall see, some later thinkers—notably Antiochus—did their best to play down the distance between the two schools. But for the protagonists of the debate, the distance seemed very real.

Arguments in the Academy

All of the Academic arguments we have considered so far have been objections to Stoic claims to knowledge. There are a number of ways in which we might interpret the motivations behind those arguments. One would be to see them simply as arguments against the Stoics, attacking the Stoics on their own terms, but without committing the Academics to any views of their own. Another way would be to see these arguments as part of a wider philosophical project directed against *all* claims to knowledge, with the ultimate aim of showing that knowledge is impossible. What, if anything, did Academics such as Arcesilaus and Carneades believe themselves and what did they think they were doing when making these arguments? These questions remain the subject of debate today, in part due to the fragmentary and second-hand nature of the surviving evidence.[66] But they were also contested issues even in the ancient Academy. In particular there was a dispute between the Academics Clitomachus and Metrodorus over the nature and extent of Carneades' scepticism. But before we turn to Carneades, it will be helpful to begin with the founder of the sceptical Academy, Arcesilaus.

As we saw in the opening chapter, Arcesilaus was the first member of the Academy to adopt a brand of scepticism, presumably inspired by reading those Platonic dialogues that undermine the claims to knowledge

---

[66] Neither Arcesilaus nor Carneades wrote any works themselves. One of our principal sources for information, Cicero's *Academica*, survives only as a composite of two fragmentary works. Another important source, Sextus Empiricus, is openly hostile towards them and so may not give a fair account. The evidence for Arcesilaus is gathered together in Mette (1984), 44–74, and for Carneades in Mette (1985), 55–109.

put forward by Socrates' interlocutors but without offering any positive answer in their place. Taking Socrates as his role model, Arcesilaus would examine the claims to knowledge held by other philosophers, raise objections, and propose arguments for opposing positions. All this was aimed at undermining any claims to knowledge.[67] Arcesilaus is reported to have claimed that he went even further than Socrates, by denying even that he knew he knew nothing:

Arcesilaus used to deny that anything could be known, not even the residual claim Socrates had allowed himself, i.e., the knowledge that he didn't know anything. He thought that everything was hidden so deeply and that nothing could be discerned or understood.[68]

Given this, he argued that one ought not to affirm or to assent to anything.

When we turn to Carneades the picture is less clear. Was he a faithful follower of Arcesilaus or did he innovate? The later Pyrrhonian sceptic Sextus Empiricus drew a clear distinction between them, labelling them heads of the 'Middle Academy' and 'New Academy' respectively, although Antiochus, who had first-hand knowledge of the Academy, saw them as both members of the same 'New Academy'. Sextus's reason for distinguishing between Arcesilaus and Carneades was that he took Carneades to have claimed that knowledge is impossible, a position Sextus characterizes as negative dogmatism. However, some modern scholars have questioned this account.[69]

A separate issue was whether Carneades thought it appropriate to hold opinions on some matters. In an argument against the Stoics, Carneades had, it seemed, proposed that a wise person might do just that. The Academics had argued against the Stoics along the following lines: 'if the sage ever assents to anything [non-kataleptic], he will sometimes hold an opinion; but he will never hold an opinion [the Stoics claimed]; so he

---

[67] For Arcesilaus's method and its Socratic inspiration see Cicero, *Fin.* 2.2 (IG III-16, LS 68J); *Acad.* 1.45 (IG III-19, LS 68A); *Nat. D.* 1.11. On its Socratic origins see Annas (1994) and Shields (1994). However, Diog. Laert. 4.33 (part IG III-1, LS 68E) quotes from both Aristo the Stoic (*SVF* 1.343) and Timon the pupil of Pyrrho, suggesting that Pyrrho had also been an influence on Arcesilaus.

[68] Cicero, *Acad.* 1.45 (IG III-19, LS 68A), trans. Brittain. The view of Socrates as a negative dogmatist seems misleading and the earlier description of his position at *Acad.* 1.16 seems closer to the mark.

[69] See e.g. Thorsrud (2010), 71.

won't ever assent to anything'.[70] Cicero tells us that Carneades sometimes offered a different second premise, so that the argument became: 'if
the wise person ever assents to anything [non-kataleptic], he will sometimes hold an opinion; he will sometimes assent; so he will sometimes
hold an opinion'. According to Cicero this was designed to offer the
Stoics a dilemma: either they accept the first version and withhold assent
or they accept the second and hold opinions.[71] In this Cicero was
following the interpretation of Carneades' pupil Clitomachus.

However, Metrodorus, another of Carneades' pupils, understood this
quite differently. He took the Carneadean premise 'the wise person will
sometimes assent' to be Carneades' own considered view, and not merely
a dialectical move in an argument against the Stoics. On that view,
Carneades was thought to have held that a wise person can hold
opinions about some things so long as they do not assent to the truth
of those opinions. Thus it is acceptable to hold opinions about things that
are plausible or persuasive. With a nod to Hume, we might say that it is
reasonable to hold the belief that the sun will rise tomorrow morning
even though we know that we have no grounds to be sure of this. Cicero
describes this as holding opinions *as* opinions, while still aware that
nothing is really knowable.[72]

This dispute over Carneades' legacy led to much debate within the
Academy about what, if anything, a sceptic might acknowledge as a
reasonable belief. The debate ultimately led to the end of the Academy's
sceptical phase, with Philo, Antiochus, and Aenesidemus all going in
different directions.

When Philo became head of the Academy he initially followed Clitomachus and the thoroughgoing scepticism that the latter had attributed
to Carneades.[73] However, he appears later to have moved away from this
position (or this interpretation of Carneades) and towards a view that
allowed the wise person to hold opinions—i.e. Metrodorus's view (or his

---

[70] Cicero, *Acad.* 2.67 (IG III-9, LS 69G), trans. Brittain modified.
[71] See Cicero, *Acad.* 2.78 (IG III-10, LS 69H). Here I follow the account in Brittain
(2001), 13–14.
[72] See Cicero, *Acad.* 2.148 (IG III-15, LS 69K); see also 2.78 (IG III-10, LS 69H) and 2.59
(IG III-8, LS 69F).
[73] See Numenius in Eusebius, *Praep. evang.* 14.8.1–15 (Philo test. 23 in Brittain
(2001), 357).

interpretation of Carneades).[74] Thus Philo's mature position, we might say, was a moderate scepticism that allowed reasonable beliefs while resisting any substantive claims to knowledge. The reports that survive suggest that Philo doubted the Stoic theory of knowledge—that is, he doubted that we can ever truly distinguish kataleptic impressions from other non-kataleptic ones. In this he followed his predecessors. However, he is also reported to have claimed that we can still know some things according to a lesser standard.[75] If Carneades had proposed that it was acceptable to hold opinions, as Metrodorus claimed, then Philo's position may have been similar to, or merely a development of, that view. If he had not, then Philo's position looks like a softening of the Academic position. Assessing Philo's contribution depends in part, then, on knowing just what Carneades thought. But, with wonderful irony, that is something we just do not and cannot know. We might also reflect on the range and extent of reasonable beliefs a sceptic could choose to hold. It is one thing to embrace everyday beliefs in order to navigate the physical world and so overcome the *apraxia* objection; it is quite another to propose complex philosophical theories, claiming that they are merely reasonable beliefs rather than firm claims to knowledge.

Unlike Arcesilaus and Carneades, Philo did write a number of philosophical works, but like so much else from the period they are lost.[76] These were probably written in response to Antiochus, Philo's renegade pupil who wanted to take the Academy in a quite different direction.[77] Antiochus referred to himself as an 'Old Academic', rejecting what he called the sceptical 'New Academy' running from Arcesilaus to Philo, instead aligning himself with the dogmatic Platonism of Plato's immediate successors (especially Polemo).[78] In epistemology he appears to have embraced a broadly Stoic view, seeing this as simply a development of Platonic doctrines.[79] This would have been anathema to his sceptical predecessors.

---

[74] See Cicero, *Acad.* 2.78 (IG III-10, LS 69H, Philo test. 25 in Brittain (2001), 358).

[75] See Sextus Empiricus, *Pyr.* 1.235 (IG III-27, **LS 68T**) and Cicero, *Acad.* 2.18 (part LS 68U).

[76] I refer to the so-called 'Roman Books', thoroughly discussed in Brittain (2001).

[77] Polito (2012), 39, challenges this image of a renegade Antiochus. He makes the point that by this stage the sceptical Academy no longer existed in any substantive sense. For more on Antiochus and his dispute with Philo see Glucker (1978), 13–120, alongside Brittain (2001) and Polito (2012).

[78] See the account in Cicero, *Acad.* 2.68–71.

[79] See Cicero, *Acad.* 2.19–21 (F5 in Sedley (2012)), with Brittain (2012).

By this point the institutional history of the Academy was already at an end (Philo and Antiochus had both fled Athens) and Antiochus's wholesale rejection of the sceptical Academy also marked the end of the distinctive Hellenistic phase of its philosophical history. His attempts to see Platonism, Aristotelianism, and Stoicism as all parts of a single, unified tradition marked the beginning of a trend that would develop throughout later antiquity.[80]

The Pyrrhonist Revival

It was in the wake of all this that the Pyrrhonist tradition was born, notwithstanding the fact that Pyrrho had died a good two centuries earlier. The sceptic Aenesidemus was dissatisfied with these developments and wanted to return to a purer form of scepticism.[81] Presumably in a desire to break with Academic wrangling altogether, he turned to the relatively obscure figure of Pyrrho as the figurehead for a new Pyrrhonist movement.[82] Pyrrho himself had lived right at the beginning of the Hellenistic period, accompanying Alexander to India, and had a student and follower, Timon. But for most of the Hellenistic period there was no Pyrrhonist tradition as such, and Aenesidemus effectively created 'Pyrrhonism' at the very close of the period in the light of the changes in the Academy. One of our sources of information for Aenesidemus's Pyrrhonism is the work of a much later Pyrrhonist, Sextus Empiricus, who offers his own version of the position. In short, there is no single version of Pyrrhonism but in fact three distinct positions that are the product of three distinct philosophers: Pyrrho himself, Aenesidemus, and Sextus Empiricus.[83] When people refer to Pyrrhonism they are often thinking of Sextus's version, as presented in

---

[80] See esp. Cicero, *Acad.* 1.17 and 1.43. For more on Antiochus see the papers in Sedley (2012).

[81] The evidence for Aenesidemus is gathered together, translated, and discussed in Polito (2014).

[82] It is unclear whether Aenesidemus was a disaffected member of the Academy. Photius, *Bibl.* 212, 169b32–5 (A1 in Polito (2014), **IG III-25, LS 71C**) implies that he was at one time an Academic but Decleva Caizzi (1992), 189, suggests that his views were 'those of an external spectator, not those of a participant in disputes internal to the Academy'. For a reply to Decleva Caizzi see Mansfeld (1995).

[83] There is also potentially a fourth position, that of Pyrrho's immediate pupil Timon. Much of our knowledge of Pyrrho comes via Timon and it is possible that it is coloured by Timon's own views. See further Bett (2000), 70–6.

his *Outlines of Pyrrhonism*, but Sextus is not our concern here, writing as he was much later, in the second century AD.

What do we know of Aenesidemus's version of scepticism? We know that he wrote a work called *Pyrrhonist Discourses* in which he contrasted his own brand of scepticism with that of the Academics.[84] In particular he appears to have been troubled by the moderate scepticism of Philo (if indeed it was still scepticism) and the increasingly conciliatory moves in the direction of Stoicism by Antiochus, which led him to brand them as 'Stoics fighting with Stoics', disagreeing only about the status of kataleptic impressions.[85] According to Aenesidemus, a true sceptic will affirm nothing, not even that he knows nothing. Thus not only were recent members of the Academy misguided in adopting some positive philosophical beliefs but so were earlier Academics such as Carneades when they claimed to know nothing or even to deny the truth of Stoic claims to knowledge. In the language that would be used later by Sextus Empiricus such claims were examples of negative dogmatism, and for the Pyrrhonists the negative dogmatism of the Academics was as questionable as the positive dogmatism of the Stoics.[86] The true sceptic, Aenesidemus suggested, believes absolutely nothing and makes no claims about knowledge at all, either positive or negative. They can and do, however, accept the content of their experiences *as* experiences, without claiming anything further about them.[87]

It was probably Aenesidemus who first formulated the 'ten modes' of Pyrrhonian scepticism.[88] These are a series of argumentative strategies aimed at generating suspension of judgement. They are supposed to work by setting in opposition perceptual experiences or value judgements that are of equal force, and so will counter-balance each other. This is said to generate a state of equipollence (*isostheneia*) that, in turn, leads to suspension of judgement (*epochê*).[89] It is important to note here

---

[84]   See Photius, *Bibl.* 212, 169b18–170b3 (B1–4 in Polito (2014), IG III-25, LS 71C).

[85]   See Photius, *Bibl.* 212, 169b18–170b3.

[86]   See Sextus Empiricus, *Pyr.* 1.1–4 (IG III-26).

[87]   See Sextus Empiricus, *Pyr.* 1.1–4; also Diog. Laert. 9.106 (B5 in Polito (2014), IG III-22, LS 71A).

[88]   For a thorough discussion, along with translations of the key sources, see Annas and Barnes (1985). Sextus Empiricus attributes the ten modes to Aenesidemus in *Math.* 7.345 (B19 in Polito (2014)) and he also credits him with a separate set of eight modes in *Pyr.* 1.180 (B14 in Polito, IG III-37, LS 72M).

[89]   See Sextus Empiricus, *Pyr.* 1.8 (IG III-26) and 1.31 (IG III-26, LS 72A).

that the sceptic does not *decide* to suspend judgement, which would be tantamount to holding the belief that the matter was unresolvable; instead, they effectively find themselves in a state of mind that makes holding any view on the subject impossible. This, in turn, is said to generate a state of tranquillity (*ataraxia*), which is presumably similar to the feeling someone has when they simply give up on some especially complex and stressful project with the thought 'I just don't care anymore, this is no longer my problem, and I feel a lot better for it'. The ideal state of the Pyrrhonian, then, is one of tranquil indifference in the face of competing and conflicting claims to knowledge.

The ten modes were effectively strategies designed to set off a chain reaction generating equipollence, suspension of judgement, and finally tranquillity. Each mode (*tropos*) refers to a different class of conflicting appearances.[90] The first mode draws attention to the fact that different species of animal experience things quite differently and are affected by the same thing in different ways. To borrow a saying from Heraclitus, seawater is 'drinkable and wholesome for fish, but undrinkable and poisonous for people'.[91] We have no real grounds for prioritizing either of these appearances over the other, and so no way to judge the nature of the seawater in itself or even to make claims about whether there is a 'seawater in itself'.[92] All we have are two conflicting appearances.

The other modes adopt the same strategy with regard to differences between human experiences; differences between the senses; differences generated by circumstances, positions, mixtures, and quantities; the relativity of experiences; the rarity of some experiences compared with others; and differences between cultural conventions. The last of these is especially interesting because it shows that Aenesidemus was not solely concerned with questions of perceptual knowledge but also tackled issues in ethics. The fact that in some cultures people bury their dead while in others they burn them calls into question the practices of both. That some countries allow men to take multiple wives while in others this is a crime likewise undermines the legitimacy of both customs. Sextus

---

[90] The modes are outlined in Sextus Empiricus, *Pyr.* 1.35–163 (IG III-35, LS 72B-K); see also Diog. Laert. 9.79–88 (IG III-22).

[91] Hippolytus, *Haer.* 9.10.5 (DK 22B61), trans. Waterfield (2000), 39.

[92] This will matter if we are trying to comprehend the nature of the seawater; but if we just want to know whether to drink it or not then naturally it will make sense to prioritize the human perspective.

Empiricus records many other examples like these,[93] all aimed at generating suspension of judgement on moral as well as perceptual issues. Once again it is worth stressing that none of this claimed to *disprove* anything; the issues remained undecided rather than undecidable and, in principle at least, the inquiry continued. However, the fact that the modes were introduced at all as a *method* for generating suspension of judgement suggests that at least some view had already been reached about the likelihood of ever attaining a firm view about anything, even if sceptics such as Sextus would deny this.

The motivation behind this new form of radical scepticism might simply have been an attempt to overcome the inherent contradiction in the emphatic form of scepticism that claims that knowledge is impossible, which is of course itself a truth claim. It might also have been an attempt to re-assert scepticism at a time when the leading members of the Academy were drifting away from it. But our evidence for Aenesidemus records another motivation which helps to explain the invocation of the long-dead Pyrrho: by suspending judgement on everything in this way, the Pyrrhonian will attain complete freedom from disturbance, i.e. tranquillity (*ataraxia*).[94] As with the Epicureans and the Stoics, the Pyrrhonists claimed that the only way to attain a calm and happy life is through a correct understanding of how the world really is, which in this case involves grasping that in fact it is impossible to say with certainty *anything* about how the world really is.

As we have seen, the much later Pyrrhonist Sextus Empiricus presented all this as an alternative to what he called the negative dogmatism of the sceptical Academy. However, there is much in common here with the early Academic scepticism of Arcesilaus. Earlier we saw Arcesilaus explicitly reject Socrates' claim to know nothing. He argued that we ought to affirm nothing at all, not even that we know nothing. According to Cicero, Arcesilaus also proposed counter-balancing arguments of equal weight against each other in order to make it easier to withhold assent.[95] A number of ancient sources describe Arcesilaus as an admirer

[93] See Sextus Empiricus, *Pyr.* 1.145–63 (IG III-35, LS 72K).
[94] See Diog. Laert. 9.107 (B21B in Polito (2014), IG III-22, LS 71A). Another source, Aristocles in Eusebius, *Praep. evang.* 14.18.4 (B21A Polito, LS 1F), says that for Aenesidemus the final outcome was pleasure (*hêdonê*) rather than tranquillity (*ataraxia*).
[95] See Cicero, *Acad.* 1.45 (LS 68A).

of Pyrrho who would have had much in common with revived Pyrrhonism; indeed, one source describes him as a Pyrrhonist in everything but name.[96] Even Sextus himself comments that the 'Middle Academy' of Arcesilaus shared much in common with Pyrrhonism and 'is practically the same as ours'.[97] (His argument, then, was with the 'New Academy' of Carneades.[98]) The contrast between Pyrrhonism and Academic scepticism, then, may not have been quite as pronounced as some traditional accounts used to suggest.[99]

Pyrrho and Timon

All this was presented by Aenesidemus in the name of Pyrrho, but Pyrrho's own view differed significantly from this 'Pyrrhonist' advocacy of suspension of judgement in the face of conflicting appearances. Pyrrho himself seems to have held the view that we ought to hold no beliefs or opinions at all, not because matters are undecided, or even undecidable, but rather because things are in themselves inherently indeterministic, and so any definite claims we make about them will be mistaken. Pyrrho himself wrote nothing and what little we do know about him comes from the now lost works of his pupil Timon. A key source reports the following:

According to Timon, Pyrrho declared that things are equally indifferent, unmeasurable, and inarbitrable. For this reason neither our sensations nor our opinions tell us truths or falsehoods. Therefore for this reason we should not put our trust in them one bit, but we should be unopinionated, uncommitted, and unwavering, saying concerning each individual thing that it no more is than is not, or it both is and is not, or it neither is nor is not.[100]

---

[96] See Numenius in Eusebius, *Praep. evang.* 14.6.4–6 (LS 68F); also Diog. Laert. 4.32–3 (IG III-1, LS 68E).

[97] Sextus Empiricus, *Pyr.* 1.232–4 (IG III-27, LS 68I).

[98] Sextus and some other ancient sources distinguish between the 'Middle Academy' of Arcesilaus and the 'New Academy' of Carneades, and also refer to the 'Fourth Academy' of Philo. However, to complicate matters, Cicero followed Antiochus in referring to all three of these sceptical phases as the 'New Academy'. Compare Sextus Empiricus, *Pyr.* 1.220 (IG III-27) and Cicero, *Acad.* 1.46 (IG III-19, LS 68A).

[99] Recent scholarship has started to highlight the continuities by examining both traditions together; see e.g. Thorsrud (2009) and Bett (2010).

[100] Aristocles in Eusebius, *Praep. evang.* 14.18.2–3 (DC 53, IG III-24, LS 1F), trans. LS. See also Diog. Laert. 9.61 (DC 1A, IG III-22, LS 1A). Part of the text of this passage has

Rather than saying we can have no knowledge at all about things in themselves, Pyrrho claims that we can know one thing, namely that they have this indeterminate nature, which invalidates any other claims we might make about them. He starts with a metaphysical claim (things are indeterminate), and moves from that to an epistemological one (therefore our sensations tell us neither truths nor falsehoods).[101] This might remind us of Heraclitus's claim that everything is constantly changing and Plato's concern that, if this were so, knowledge would become impossible.[102] It is unclear whether Pyrrho was influenced by Heraclitus, but there is evidence to suggest that Aenesidemus might have been.[103] Even if they both were, there remain significant differences between the philosophical positions of Pyrrho and Aenesidemus. In particular, there seems to be no reason to think that Pyrrho would have been concerned with the later 'Pyrrhonist' method of generating suspension of judgement (*epochê*). While the later Pyrrhonists continue the search for knowledge, Pyrrho does not; he already knows that matters are undecidable because things are in themselves indeterminate.

Much of what we know of Pyrrho derives ultimately from his pupil Timon. There is always the possibility that Timon's account of Pyrrho owed as much to Timon's own views as it did to Pyrrho's. Reports suggest that Timon attracted a few pupils, but no real school of Pyrrhonism seems to have established itself after his death.[104] That would have to wait for Aenesidemus; but as we have just seen, it is far from clear that Pyrrho would himself have been a Pyrrhonist.

*   *   *

been disputed; here I follow DC, IG, and LS in accepting the MS reading of *dia touto* ('for this reason'), rather than the emendation of *dia to* ('because') proposed by Zeller (1870), 493. See further Bett (2000), 25. In general I follow the interpretation in Bett (2000), already adopted in Long and Sedley (1987), 16–17.

[101] It is worth noting that the textual emendation proposed by Zeller (see previous note) would reverse the order here, with the epistemological claim coming first (our sensations tell us neither truths nor falsehoods) and the metaphysical one being its consequence (therefore things are indeterminate). Naturally that has significant implications for the interpretation of Pyrrho's philosophy. See again Bett (2000), 25. For a defence of the alternative reading and the epistemological interpretation of Pyrrho see Annas (1993a), 203.

[102] See Plato, *Cratylus* 402a (DK 22A6); cf. Aristotle, *Metaph.* 4.5, 1010a7–15.

[103] See further Bett (2000), 223–32; Schofield (2007); Polito (2004).

[104] See Diog. Laert. 9.115 (IG III-23).

On questions concerning knowledge, there was a clear division between, on the one hand, Epicureans and Stoics, who in different ways affirmed the reliability of the senses, and, on the other, a variety of sceptics doubtful about almost all claims to knowledge. What philosophers on both sides of the divide shared, though, was the view that false beliefs can be pernicious and will ultimately lead to suffering. On that point, at least, there was broad agreement.

3

Nature

In the last chapter we saw that, despite their differences, the Epicureans and Stoics shared some philosophical common ground in so far as they were both committed to versions of empiricism. In this chapter we shall consider their competing conceptions of the physical world, and again, despite significant differences, both schools do at least share something in common: they are both committed to versions of materialism. As in the last chapter, we shall also consider some sceptical objections to both schools, in particular objections to their quite different theologies.

Hellenistic Metaphysics

Before turning to the specifics of Stoic and Epicurean physical theory, it might be worth beginning with some wider comments about metaphysics, the study of what exists. The part of philosophy we now know as metaphysics was formalized just before the Hellenistic period by Aristotle, although the story goes that the word was not coined until much later, around the end of the Hellenistic period, by Andronicus of Rhodes when he placed certain of Aristotle's books *meta ta phusika*, 'after the [books on] physics'.[1] What we now call metaphysics Aristotle called 'first philosophy' (*philosophia prôtê*) and it involved the study of the nature of existence or being—of being *qua* being.[2] To be more precise, we might

---

[1] The role of Andronicus is contested; see further Barnes (1997) and Griffin (2015), esp. 23–32. Alexander of Aphrodisias, *in Metaph.* 171,5–7, suggests that the title does go back to Aristotle, and that it reflects the fact that the study of first philosophy should come after the study of physics, in a philosophical curriculum that culminates with the highest form of knowledge.

[2] See Aristotle, *Metaph.* 4.1, 1003a20–6. I use the word 'existence' here conscious that it may not be wholly appropriate. According to Kahn (2009), 3, the notion of 'being' in Greek philosophy is better understood 'as a verb of predication rather than as an expression of existence'. See further Kahn (1976), reprinted in Kahn (2009), 62–74.

say that it is concerned with what can be said about beings simply in virtue of their being beings. Because entities in the physical world are continually changing and so, on Aristotle's account, are never fully actualized, a central preoccupation of Aristotle's first philosophy is the search for a fully actualized being, an unchanging being. Aristotle thinks there is such an 'unmoved mover' and first philosophy studies this as well, and so includes theology.[3] So, metaphysics studies the nature of what exists (i.e. what can be said about things that exist simply in virtue of their existence) but, as it turns out, what really exists stands in some sense outside of and prior to the changing world of nature, the study of which is reserved for a separate discipline, physics.

The study of metaphysics seems to have continued in the Lyceum during the Hellenistic period, at least at the beginning. Aristotle's immediate successor, Theophrastus, wrote a short treatise on first philosophy (traditionally known under the title *Metaphysics*) in which he broadly follows Aristotle's approach to the subject, but also engages critically with his old teacher's position.[4] Perhaps most interesting, though, is the way in which Theophrastus subtly shifts the focus of debate. Whereas his predecessors defined first philosophy as the study of objects of reason (*noêtoi*) rather than objects of sense (*aisthêtoi*), 'on the ground that these are unmovable and unchangeable', Theophrastus says that he is more concerned with trying to understand the nature of the relationship between these two classes of objects.[5] Dismissive of the idea that mathematical objects have an autonomous existence, or even if they did that they would have much direct connection with Nature, Theophrastus suggests that the fundamental principle apprehended by reason rather than the senses is Aristotle's prime mover, the cause of all movement that is itself unmovable.[6] Thus the task of first philosophy becomes to explain how this unmoving first principle connects with the natural world and generates the change that is Nature's defining feature. As he puts it right at the end of his treatise, 'this is the beginning of the inquiry about the

---

[3] See further Aristotle, *Metaph.* 6.1, esp. 1026a10–32, and 12.8. Inevitably these brief comments cannot begin to do justice to the complexities of Aristotle's account, which among other things admits more than one unmoved mover.

[4] For Theophrastus's *Metaphysics* see Ross and Fobes (1929), Raalte (1993), and Gutas (2010), all containing translations into English. Translations in what follows come from Ross and Fobes, somewhat modified.

[5] See Theophrastus, *Metaph.* 1.1–2.   [6] Theophrastus, *Metaph.* 1.5.

universe (*sumpas*), namely the effort to determine the conditions on which existing things (*ta onta*) depend and the relations in which they stand to one another'.[7] However, in this short text Theophrastus is more concerned with raising questions that need to be considered when doing first philosophy than specifying precisely what he thinks counts as an existing thing.

It is difficult to know to what extent Aristotle's or Theophrastus's writings on first philosophy circulated and how much members of the Lyceum debated with philosophers outside their own school. One thing does seem clear, though: neither Stoic nor Epicurean reflections on metaphysical questions engage very much with the Aristotelian tradition.[8] Instead they draw on earlier Presocratic discussions by philosophers such as Heraclitus, Parmenides, and Democritus.[9] While Theophrastus was grappling with the Platonic-Aristotelian tradition of trying to explain changing Nature by reference to some more fundamental unchanging principle, the metaphysical views of the Stoics and Epicureans deny the existence of any foundational principle outside of Nature. Instead, both schools shift the focus of attention to the idea that only material bodies really exist, although in both cases that big generalization needs to be qualified in different ways.

For the Stoics, only bodies exist.[10] There are no immaterial entities, no universal concepts, only material bodies. Only bodies, they say, can act or be acted upon, and so consequently anything that acts or is acted upon must be a body. That means that even the soul, assumed by some earlier philosophers to be immaterial, must be a body.[11] However, there were a few things that the Stoics acknowledged must exist in some sense even though they clearly cannot be counted as physical bodies. These were

[7] Theophrastus, *Metaph.* 9.34.

[8] Only much later do we see some interaction, right at the end of the period, with the Stoics Athenodorus and Cornutus commenting on Aristotle's *Categories*; see further Griffin (2015), 129–73.

[9] For the Stoic debt to Heraclitus see Long (1975); for the Epicurean debt to Democritus see Bailey (1928).

[10] See e.g. Cicero, *Acad.* 1.39 (*SVF* 1.90, IG II-29, LS 45A) and Sextus Empiricus, *Math.* 10.218 (*SVF* 2.331, IG II-34, LS 27D), although neither quite states it explicitly. The clearest expression, which only alludes to the Stoics rather than naming them, is perhaps Plutarch, *Adv. Col.* 1116b.

[11] See Cicero, *Acad.* 1.39 (LS 45A) and Nemesius, *Nat. hom.* 21,7–10 (*SVF* 1.518, IG II-72, LS 45C).

time, place, void, and meaning or sense.[12] These entities, the Stoics say, do not strictly speaking exist, because they are not bodies, but they are nevertheless in some sense real. They fall under the ontological category of being 'something' (*ti*), which includes both existing bodies and these 'subsisting' incorporeals. The defining characteristic of being 'something' appears to have been being something particular, an individual.[13] So, individual bodies exist, and individual times and places subsist, but universal concepts fall outside this highest ontological category of 'something'. In this way, the Stoics deny the existence or even subsistence of Platonic Ideas or Forms. This puts the Stoics starkly at odds with the Platonic-Aristotelian approach to metaphysics.[14]

The Epicureans also insisted that bodies exist, but alongside this they admitted the existence of void. As Epicurus put it, 'the totality of things is bodies and void'.[15] The bodies that exist for the Epicureans are made up of atoms, the material constituents of all physical objects. To understand the foundations of Epicurean metaphysics we must turn to a quite different philosopher, the Presocratic Parmenides. In what is the foundational text for rationalist metaphysics, Parmenides had argued that what exists must have always existed, because there is no way in which it could have been created out of nothing.[16] Similarly, there is no way in which it could be destroyed into nothing, in part because there is no such thing as nothing. According to Parmenides, the idea of nothing or what 'is-not' is incoherent because, as soon as we try to think of it, it becomes something, namely an object of thought.[17] It is literally impossible to think or speak about nothing, Parmenides claimed. There is only existence, unchanging and eternal. These reflections on the nature of existence or being led Parmenides to deny the reality of movement, change, and plurality.

Atomism developed in response to Parmenides. The earliest atomists, Leucippus and Democritus, embraced some of Parmenides' claims but

---

[12] See Sextus Empiricus, *Math.* 10.218 (*SVF* 2.331, **IG II-34**, **LS 27D**).

[13] See e.g. Syrianus, *in Metaph.* 104,17–21 (**LS 30G**).

[14] On Stoic metaphysics, see further Brunschwig (1994), 92–157, Caston (1999), and Brunschwig (2003).

[15] Epicurus, *Ep. Hdt.* 39 (**IG I-2**, **LS 5A**).

[16] See the fragment of Parmenides' poem in Simplicius, *in Phys.* 145,1–13 (DK 28B8), translated in Waterfield (2000), 59. Compare with Epicurus, *Ep. Hdt.* 38 (**IG I-2**, LS 4A) and Lucretius 1.150.

[17] Parmenides, in Simplicius, *in Phys.* 145,1–13 (DK 28B8).

were not prepared to abandon completely the testimony of the senses. The world we experience is indeed one of plurality and movement, generation and destruction. Is it possible to reconcile this world of experience with Parmenides' insights about the nature of existence? The atomists thought it was if we make one modification: admit the possibility of what 'is-not', i.e. nothingness or void.[18] By positing the reality of void, the atomists were able to reintroduce plurality into the Parmenidean world, for there could be empty spaces between a multiplicity of existing things, which they called 'atoms' (*atomoi*, literally 'uncuttables'). These atoms have the characteristics that Parmenides attributed to existing things: they are ungenerated and indestructible. For the early atomists, then, there are both atoms and void, and the world of plurality and change that we experience via the senses is the product of atoms of different shapes coming together to form aggregates in a variety of arrangements.[19]

A central claim in early atomist and Epicurean metaphysics, then, is the seemingly paradoxical statement that what 'is-not' is, that 'nothing' is in fact something. This is the claim that Parmenides dismissed as nonsensical. We might try to salvage it from obvious self-contradiction by saying something like this: 'nothing' cannot exist in the same sense that 'existence' exists, but it is nevertheless real in some weaker sense. Unfortunately the ancient evidence for both the early atomists and the Epicureans counts against that line of interpretation. Summarizing the early atomists, Aristotle wrote 'what-is (*to on*) has no more existence than what-is-not (*to mê on*), because void exists just as much as solidity (or body, *sôma*)'.[20] Whereas the Stoics were happy to introduce a distinction between existing and subsisting things, placing void among the things that subsist, the atomists insisted on ontological parity between atoms and void.

Our fullest account of Epicurean metaphysics fleshes out the distinction between atoms and void in another way too.[21] Lucretius says that all of Nature comprises two things: bodies and void. That bodies exist we know via the senses. As for void, Lucretius adds that were there not the

---

[18] See Aristotle, *Metaph.* 1.3, 984b4–20 (DK 67A6), trans. in Waterfield (2000), 172.
[19] Aristotle, *Metaph.* 1.3, 984b4–20 (DK 67A6).
[20] Aristotle, *Metaph.* 1.4, 985b7–9, trans. Waterfield (2000), 172.
[21] I refer to Book 1 of Lucretius, esp. 1.146–634.

place and empty space that we call void, bodies would have no location and not be able to move, so void is absolutely necessary.[22] We might say that there must *be* void, and so in one sense nothingness *is*, it exists. But it is clearly a very different sort of thing from bodies. To borrow a distinction from Theophrastus, while bodies are objects of sense, void is an object of reason, that is, not something that we perceive, but something we reason that must exist in the light of what we perceive. In the world of Platonic-Aristotelian metaphysics, objects of reason are accorded a higher status than objects of sense; for the Epicureans, bodies and void are always presented as equally basic and fundamental principles, even if void might have a somewhat paradoxical status of existing nothingness. According to one source, Epicurus called it 'intangible substance' (*anaphês phusis*).[23]

One important way in which Epicurean metaphysics differed from earlier atomism was in its approach to properties of bodies, such as colour, taste, or temperature.[24] Democritus had famously proclaimed 'by convention hot, by convention cold; in reality atoms and void'.[25] That implies that properties such as temperature—and, by extension, colour and taste and so on—are not properties that exist within objects, but rather exist only within our sense-perceptions. Epicurus rejected that view, insisting instead on the reality of these properties of bodies. This is reflected in his move from the Democritean claims that only *atoms* and void exist to his own view that *bodies* and void exist. It is also echoed in his more positive attitude towards the content of our sense-perceptions.[26]

Both the Stoics and Epicureans develop metaphysical positions based on the claim that only material bodies exist, but both also admit the presence/reality/subsistence of some non-material entities as well. However, both reject the Platonic tradition of realism about universals and the idea that changing nature must be underpinned by some external unchanging principle.

---

[22] See Lucretius 1.418–34 (LS 5B) and note also Epicurus, *Ep. Hdt.* 39–40 (IG I-2, LS 5A).
[23] Sextus Empiricus, *Math.* 10.2 (IG I-80, LS 5D), trans. LS.
[24] On this topic see further O'Keefe (2010), 33–40.
[25] Diog. Laert. 9.72 (DK 68B117, IG III-22); cf. Sextus Empiricus, *Math.* 7.135 (DK 68B9).
[26] See Ch. 2 above.

The Stoic Cosmos

In the light of these fundamental metaphysical claims, we can now turn to consider the conceptions of Nature that the Stoics and Epicureans built upon these foundations, beginning with the Stoics.[27]

Because the vast majority of the works written by Stoics in the Hellenistic period are lost, we have to rely on later reports and summaries to get a sense of what they thought. One of the longest and most important of these is in Book 7 of the *Lives and Opinions of the Philosophers* written by Diogenes Laertius, probably sometime in the third century AD. Diogenes offers us a fairly full account of Stoic physics and is a good place to start.[28] He also names many of the now lost works by Zeno, Cleanthes, Chrysippus, and Posidonius upon which his account is based.[29]

The central principle of Stoic physics is the claim that there are two principles (*archai*) in Nature: the active and the passive.[30] These principles are identified with reason (*logos*) and matter (*hulê*) respectively. The active reason within Nature is also identified with God and with fate (*heimarmenê*). Diogenes reports that God created the four traditional elements—fire, water, air, and earth—which together constitute matter.[31] That implies that the active principle in Nature (God, reason) effectively created the passive principle (matter). Indeed, Diogenes goes on to say that at certain times God reabsorbs matter and then generates the world again, in a series of cyclical recurrences.[32]

The cosmos, then, is created and governed by this active, rational principle, identified with God, fate, and also providence (*pronoia*). This rational principle pervades everything, including us. The part of this rational principle that pervades our body is our soul, and so our soul is but a fragment of the divine soul in Nature. Just as they thought there

---

[27] On Stoic physics I note the older studies in Sambursky (1959) and Hahm (1977), the essays by Todd (1978) and Lapidge (1978), both in Rist (1978), the more recent collection of essays in Salles (2009), and the briefer overview in White (2003).

[28] Diog. Laert. 7.132–60 (in full in IG II-20 and extracts in LS 43–54).

[29] See e.g. Diog. Laert. 7.134 (IG II-20). It seems unlikely that all of these works would have been readily available in Diogenes' day, so he was probably relying on an intermediate source.

[30] See Diog. Laert. 7.134 (IG II-20, LS 44B).

[31] See Diog. Laert. 7.136–7 (IG II-20, LS 46B).

[32] See Diog. Laert. 7.137 (IG II-20).

was a central location for the human soul where the mind resides (thought to be the heart, although some did suggest the brain), so too they thought that there was a central location for the ruling part (*hêge-monikon*) of the divine soul permeating Nature, and this was usually taken to be the heaven.[33] The cosmos, then, is a living being, an animal (*zôion*) with a soul (*psuchê*) and reason (*logos*).[34]

The cosmos, conceived as a living being, is a single unified entity and spherical in shape. It is surrounded by an infinite void but there is no void or empty space within it.[35] As we have seen, it had a beginning, and it will also have an end, before being created again. Thus the cosmos as a living being has a life cycle marked by birth, death, and then re-birth.[36] Diogenes reports just one argument that the Stoics made in support of these claims:

> An animal is better than a non-animal;
> nothing is better than the cosmos;
> therefore, the cosmos is an animal.[37]

Other sources report similar arguments that the Stoics made, such as:

> Nothing that is inanimate and irrational can give birth to an animate
>   and rational being;
> but the world does give birth to animate and rational beings;
> therefore the world is animate and rational.[38]

What these arguments tend to have in common is the claim that the cosmos as a whole is the greatest thing there is. Any property that we can find in some part of Nature must therefore also be a property of Nature as a whole, for no part can have greater perfection than the whole. So, if we are intelligent, then so is Nature.[39] These are effectively arguments against what modern philosophers call emergent properties. Consciousness

---

[33] See Diog. Laert. 7.138–9 (*SVF* 1.499, 2.644, EK F23, **IG II-20, LS 47O**). Chrysippus and Posidonius say the heaven; Cleanthes was more specific in suggesting the sun.

[34] See Diog. Laert. 7.139; see also 7.142–3, 7.147 (all **IG II-20**, the last **LS 54A**).

[35] See Diog. Laert. 7.140 (**IG II-20**).

[36] See Diog. Laert. 7.141 (**IG II-20, LS 46J**). However, Panaetius disputed this, claiming that the cosmos is indestructible (7.142), and Boethus denied that the cosmos is a living animal (7.143).

[37] Diog. Laert. 7.143 (**IG II-20**), trans. IG, slightly modified.

[38] Cicero, *Nat. D.* 2.22 (*SVF* 1.112–14, **IG II-23, LS 54G**). Cicero attributes this argument to Zeno.

[39] See Diog. Laert. 7.143 (**IG II-20, LS 53X**).

cannot simply come about through the interaction of unconscious matter, so this line of thought goes, no matter how complex its structure might be. The Stoics never used the word 'consciousness' of course, but it seems implied by their references to sensation (*aisthêsis*) and reason (*logos*), and it is also implied by the general structure of the arguments they used such as the ones quoted above.[40]

Diogenes goes on to report that the Stoics identified the active, rational principle with both fire (*pur*) and breath (*pneuma*).[41] The connection with fire may reflect the influence of Heraclitus, who described the cosmos as an 'everliving fire' (*pur aeizôon*).[42] The identification with breath reflects a common and very old idea about a connection between breath and life, to which we shall return in the next chapter. If there are two characteristics that distinguish a living person from a dead one, they are that a living person breathes and is warm. Thus breath and fire (i.e. heat) became, for the Stoics and others, synonyms for soul understood as that which distinguishes the living from the dead. The fire-breath-soul-reason-active principle of the cosmos permeates everything, as we have seen, which is to say that it is part of a mixture with matter. According to Chrysippus, these two principles are in a complete mixture or blend, and not merely juxtaposed to one another.[43] Diogenes reports the example of a drop of wine poured into the sea, which will become completely blended with the sea to the point of being indistinguishable from it.[44]

This claim raises a number of problems for the Stoics. At first glance it looks as if the two principles effectively lose their own identities and blend to form a new, third entity. That is not problematic in itself, for we never experience undifferentiated matter or soul on their own, only in combination. But it is a problem if the Stoics want to insist, as many of them did, that at certain moments the cosmos comes to the end of its life

---

[40] The English word 'consciousness' may well have been coined in a discussion of this very issue by Ralph Cudworth, in his *The True Intellectual System*, first published in 1678. See further Sellars (2012).

[41] See Diog. Laert. 7.156–7 (**IG II-20**).

[42] Heraclitus, in Clement of Alexandria, *Strom.* 5.105 (DK 22B30). The Stoic Cleanthes wrote a four-volume commentary on Heraclitus; see Diog. Laert. 7.174 (*SVF* 1.481). On Heraclitus and Stoicism see Long (1975).

[43] See Diog. Laert. 7.151 (*SVF* 2.479, **IG II-20, LS 48A**), reporting Book 3 of Chrysippus's lost *Physics*.

[44] Diog. Laert. 7.151. As we shall see, Diogenes may not be quite right to put it this way. See the note in Cherniss (1976), 810.

cycle and all matter is resolved back into the divine soul out of which it was originally created. Indeed, how can the divine soul be the guiding intelligence ruling the cosmos if effectively it no longer exists as a distinguishable entity? We need not worry as much about the second concern: the cosmos is (except at the moment of conflagration) a unified living animal rather than a combination of separable material body and divine soul. But what about the first?

The Stoics addressed this problem by drawing a threefold distinction between i) juxtaposition, ii) fusion, and iii) a mixture or blend.[45] A juxtaposition (*parathesis*) is where the tiny particles of two ingredients that are combined together sit side by side, as the atomists might propose. This is distinct from a fusion (*sunchusis*) in which the ingredients are effectively destroyed and a new entity is created (as, for example, when making bread). The Stoics rejected both of these models by proposing a third model that they called mixture (*mixis*) or, in the case of liquids, blend (*krasis*), in which two ingredients continue to exist and retain their individual qualities.[46] The problem with this third model is that it seems to imply that the two ingredients actually exist in the same place, retaining all their individual qualities, and remaining able to be re-separated in the future. Chrysippus argued, against Aristotle, that a drop of wine in the ocean would survive the process of blending and could, in principle, be extracted from the ocean later.[47] One ancient source reports that it is indeed possible to extract wine from a blend of wine and water by using an oil-drenched sponge.[48] It is this sort of mixture or blend that characterizes the relationship between *pneuma* and matter, the Stoics suggested. It thoroughly permeates things while retaining its

---

[45] Some of the key sources for this are gathered together in LS 48; note in particular Alexander of Aphrodisias, *Mixt.* 216,14–218,6 (*SVF* 2.473, LS 48C). Alexander's treatise is edited and translated in full in Todd (1976). Another key source, Arius Didymus, taken from Stobaeus 1,153,24–155,14 (*Fr. Phys.* 28 in Diels (1879), 463,14–464,8, *SVF* 2.471), is not translated in full in IG or LS (part LS 48D), but can be found translated in Sorabji (1988), 82–3. For further discussion see Sorabji (1988), 79–105.

[46] On the distinction between 'mixture' and 'blend' see Arius Didymus, *Fr. Phys.* 28, in the previous note.

[47] For Chrysippus, see Plutarch, *Comm. not.* 1078e (*SVF* 2.480, LS 48B); for Aristotle's opposed view see *Gen. corr.* 1.10, 328a23–8. There has been some debate about whether Chrysippus was consciously responding to Aristotle, on which see Sorabji (1988), 80–1.

[48] See Stobaeus 1,155,5–11 (part of Arius Didymus, *Fr. Phys.* 28, LS 48D). See also Sorabji (1988), 103, who reports that this has been tested with success in his presence.

own qualities and identity, and can be re-separated at the moment of cosmic conflagration.

Not all Stoics accepted the foregoing account of Nature in all its details. A number of later Hellenistic Stoics, including Diogenes of Babylon, Boethus of Sidon, and Panaetius, rejected the idea of periodic conflagration, perhaps due to some of the difficulties we have just considered. Our source, Philo, claims that they changed their mind away from the orthodox Stoic view under pressure from arguments made by their opponents.[49] Although on its own that might seem like a minor detail, it has potentially far-reaching consequences for the Stoic worldview. If conflagration is denied then the cosmos exists eternally, without birth or death. If that is so, then the whole image of Nature as a living being is called into question, or at least requires radical revision. Indeed, Boethus of Sidon is reported also to have denied that the cosmos is a living being,[50] which looks like a consequence or at least a counterpart of the denial of periodic conflagration and cyclical recurrence. He also located God in the sphere of the fixed stars, although it is not clear if by this he meant simply the ruling part of the divine soul or all of God.[51] Might all of this reflect Peripatetic influence? When Philo refers to the arguments of opponents winning over some Stoics, he is certainly thinking of Peripatetic arguments: immediately before reporting the heterodox views of Diogenes, Boethus, and Panaetius, Philo discusses the views of the Peripatetic Critolaus, and later on in the same work he considers Theophrastus's objections to the Stoic view.[52]

Peripatetic Objections

What arguments did the Peripatetics make against Stoic claims regarding periodic conflagration of the world? Philo reports a number of them,

---

[49] See Philo, *Aet. mund.* 76–8 (part **LS 46P**). Note that this is not the Academic Philo of Larissa, but the Jewish philosopher active in Alexandria in the first century AD.

[50] See Diog. Laert. 7.143 (*SVF* 3.Boeth.6, IG II-20).

[51] See Diog. Laert. 7.148 (**IG II-20, LS 43A**), which refers to the substance of God (*ousia theou*). In the same section Zeno is said to have identified the substance of God with the whole cosmos and the heaven. The implication is that Boethus is saying something quite different, namely that God is only located in the sphere of the fixed stars.

[52] See Philo, *Aet. mund.* 55–75 (parts frr. 12–13 in Wehrli (1969d)) and 117–49 (FHSG 184).

a couple of which I shall discuss here. Critolaus is said to have argued along the following lines:

If the cosmos has been created, the earth must have been so too, and if the earth was created, so certainly must have been the human race, but man is uncreated and his race has existed from everlasting as will be shown, therefore the cosmos also is everlasting.[53]

As a Peripatetic, Critolaus was committed to the view that the human race has existed eternally, each generation having been preceded by their parents, and them by their parents, and so on ad infinitum. He could not conceive how the human race might have developed and evolved out of something else: 'man begets man', as Aristotle said in a number of places,[54] and if that is taken strictly then there is no possibility of evolution from something more primitive. Earlier philosophers, such as Anaximander and Empedocles, had proposed theories of human evolution, but Aristotle was unconvinced and so was Critolaus.[55]

Critolaus took the alternative view to be that humans are a later work of Nature and ultimately generated from the earth. But rather than grapple seriously with the question of whether biological life can develop out of inert matter (a view that, as we have seen, the Stoics rejected), or whether humans could have evolved out of lower animals, he instead refers to an early Greek myth about humans springing from the ground fully grown and wearing armour.[56] Critolaus dismissed this as a mythical fiction, which it clearly is, and no doubt the Stoics would have agreed. Although the opening line of argument is well made, it is hard to take the rest seriously.

A more plausible line of attack attributed to Critolaus—and one that goes to the heart of Stoic claims about God and Nature—goes like this: if the cosmos is indeed an animal with a life cycle involving birth, development, decline, and then momentary death, we ought to expect both physical and mental periods of immaturity followed by maturity. Human

---

[53] Philo, *Aet. mund.* 55 (fr. 13 in Wehrli (1969d); 20A in Sharples (2010)), trans. Colson (LCL), modified.
[54] See Aristotle, *Phys.* 2.1, 193b8; 2.2, 194b13; 2.7, 198a26–7; 3.2, 202a11–12; *Metaph.* 12.3, 1070a27–8.
[55] For Anaximander see DK 12A30 (translated in Waterfield (2000), 17), for Empedocles DK 31B62 (in Waterfield (2000), 152–3), with Aristotle's doubts in *Phys.* 2.8.
[56] See Philo, *Aet. mund.* 57.

beings are born irrational, but grow and develop into rational beings later on. The same must apply to the cosmos as a whole. In other words, in the early stages of each cosmic life cycle one would expect the Stoic God to be irrational and only develop into a perfectly rational being later on.[57] Yet this is clearly something they do not accept. There is a tension, then, between the Stoics' account of God-Nature as a living being and their desire to present God as perfectly rational and everlasting. Perhaps Boethus and the other later Stoics were right to drop the former claim and focus on the latter.

Can we defend the Stoic position against this sort of objection? The way to do it would be to distinguish between i) God conceived as the active rational principle in Nature and ii) the cosmos conceived as a living being made up of divine soul and matter. It is the cosmos that goes through cycles of birth, life, and death, but God is unaffected by those cycles and persists from one to the next, immortal and perfectly rational.[58] At the moment of conflagration all matter is consumed and converted into active principle—i.e. into God—who then creates the cosmos anew. For this to be possible, God must transcend each cosmic life cycle. God's rationality, then, is not subject to the development and decline that marks the life of the cosmos.

Philo records further objections by Critolaus against the Stoic position, such as how the next cosmic cycle begins if everything has been destroyed and nothing remains.[59] His objections bring out some of the tensions that seem to be inherent in Stoic physics. The Stoic desire to posit an immortal and perfectly rational God *within* a dynamic, material Nature generates a whole host of philosophical problems that are not easily resolved. No doubt much time was spent working through these but, alas, the relevant texts are all lost. One thing seems clear, though: there was vibrant debate both within the Stoa and between Stoics and Peripatetics about just how this pantheistic conception of Nature was supposed to work.

Before departing the Peripatetics we might also briefly mention Strato, referred to in antiquity as 'the physicist'.[60] Cicero tells us that he located

---

[57] See Philo, *Aet. mund.* 72–3.
[58] For the Stoic God's immortality see Diog. Laert. 7.147 (**IG II-20, LS 54A**).
[59] See further Philo, *Aet. mund.* 85–8.
[60] See e.g. Diog. Laert. 5.58 (fr. 1 in Sharples (2011)).

divine power in Nature, which might remind us of the Stoic view.[61] However, he claimed that this God within Nature was without sensation, echoing the view of the heterodox Stoic Boethus, and leading a later Stoic to comment that this left God without a mind.[62] At the same time, he agreed with the Epicureans—against both Aristotle and the Stoics—that there could be void within the cosmos, and he appears to have adopted a theory of elements that shared something in common with atomism.[63] Yet he also distinguished his own view from the atomism of Democritus.[64] The evidence is all too fragmentary, but it does seem clear that the Peripatetics were active participants in Hellenistic debates about Nature.

Epicurean Physics

As we saw earlier, Diogenes Laertius is an important source of information about Stoic physics; he is also an invaluable source of knowledge for Epicureanism. In his life of Epicurus in Book 10, Diogenes transcribes a number of letters by Epicurus, one of which gives a summary of Epicurus's physics and was conceived as an epitome of his much longer work *On Nature*. This is the *Letter to Herodotus* and is the obvious place to start.[65]

Our knowledge of Nature comes via the senses, Epicurus says, just as we would expect given his empiricism. This is how we know that bodies exist. Our experience of a plurality of bodies in motion enables us to infer the existence of void. We have no direct experience of void, but the experiences that we do have make it possible and indeed necessary to posit its existence.[66] Fundamentally this is all that there is—bodies and void—and everything that there is in Nature can be explained with reference to these two basic things.

---

[61] See Cicero, *Nat. D.* 1.35 (fr. 33 in Wehrli (1969b), 19A in Sharples (2011)).

[62] See Seneca, quoted in Augustine, *Civ. Dei* 6.10 (fr. 37 in Wehrli (1969b), 22 in Sharples (2011)).

[63] See Stobaeus 1,156,4–6 (fr. 55 in Wehrli (1969b), 26B in Sharples (2011)). On his corpuscular theory see Simplicius, *in Phys.* 788,33–790,29 (fr. 75–7 in Wehrli (1969b), 31 in Sharples (2011)).

[64] See Cicero, *Acad.* 2.121 (fr. 32 in Wehrli (1969b), 18 in Sharples (2011)).

[65] Epicurus, *Ep. Hdt.* (in Diog. Laert. 10.35–83), translated in **IG I-2**, with extracts in **LS 4–19**. On Epicurean physics I note the older studies by Bailey (1928) and Furley (1967) and the more recent overview in Morel (2009).

[66] See Epicurus, *Ep. Hdt.* 39–40 (**IG I-2**, **LS 5A**). Of course some would deny the claim that void is necessary to explain movement, most famously Aristotle who argued against the earlier atomists on this point in *Phys.* 4.6–9.

Bodies are composed of indestructible atoms. The generation and destruction of bodies that we experience is of compounds of atoms, not the atoms themselves, which survive such changes and go on to become constituents of other compounds. The void in which the atoms move about is unlimited in extent, for there is nothing (apart from more atoms and void) that could form a limit to it. The number of atoms within the void is also unlimited, for a finite number in an infinite void would be spread infinitely thin, which would make the formation of compounds impossible.[67]

The variety of different types of bodies that we experience suggests a variety of shapes of atoms, and there are an unlimited number of atoms of each shape.[68] As well as shape, atoms vary in weight and size; they also have a minimum size.[69] Everything that exists is thus a compound of atoms of varying size, shape, and weight. The infinite variety of Nature can be explained by the fact that there are an unlimited number of possible compounds within the unlimited void. Even the cosmos, Epicurus says, which in this context we might take to mean our galaxy, is but one among many possible worlds in the infinite void.[70] However, these are not hypothetical possible worlds; they actually exist somewhere in the far reaches of outer space.

Epicurus's letter offers us a summary of his thinking about Nature. His fuller account was laid out in his major work *On Nature*, which for many centuries was lost, but fragments of which have been recovered from the papyri excavated in Herculaneum.[71] The process of reconstructing and deciphering these fragments is painstaking and we shall not look closely at any here, but one conclusion that scholars have drawn from what they have been able to decipher is that Lucretius's great Epicurean poem, *On*

---

[67] See Epicurus, *Ep. Hdt.* 41–2 (IG I-2, LS 10A).

[68] See Epicurus, *Ep. Hdt.* 42 (IG I-2, LS 12B).

[69] See Epicurus, *Ep. Hdt.* 54 (IG I-2, LS 12D) and 57 (IG I-2, LS 9A). On atoms having a minimum size, see also Lucretius 1.599–634 (LS 9C), who argues that this is necessary to avoid infinite divisibility, which if embraced would unleash some of Zeno of Elea's paradoxes of motion.

[70] See Epicurus, *Ep. Hdt.* 45 (IG I-2, LS 13A). On the plurality of worlds see Warren (2004b).

[71] For an introduction to *On Nature* see Sedley (1998), 94–133. The first fragments were recovered by John Hayter during 1802–6 and there have been many publications since. There is a selection in Arrighetti (1973), 189–418 (i.e. Ar. 23–39), with an Italian translation. Leone (2012) reconstructs Book 2 of *On Nature* with an extensive introduction and a bibliography of further work on the papyri.

the Nature of Things, follows the structure and content of Epicurus's *On Nature* closely.[72] Consequently it looks as if we can be fairly confident that Lucretius's poem offers us a faithful account of Epicurean thought.

Beyond what we have already seen, Lucretius insists on the perpetual movement of atoms, saying that they never come to a rest: everything is in a continual state of change.[73] This movement leads to collisions between atoms and sometimes, if the atoms have complex shapes, they get stuck to each other, generating larger compounds. For an image of what this atomic motion looks like, Lucretius suggests we observe the chaotic movements of dust particles when light shines on them through a window.[74] This, he says, gives us a glimpse of the hidden movements of matter.

The density of atoms is unchanging, with no additions to or subtractions from the total quantity of matter. Consequently the totality of things has never and will never differ dramatically from how it is at the moment.[75] However, that total quantity is unlimited, and within it there is a vast variety of atomic shapes, akin to the variety we see between species and individual animals in the natural world.[76] The number of types of atom must be finite, for an unlimited number of shapes and sizes would entail no upper limit to the size of atoms. Given that, and that the total number of atoms is unlimited, the number of each type of atom must also be unlimited.[77]

Lucretius refers to a number of observable phenomena that he thinks can be explained by reference to the size or shape of atoms: light can shine through translucent materials, whereas water is repelled because light atoms are smaller and can pass through the seemingly solid compound; water flows faster than oil because oil atoms are either larger or have a more complex shape that impedes their movement; and so on.[78] The same works for the other senses too, such as taste: smooth atoms please the tongue while rough ones taste bitter and harsh. Lucretius goes on to offer further examples for sound and smell too, coming to the general conclusion that all pleasant experiences are due to smooth atoms, while anything unpleasant or painful must be due to atoms that are

---

[72] See Sedley (1998), 134–65.   [73] See Lucretius 2.80–111 (**LS 11B**).
[74] See Lucretius 2.112–24 (**LS 11B**).   [75] See Lucretius 2.294–307.
[76] See Lucretius 2.333–80.   [77] See Lucretius 2.478–531 (**LS 12C**).
[78] See Lucretius 2.381–97 (**LS 12F**).

rough in texture.[79] Indeed, all of our sensory experiences ultimately come down to touch, to physical interaction with atoms.[80] The atoms themselves, as we saw with Epicurus, vary in size, shape, and weight, but they do not possess any further qualities. In particular they have no colour, our experience of which is generated by the interaction between the primary qualities of the atoms and our sense organs. The same goes for heat, sound, taste, and smell.[81]

The natural world, then, is simply the product of chance collisions between inert atoms of varying shapes and sizes. As Lucretius puts it,

> . . . nature made this world. The seeds of things
> In random and spontaneous collision
> In countless ways clashed, heedless, purposeless, in vain
> Until at last such particles combined
> As suddenly united could become
> The origins always of mighty things,
> Of earth, sky, sea, and breeds of living creatures.[82]

Given this, Lucretius continues, there is no reason to think that Nature is governed by any kind of divine being.[83] He says that Nature acts by itself, although in the light of what we have seen it would be a mistake to take his personified references to Nature too literally, for there is no single unified Nature in the Epicurean universe, just a plurality of dead atoms in an infinite void.

The Epicurean gods, in order to exist, must be bodies composed of atoms. This is precisely what the Epicureans claimed. Later in his poem Lucretius says that the gods live well beyond the limits of our world, existing as thin films of atoms in a place equally thinly made (another source describes them as 'quasi-corporeal').[84] That thinness makes the gods unable to touch, and so interact with, our world.[85] They have a human form, like the traditional pagan gods, and they live a life of perfect blessedness and tranquillity, uninterested in human affairs and unable to intervene in them, even if they wished.[86] Their tranquillity forms for us

---

[79] See Lucretius 2.422–5.   [80] See Lucretius 2.434–5.
[81] See Lucretius 2.730–864 (part LS 12E).   [82] Lucretius 2.1058–63, trans. Melville.
[83] See Lucretius 2.1090–2 (LS 13D).   [84] See Cicero, *Nat. D.* 1.49 (LS 23E).
[85] See Lucretius 5.146–55 (LS 23L).
[86] See Cicero, *Nat. D.* 1.45–6 (LS 23E); note also (on their tranquillity) Lucretius 6.68–79 (LS 23D).

an image of an ideal life of freedom from care and disturbance. They are certainly nothing to be feared.

One striking feature of Lucretius's account of Epicurean physics is his insistence that the study of Nature will enable people to live happier lives. At the beginning of Book 1 and also in the openings of subsequent books he argues that the study of Nature undermines those traditional superstitious beliefs that generate anxiety and fear in people, such as fear of death or belief in vengeful gods.[87] Atomic theory, then, is an integral part of the Epicurean project of trying to achieve a calm and tranquil life—a life like that of the Epicurean gods.[88]

Hellenistic Theology and Academic Objections

Theology features prominently in Stoic and Epicurean physics, albeit in different ways. For the Stoics, there is no fundamental division between physics and theology, in so far as they are dealing with the same thing. For the Epicureans, a central task of physics is to recast our conception of the gods. Both approaches faced criticisms from the sceptical Academy, many of which are recorded in Cicero's dialogue *On the Nature of the Gods*.[89] There, Cicero allows an Epicurean and a Stoic to outline their views about the gods but subjects both accounts to Academic criticism. The Epicurean and Stoic spokesmen not only outline their own views but also attack each other, and criticize the theological views of earlier philosophers.[90] The Academic spokesman Cotta, presumably reflecting Cicero's own views in part, advances no positive views, as one would expect. The result is a discussion that is dominated by criticism of existing conceptions of the gods, to the point that one might mistake it for a sustained argument for atheism, even though it is highly unlikely that Cicero intended it to be read that way.

---

[87] See e.g. Lucretius 1.62–148, 2.53–4 (LS 21W), 3.14–16, 4.24–5, 5.1–21, 6.43–95 (part LS 23D).

[88] We shall return to the therapeutic role of Epicurean physics in Ch. 9.

[89] Cicero's *Nat. D.* is translated in Walsh (1997), based on the text in Plasberg and Ax (1933). There are important annotated editions of the Latin text in Mayor (1880–5) and Pease (1955–8).

[90] See especially the Epicurean Velleius's lengthy criticisms at *Nat. D.* 1.18–42 (part LS 13G).

Cicero's discussion opens with Epicureanism. Epicurus has often been judged to be a closet atheist, retaining the gods within his philosophy simply for the sake of appearances. Even in antiquity, others such as the Stoic Posidonius accused Epicurus of being an atheist.[91] His extant letters say relatively little about the gods and the same goes for Lucretius's *On the Nature of Things*, which refers to them only to insist that they are not responsible for either the creation or the management of the cosmos.[92] That, combined with the repeated warnings against superstitious beliefs about the gods (*religio*), has led some to see Lucretius's poem as practically a hymn to atheism, even if on paper at least the gods are still there, albeit doing very little.[93] Cicero's account of Epicurean attitudes towards the gods is more complex. It opens with the Epicurean spokesman Velleius dismissing all previous philosophical accounts of divine being(s) as nonsensical.[94] Much of this is directed against the Stoics, but various Presocratics, Plato, and Aristotle are all targeted. By the end one might expect Velleius to conclude—in harmony with the image of Epicureans as closet atheists—that all notions of a divine being are incoherent.

In fact, Velleius continues by insisting that *everyone* believes in the gods. We all have a natural conception of the gods—an innate idea (in Epicurean technical vocabulary, a *prolêpsis*)—and the ubiquity of this belief, Epicurus had argued, suggests that the gods do in fact exist.[95] A similar appeal to widespread popular opinion is made in determining the essential characteristics of divine beings: everyone agrees that they are blessed and immortal, and everyone agrees that they possess human form.[96] It is on the basis of accepting these widely held views that the Epicureans then elaborate their own conception of the gods. If they are blessed then they are tranquil, which counts against them playing an active role in the management of the cosmos. If they have human form— which is plausible if they are rational beings, given that humans are the only rational creatures with which we are familiar—then they will have

---

[91] See Cicero, *Nat. D.* 1.123 (EK F22a); note also, later, Sextus Empiricus, *Math.* 9.58.

[92] See e.g. Lucretius 2.167–83 and 1090–1104 (LS 13D).

[93] If one defines atheism—as many would today—as the denial of the existence of *supernatural* beings, then the Epicureans were atheists, for their gods were physical creatures, albeit immortal ones.

[94] See Cicero, *Nat. D.* 1.18–42 (part LS 13G).

[95] See Cicero, *Nat. D.* 1.43–4 (IG I-16, LS 23E).

[96] See Cicero, *Nat. D.* 1.45–6 (IG I-16, LS 23E).

bodies of flesh and blood made out of atoms, similar to ours.[97] Perhaps unexpectedly, there will be as many gods as there are mortal beings, in order to maintain a balance between the two.[98]

It is difficult to know what to make of the Epicurean view. The only argument made *for* the existence of the gods is from widespread popular opinion. That is a deeply unsatisfactory way to argue for something. In any case, as Cotta is quick to point out, it is not true that *everyone* believes in the gods, a point illustrated by some of Velleius's own earlier examples.[99] It is interesting to note that here Cotta refers to the agnosticism of Protagoras, who is reported to have said, 'I cannot say whether gods exist or not'.[100] Cotta quickly adds that for this cautious scepticism Protagoras was banished by the Athenians, and then he says, 'I personally think that this precedent induced many to be more reluctant to declare similar convictions, for mere expressions of doubt could not guarantee them immunity from punishment'.[101] Should we take this as a comment on Epicurus? Whatever Epicurus himself may have thought about the gods, perhaps he had no choice but to affirm their existence. That might explain why the only argument given for their existence is from widespread popular belief. Cotta, for his part, and by extension perhaps Cicero himself, repeats the view that 'Epicurus gave merely nominal assent to the gods' existence, while dispensing with them in reality, to avoid incurring the Athenians' displeasure'.[102] But he concludes by rejecting this assessment and puts the difficulties with Epicurean theology down to philosophical ineptitude rather than political caution. That should not surprise us, given that Cotta is engaged in a polemic against Epicureanism, but the fact he felt the need explicitly to reject the 'closet atheist' interpretation suggests that it was already in circulation (it was at least voiced by Posidonius, as we have seen).

Cicero's contemporary, the Epicurean Philodemus, wrote an extended defence of Epicurus against charges of impiety, a work on which Cicero

---

[97] We are told that they are 'quasi-corporeal', containing 'quasi-blood'; see Cicero, *Nat. D.* 1.49 (IG I-16, LS 23E). For further discussion of Epicurean theology see the contrasting views in Konstan (2011) and Sedley (2011), both in Fish and Sanders (2011).

[98] See Cicero, *Nat. D.* 1.50 (IG I-16).   [99] See Cicero, *Nat. D.* 1.62–3.

[100] Cicero, *Nat. D.* 1.63 (DK 80A23); for Protagoras see also Diog. Laert. 9.51 (DK 80B4); Sextus Empiricus, *Math.* 9.56 (DK 80A12); Plato, *Theaetetus* 162d–e (DK 80A23).

[101] Cicero, *Nat. D.* 1.63.   [102] Cicero, *Nat. D.* 1.85.

may have drawn when writing *On the Nature of the Gods*.[103] It is called
On Piety and probably drew on the work of Philodemus's Epicurean
teacher in Athens, Zeno of Sidon.[104] It includes an extended discussion
from an Epicurean perspective of the nature of the gods and responds to
charges that Epicurus was an atheist. Philodemus reports that in Book 12
of his *On Nature*, Epicurus reproached Prodicus, Diagoras, and Critias
(all of whom had reputations as *atheoi* in antiquity) for their disbelief.
According to Philodemus, Epicurus said that these atheists 'rave like
lunatics', and he admonished them 'not to trouble or disturb us'.[105] This
perhaps offers a key to understanding Epicurus's attitude. Holding
controversial beliefs that stand against widespread popular opinion
runs the risk of generating suspicion, conflict, and in the worse cases
banishment (Protagoras), or even execution (Socrates, charged with
introducing new gods). None of this is conducive to or compatible
with a life of Epicurean tranquillity. As we shall see later, Epicurus
argued that one ought not to break the law even when it seems possible
to do so without detection, because the anxiety of being caught at some
point in the future will be too unsettling.[106] One can imagine him making
a similar argument about holding heterodox religious views.[107] (It is
worth remembering that in antiquity religion was a public and social
affair, and not merely a matter of private belief.)

The Stoics, by contrast, were on less ambiguous theological ground,
although, as we shall see, their position was also not without its problems.[108] Cicero's Stoic spokesman, Balbus, opens like his Epicurean
counterpart by asserting that there is general agreement that the gods
exist.[109] However, his exposition quickly shifts without comment from

[103] In the nineteenth century Hermann Diels printed the two works in parallel columns
to highlight their similarities. One may have drawn on the other or they may both have
relied on a common source. See Diels (1879), 529–50.
[104] The text was recovered from the papyri at Herculaneum. For a painstaking reconstruction of the fragmentary text, along with a translation and commentary, see Obbink
(1996), and esp. 1–23 for a discussion of Epicurus and religion. On Philodemus's debt to
Zeno see 17–18.
[105] Philodemus, *Piet.* 19,519–33 (Obbink (1996), 142–3; cf. Us. 87, Ar. 27.2, **LS 23H**).
[106] See Ch. 8 below.
[107] However, it is worth noting that in *Ep. Men.* 123 (**IG I-4, LS 23B**) Epicurus asserts
that the gods are *not* as most people conceive them.
[108] On Stoic theology see Algra (2003) and, more fully, Meijer (2007).
[109] See Cicero, *Nat. D.* 2.12 (**IG II-23, LS 54C**); in 2.13–15 he outlines four reasons for
this, which he credits to Cleanthes (and so is *SVF* 1.528).

the gods of traditional pagan religion to a single god. We are offered a number of arguments in support of the claim that some kind of creator god must exist. According to Chrysippus, things in Nature that could not have been created by humans, such as heavenly bodies, must have been created by some superior being. Moreover, Nature as a whole is beautiful and well organized, exhibiting all the characteristics of having been designed.[110] Balbus also offers the following argument:

Yet beyond all doubt no existing thing is better, more outstanding, or more beautiful than the universe, indeed, not only is there nothing better, but there is nothing conceivably better. Now if there is nothing better than reason and wisdom, these qualities must exist in that which we concede is best of all.[111]

At first glance this looks like an ontological argument, prefiguring the famous ontological argument of Saint Anselm that defines God as 'something than which nothing greater can be thought'.[112] Anselm's aim was to show that once we grasp the concept of God we shall be unable to deny his existence. The argument that Balbus presents is different: we already know that the universe (*mundus*, i.e. *kosmos*) exists; but if the universe is, by definition, the greatest thing there is (and so nothing greater can be thought), then it must possess all the features that belong to superior things. Thus the universe must be wise and rational; by extension it must also be alive and possess sensation.[113] So, whereas Anselm's argument is about establishing the existence of something, Balbus's Stoic argument is about attributing properties to something we already know to exist.

Despite that difference, the Stoics have also been credited with devising an Anselm-style ontological argument. In particular, Diogenes of Babylon has been proposed as the inventor of the traditional ontological argument. He appears to have argued that i) it is reasonable to honour the gods, and ii) it would not be reasonable to honour 'those who are not of such a nature to exist', so iii) the gods *are* of such a nature to exist.[114]

---

[110] See Cicero, *Nat. D.* 2.16–17 (*SVF* 2.1012, **IG II-23**).
[111] Cicero, *Nat. D.* 2.18 (**IG II-23**).
[112] Anselm, *Proslogion* 2, in Charlesworth (1965), 117.
[113] See Cicero, *Nat. D.* 2.22 (*SVF* 1.112–14, **IG II-23, LS 54G**).
[114] See Sextus Empiricus, *Math.* 9.133–6 (**LS 54D**), which I paraphrase here, drawing on the analysis in Brunschwig (1994), 170–89, esp. 172–3. See also, more recently, Papazian (2007).

The text reporting Diogenes' argument is especially complex and scholars have yet to reach a consensus about it.[115] We might note that it does not quite take the extra step from 'the gods are of such a nature to exist' to 'therefore the gods do exist', although perhaps this was thought to be implicitly obvious. It is also noteworthy that this argument is about the gods (plural) and not a single supreme entity nothing greater than which can be thought.

Stoic theology, then, begins with the self-evident fact of the existence of the universe and proceeds to deify it by attributing superlative qualities to it using the argument that the universe is, by definition, the greatest thing there is. Balbus continues his exposition by reporting a number of arguments he attributes to Zeno and Chrysippus that lead to the identification of God with Nature. These include some of the arguments that we saw earlier aimed at denying the existence of emergent properties. If nothing is better than Nature as a whole, and human attributes such as sensation, reason, wisdom, and virtue are better than their opposites, then Nature must possess these attributes too. If we distinguish living things from inanimate objects by the fact that the former are self-moving and the latter require an external force to propel them, then the universe must be alive, given that there are no forces external to it.[116] Thus, if anything deserves the name 'God', it is Nature; there are no other plausible candidates.

Beyond this identification of Nature with God, the Stoics also described the stars as gods. The consistent and regular movement of heavenly bodies suggests that they are guided by reason, not chance, Balbus argues.[117] They also held on to the traditional pantheon of pagan gods, but rejected traditional myths about them and tried to re-describe them in terms of natural processes.[118] On this, the Stoics were close to the Epicureans, rejecting superstitious beliefs but holding on to the traditional gods transformed to accord with their own philosophical system. Balbus also insists that the universe is ordered by divine intelligence 'for the welfare and preservation of all'.[119] However, the ensuing description of the providential ordering of Nature makes it clear that humans are the

---

[115] See Brunschwig (1994) for a survey of earlier opinions. It is worth noting that Brunschwig himself denies that it is a genuinely ontological argument.
[116] See Cicero, *Nat. D.* 2.31–2.   [117] See Cicero, *Nat. D.* 2.43 (IG II-23).
[118] See Cicero, *Nat. D.* 2.63–4.   [119] Cicero, *Nat. D.* 2.132 (IG II-23).

principal beneficiaries: 'As for the pig, what role has it other than to become our food?'[120] All these things have been provided for us by 'the gods', Balbus asserts, although by this point it is far from clear which gods he means. Perhaps he is referring to the traditional gods, re-interpreted as natural processes, which are in turn expressions of divine Nature.

Cotta's response to all this is unsurprisingly dismissive. He is sceptical about the whole enterprise of trying to provide rational foundations for belief in God, insisting instead that one ought simply to accept the beliefs of one's forebears. He is also unimpressed by the Stoic arguments attributing reason and sensation to Nature; after all, that kind of argument could be used to attribute any and every characteristic imaginable to Nature, from literacy to musical talent.[121] The idea that the gods must be responsible for the coherence and harmony in Nature he also rejects, suggesting instead that these might be the product of the force of Nature itself. Of course this misses the central point of the Stoic account of God, namely that he *is* the force within Nature that brings these things about. Balbus's attempt to recount the Stoic conception of God and to address the role of the traditional gods in tandem has no doubt generated some confusion.

The most philosophically interesting objections, though, are those that Cotta attributes to Carneades, who questioned the consistency of claiming both that God is immortal and a body. By definition, no physical entity can be everlasting, because all bodies are composed of elements and prone to division and ultimately destruction. Consequently no body can be immortal. If God is immortal (as the Stoics claim), then it cannot be identified with Nature, a body.[122] The same applies to living creatures: how can the Stoic God be both immortal and a biological organism? Cotta writes, 'we cannot encounter any living creature which was never born and which will live for ever',[123] although this fails to take into account that the Stoic God does have its life cycle between periodic conflagrations. But he has separate concerns about that doctrine, not least how it is that the Stoic God can create the universe effectively out of himself, given that at the point of conflagration all matter is supposedly converted into divine breath (*pneuma*).[124] Cotta is equally dismissive of the Stoic attempts to explain the traditional gods with reference to

---

[120] Cicero, *Nat. D.* 2.160 (IG II-23).   [121] See Cicero, *Nat. D.* 3.23.
[122] See Cicero, *Nat. D.* 3.29–31.   [123] Cicero, *Nat. D.* 3.32.
[124] See Cicero, *Nat. D.* 3, a fragment preserved in Lactantius, *Div. inst.* 2.9.14.

natural processes. He suggests that Zeno, Cleanthes, and Chrysippus generated for themselves 'unnecessary difficulties in seeking to make sense of lying fables'.[125] Again, it seems that the attempt to accommodate the traditional gods alongside the single Stoic God probably generated more problems than it solved.

The Stoic approach to theology, as it is presented by Cicero at least, looks hopelessly confused. The formal philosophical arguments attribute life and intelligence to Nature: Nature *is* God. But the order and beauty of Nature show that it must have been designed by God, so Nature was created *by* God. Within Nature the heavenly bodies are gods, so there are gods *within* God. The gods that most people talk about—and the ones with which Cicero's dialogue is concerned—are merely superstitious names for natural entities and processes; those gods do not really exist at all. What are we to make of this? The later Platonist Plotinus accused the Stoics of bringing God into their philosophy simply for the sake of appearances.[126] That may be true to the extent that the name 'God' is not essential to their thinking, but it is beyond doubt that the Stoics held that Nature is alive and intelligent, organizing and directing things according to a rational and providential plan. Given those attributes, it is unsurprising that Chrysippus said, 'what better name can be ascribed to this than God?'.[127]

There are, however, further complications we ought to take into account. The perfection of the Stoic God means that whatever happens is an expression of that perfection and could not happen other than it does. The providential ordering of Nature may be an expression of God's will, but it is also deterministic to the point that the Stoic God is unable to act otherwise.[128] When put in those terms, the Stoic view sounds decidedly odd, but if we remember that God is simply another name for Nature, then we can, if we choose, drop all reference to God and talk simply in terms of natural processes instead. The 'divine providence' that pervades Nature is merely another name for the chain of physical causes. Nature is an intelligent, dynamic system, fundamentally alive rather than inert, but perhaps not really divine in any sense that would be meaningful to theologians then or since.

---

[125] Cicero, *Nat. D.* 3.63.   [126] See Plotinus, *Enn.* 6.1.27 (*SVF* 2.314).
[127] Cicero, *Nat. D.* 2.16 (*SVF* 2.1012, **IG II-23**, **LS 54E**).
[128] See Seneca, *QNat.* 1 Praef. 3 for a later Stoic comment on this.

Cicero on the Gods

What about Cicero's own views on all this? In the opening prologue of *On the Nature of the Gods* in which he speaks in his own voice, he explicitly identifies himself as an Academic.[129] Although he also says there that he is happy to embrace what is plausible,[130] even if not demonstrably true (following one interpretation of Carneades), in the ensuing dialogue the Academic Cotta repeatedly says that the issue is too complex for him to hold any view at all.[131] However, in the final line of the whole work Cicero concludes in his own voice by saying that the Stoic view 'seemed to come more closely to a semblance of the truth'.[132] Is he saying that the Stoic position is plausible enough to embrace? It is not entirely clear whether Cicero himself thought that the gods' existence (Stoic or otherwise) was plausible, or that the matter was simply too opaque to make any kind of judgement. What is much clearer, though, is that he thought that religion had a useful social function. In his own voice he says that 'it is conceivable that, if reverence for the gods is removed, trust and the social bond between men and the uniquely pre-eminent virtue of justice will disappear'.[133] Later, in a passage that might conceivably reveal his own view, he has Cotta say:

> though I believe that our ritual and our state-observances should be most religiously maintained, I should certainly like to be persuaded of the fundamental issue that gods exist, not merely as an expression of opinion but as a statement of truth; for many troubling considerations occur to me which sometimes lead me to think that they do not exist at all.[134]

Cicero the sceptic may have his doubts; Cicero the politician thinks that such doubts ought to remain firmly in the private sphere.

*   *   *

In the Introduction I commented that both the Stoics and Epicureans can sometimes look surprisingly modern, given their commitments to both empiricism and materialism. That impression is tempered somewhat by

---

[129] See Cicero, *Nat. D.* 1.12.

[130] Cicero uses the word *probabilis*, which Rackham (LCL) and Walsh (1997) both translate as 'probable'. But if Cicero has the Greek word *pithanos* in the back of his mind, then 'plausible' or 'persuasive' may be more appropriate.

[131] See e.g. Cicero, *Nat. D.* 1.60, 2.2.   [132] Cicero, *Nat. D.* 3.95.

[133] Cicero, *Nat. D.* 1.4.   [134] Cicero, *Nat. D.* 1.61.

their theological views, quite different from each other but equally striking to modern readers, and both taking the existence of gods to be self-
evident. Carneades' scepticism towards these views may also strike some
as surprisingly modern, perhaps more so than the views of his dogmatic
adversaries, and the sort of thing one might not expect to encounter until
the eighteenth-century Enlightenment. Indeed, one of the most famous
discussions of religion in the eighteenth century, David Hume's *Dialogues
Concerning Natural Religion*, was inspired by Cicero's *On the Nature of
the Gods*, and there Hume debates the views of the Hellenistic schools.[135]
Via Hume and others, these Hellenistic ideas were vital sources in shaping
what we now think of as very modern attitudes towards both the natural
world and religion.

---

[135] See Hume (1779). Hume's characters in the dialogue include 'Cleanthes' and
'Philo'.

4

The Self

It might seem potentially anachronistic to talk about the way in which Hellenistic philosophers thought about the 'self'. We might more naturally ask the question how they conceived the 'soul'.[1] But the language of 'souls' does not fit comfortably with debates in contemporary philosophy and can often sound outdated, if not irrelevant, as well as having religious connotations that might distract us. Consequently some scholars of ancient philosophy prefer to talk about Hellenistic 'philosophy of mind'.[2] In many ways, this makes good sense and shows how Hellenistic philosophers contributed answers to problems that still preoccupy philosophers today. However, one problem with talking about 'philosophy of mind' in this period is that, for the Stoics and Epicureans at least, the discussion is as much about the body as it is about the mind (this is also true for some modern philosophers whose work gets classified in the same way). Moreover, thinking about the 'self' gives the opportunity to consider a broader range of topics than are usually considered in philosophy of mind. So, in what follows we shall consider a loosely related set of questions about the nature of human beings, the relationship between mind and body, and what it means to be a person.

What does it mean to be a person, to be a human being, to be conscious, to be alive? Ancient discussions of these sorts of questions make reference to the role of *psuchê*, traditionally translated as 'soul'. Given the religious connotations that 'soul' can have in English, this may

---

[1] When Socrates exhorted people 'to take care of the self' he either used the reflexive 'oneself' (*heautou*) or referred to the 'soul' (*psuchê*). See e.g. Plato, *Alcibiades I* 127e and *Apology* 30a–b, with discussion in Sellars (2003), 36–9.

[2] See e.g. Annas (1992). Despite my passing aside about the title, this book is highly recommended. Another book I highly recommend is Gill (2006), who opts for 'self' when discussing these topics.

not be the best translation. For some ancient philosophers, in particular Platonists, that might not cause too many problems. However, for the Epicureans and Stoics, translating *psuchê* as 'soul' runs the risk of introducing all sorts of confusions, although, like many other modern commentators, I shall continue to use it given the lack of a better alternative. But before we turn to them, it might be useful to examine this term *psuchê* a little more.

The term *psuchê* refers to that by virtue of which a living being is alive. It is that which animates a living being. In fact, the English word 'animate' comes from the Latin *anima*, which is the usual Latin equivalent for *psuchê*, and 'animator' has been proposed as an English translation of *psuchê*.[3] So *psuchê* is much broader than 'soul' or 'mind', as it is something shared by all living beings, whether conscious or not. (As we shall see, for the Stoics it is broader still.) If it is that by virtue of which a living being is alive, then death is the product of its destruction or departure from the body. A corpse is a body without *psuchê*. In early Greek thought the *psuchê* was thought to be immortal, living on after its departure from the body.[4] Consequently it came to be associated with what we might call the 'essential self'. Among early Greek philosophers, Pythagoras is reported to have held this view,[5] and it was repeated by Plato.[6] In this tradition, the *psuchê* is something different in kind from the body, incorporeal and immortal. We are not our bodies.

The Epicureans and Stoics take a quite different view. As we have already seen, both schools hold that only physical things exist, whether atoms moving within a void or bodies conceived as parts of a larger continuum of matter. Consequently both schools face the challenge of trying to define what distinguishes a living being from a dead being in purely physical terms. But it also means that, whatever solution they come up with, there is no reason in principle why the body cannot itself be part of what we are as human beings.

---

[3] See e.g. Barnes (1982), 65, with reference to Aristotle.

[4] On early Greek thoughts about *psuchê*, death, and immortality see Rohde (1925) and Onians (1951). For a briefer and more recent overview, see Long (2015).

[5] See e.g. Porphyry, *Vit. Pyth.* 19,6–13 (DK 14A8a), translated in Waterfield (2000), 98–9.

[6] See e.g. Plato, *Phaedo* 105c–e.

Epicurean Souls

For Epicurus, whatever 'we' are, we are made of atoms.[7] Our bodies are nothing more than conglomerations of atoms. The difference between a living human body and a dead one will either come down to a difference in the way in which the atoms that make up the body are arranged, or to the absence or presence of some element that must also ultimately be made of atoms. Epicurus, as he tells us himself in his *Letter to Herodotus*, opted for the second of these:

The soul is a body [made up of] fine parts distributed throughout the entire aggregate, and most closely resembling breath with a certain admixture of heat, in one way resembling breath and in another resembling heat.[8]

He goes on:

There is also the part which is much finer than even these [components] and because of this is more closely in harmony with the rest of the aggregate too.[9]

So, the soul is made up of fine atoms that resemble breath and heat, with some atoms that are even finer. On its own, this does not tell us very much. Another source adds some detail by saying that the soul is a blend of four things, presumably four types of atom.[10] These are 'fire-like', 'air-like', 'wind-like', and the fourth is unlike anything else and remains unnamed. It is this last type that is responsible for sensation. Presumably 'fire-like' atoms are responsible for the heat mentioned by Epicurus and 'air-like' and 'wind-like' might both provide the breathy characteristics. That leaves the fourth type, which are presumably the finest atoms that Epicurus mentions last. These four types of atom come together in a special blend generating a single nature.[11] It is this blended single nature that is distributed throughout the body, giving it heat, breath, and sensation—the essential features that distinguish a living human body

---

[7] For further reading on the Epicurean theory of the soul see e.g. Annas (1992), 123–56; Everson (1999); Gill (2006), 46–66; Konstan (2008); Németh (2017).

[8] Epicurus, *Ep. Hdt.* 63 (**IG I-2, LS 14A**), trans. IG.

[9] Epicurus, *Ep. Hdt.* 63. I omit IG's '<third>', which translates a conjecture by Diels, printed in the OCT edition of Diogenes Laertius, but omitted from the more recent edition in Dorandi (2013).

[10] See Aetius 4.3.11 (Us. 315, **IG I-95, LS 14C**). See also Plutarch, *Adv. Col.* 1118d–e (Us. 314, **IG I-29**).

[11] See Lucretius 3.265, 270 (**LS 14D**).

from a dead one. The things that we might associate with soul or mind—
sensation, consciousness—are due to the presence of the unnamed
fourth type of soul atom. Thus, the properties that a body has reflect
its underlying atomic composition.

In his own brief account, Epicurus focuses on the blended soul rather
than its constituents, and he says that the soul as a whole is responsible
for sensation (*aisthêsis*). When the soul departs the body, the body no
longer has sensation, and in principle the soul could take its power of
sensation with it, if it could survive the body. In fact, however, the soul is
destroyed along with the body. When the aggregate of atoms forming the
body is destroyed, the fine atoms of the soul spread throughout it are
dispersed along with the rest.[12] In any case, Epicurus says that it is
impossible to imagine what sensation would be like for a soul separated
from the body's sense organs.[13]

To those who insist that the soul must be incorporeal, Epicurus replies
by saying that the only thing we can conceive of that is not corporeal is
the void. But the void cannot act or be acted upon in the way the soul
can. Therefore the soul cannot be incorporeal.[14] (The unstated premise
here is that only bodies can act or be acted upon, a view shared by the
Stoics.) Indeed, not only can the soul act and be acted upon, but it acts
upon our body and is in turn altered by our body, and the simplest
explanation of how this is possible is that the soul is also a body.[15]

Lucretius on Mind-Soul-Body

Epicurus's own account amounts to little more than a couple of paragraphs in his *Letter to Herodotus*. Fortunately we have a much fuller
account that survives intact in Book 3 of Lucretius's *On the Nature of
Things*.[16] Lucretius's principal concern throughout his poem is to remove
human suffering caused by superstitions concerning the gods and fear of

---

[12] See Epicurus, *Ep. Hdt.* 63–5 (IG I-2, **LS 14A**).
[13] See Epicurus, *Ep. Hdt.* 66 (IG I-2, **LS 14A**). Epicurus does not explicitly mention the
sense organs but it seems obvious that this is part of what is implied. Lucretius does
mention them explicitly at 3.624–33 (**LS 14G**).
[14] See Epicurus, *Ep. Hdt.* 67 (IG I-2, **LS 14A**).
[15] See Lucretius 3.161–76 (**LS 14B**).
[16] See esp. Lucretius 3.94–829. The remainder of Book 3, lines 830–1094, deals with fear
of death, a topic we shall discuss in Ch. 7.

death, and he is explicit about this therapeutic goal more than once. It is within this context that he discusses the nature of the human soul. He opens by insisting on the soul's materiality, has an extended discussion of its mortality, and concludes by challenging traditional fears about death. The mind (*animus*, *mens*), he says, is a part of a human being in the same way that a hand or a foot is a part.[17] It is not, despite what some other philosophers might claim, a feature of the human being as a whole, without specific location.[18] It is worth noting here that Lucretius is not talking about the soul (*anima*) as a whole but rather just the mind (*animus*), which is a part of the soul. Although the soul is distributed throughout the body, the mind, Lucretius says, has a specific location within the human body, and that location is the chest. Although now we might be more inclined to locate it in the head, in antiquity it was far more common to locate the mind in the chest, associating it with the heart rather than the brain, because the heart was taken to be the seat of the emotions.

The mind (*animus*), then, is located in the chest and is that by virtue of which we experience and think; the soul (*anima*) is distributed throughout the body and is that by virtue of which we are alive. Neither is the product of 'harmony', he says, which we might gloss as the structure or organization of the matter that makes up the body;[19] instead both are substantial entities, which is to say they are made out of atoms. Indeed, they are, he suggests, better considered as a single entity (*una natura*), with the mind being the commanding part of the soul.[20]

The mind and soul must be material, Lucretius says, because they act on and are acted upon by the body. This echoes the argument we saw earlier in Epicurus. Here the argument is slightly expanded, though, because it makes specific reference to touch. Things act and are acted upon by touch; only material things can touch one another; the mind-soul acts and is acted upon; therefore, the mind-soul is a material thing.[21] The atoms that make up the mind and soul must be especially smooth and small, he suggests: smooth to enable them to move very quickly

---

[17] See Lucretius 3.94–7.
[18] Here Lucretius may be responding to certain Peripatetics, perhaps Aristoxenus; see Bailey (1947), ii, 1003–5.
[19] See Lucretius 3.100 and 118.
[20] See Lucretius 3.136–7 (**LS 14B**) and 421–4 (**LS 14F**).
[21] See Lucretius 3.161–76 (**LS 14B**).

through the body, given how quickly the mind works; and small because when someone dies and the soul escapes the body there is no noticeable loss of weight. Of course, the fact that there is no noticeable reduction in the body at death might be taken as a very good reason to reject Lucretius's claim that the soul is a material component within the body. Although his attempt to get round this may seem a bit weak, he was at least conscious that it was an objection that needed answering.

The material mind-soul is a unity, but it is made up out of different types of atoms. Lucretius mentions heat, breath, and air, along with a fourth unnamed element, which is responsible for sensation.[22] This, of course, echoes the account we saw attributed to Epicurus earlier. The fourth nameless element Lucretius describes as a soul within a soul.[23] It is the component of the soul that is essential for the soul's most characteristic feature—sensation—just as the soul is essential for a living being's most obvious feature—being alive. Lucretius can offer no empirical evidence for the presence of this special type of atom within the material soul, so what type of argument, if any, does he give for its existence? His line of reasoning goes something like this. We have a whole series of good reasons to suppose that everything, including human beings, is made up of atoms and nothing else; human beings have the power of sensation; it is not credible to think that sensation arises from the mere organization of atoms; therefore, there must be a special type of atom that makes sensation possible. It is the fact of sensation combined with his pre-existing commitment to atomism that leads him to posit the existence of this otherwise mysterious and unnamed fourth element in the soul.

Lucretius also repeats Epicurus's claim that the soul and body cannot be split apart, or at least not without death for both.[24] The soul is not immortal—it is born with and it dies with the body. The fact that the soul is affected by illness and old age, just as the body is, suggests that the soul too is corruptible and ultimately mortal. If the mind in particular could be separated from the body, it would in any case not be able to experience anything, for it would not have the body's sense organs on which it depends. If it were immortal, we might expect some trace memory of past lives, but Lucretius insists there is no trace. Without any continuity

---

[22] See Lucretius 3.228–42.   [23] See Lucretius 3.280–1 (LS 14D).
[24] See Lucretius 3.323–36, 548–57.

of memory, we might as well say that the previous soul has died and a new one has been created.[25] In total Lucretius offers over a dozen distinct arguments for the mortality of the soul.[26] It is possible that all of these ultimately come from Epicurus himself. What is clear, though, is that Lucretius thought proving this was an important part of his philosophical project, namely overcoming the fear of some unknown post-mortem existence.

The foregoing references to 'soul atoms' might lead one to think these atoms have some special, magical property that makes consciousness possible, but they do not. They are as dead as all the other atoms. Consciousness, and indeed life itself, is an emergent property generated by the interaction of inert matter. As Lucretius put it, 'living things are born from insentient atoms'.[27] That suggests that we are dealing with an explanation of life based primarily on matter being arranged in a certain way, albeit one that requires a very specific set of ingredients. It is not clear just how this is supposed to work, but we can see Lucretius doing his best with the information available to him to give a thoroughly naturalistic and scientific explanation of life.

Epicurus Contra Democritus

For the Epicureans, then, there is no fundamental difference between soul (*psuchê*) and body (*sôma*), for both are ultimately made of atoms. That is not to say that the mind (as we use the term today) does not really exist, and in fact Epicurus wanted to resist the reductive aspect of Democritus's atomism that insisted that *nothing* exists except atoms and void.[28] What we call the mind *does* exist for Epicurus, as do all of our experiences, and they should not be dismissed as the mere epiphenomena of atomic interactions.

But precisely how best to understand Epicurus's position here is far from clear, and scholars have disagreed. The traditional view has held that Epicurus was more or less in agreement with Democritus, apart

[25] See Lucretius 3.670–8.
[26] These fill Lucretius 3.425–829. Bailey (1947), ii, 1065–131, counts a total of twenty-nine proofs against the pre-existence and immortality of the soul; Leonard and Smith (1942), 418–19, count seventeen.
[27] Lucretius 2.870.
[28] See e.g. Sextus Empiricus, *Math.* 7.135 (DK 68B9), in Waterfield (2000), 176.

from a few modifications. On that view, atoms are foundational for Epicurus, as they were for Democritus, with the implication that phenomenal properties such as colours, and mental properties such as feelings, desires, and experiences, are mere by-products of atomic interactions. But others have pointed out that in his summary of physics Epicurus begins the exposition by referring to bodies, not atoms, the difference being that bodies are physical entities we know via sense-perception.[29] Atoms, by contrast, are imperceptible entities proposed in order to explain the phenomenal world we know via the senses. For Epicurus, then, atoms function as part of an explanation of the very real phenomenal world, whereas for Democritus atoms are the only things that really exist.

This inevitably has important consequences for how Epicurus understood mental properties. What we call the mind is thus not merely the by-product of the interaction of atoms, even if it is ultimately the product of those interactions. Mental processes such as decision-making cannot be dismissed as illusory, and Epicurus was explicit in his rejection of physical determinism.[30] We can and do make decisions and then act freely, and those actions have consequences in the world. For that to be the case, it must be that mental processes such as choosing one option over another can affect the subsequent movement of bodies composed of atoms. The mind, then, on this interpretation, is something very real, produced by the interaction of atoms, rather than a mere epiphenomenon. It quite literally takes on a life of its own.

In these ancient discussions, as we have seen, references to the mind and soul refer not to the sorts of things we now refer to as 'mental' but rather to physical entities that explain the presence of psychological and biological properties of bodies. It seems clear that Epicurus conceived the human being as a psychophysical whole.[31] By that I mean that the body and soul function together as a single organized system. As we have seen, Epicurus and Lucretius argued that the soul cannot survive without the body and that, without the soul, the body is merely a corpse. A living human being is a unity composed of both, and given that both are composed of atoms, we might equally say that a living human being is simply a complex aggregate of atoms, discarding the division between soul

---

[29] See Epicurus, *Ep. Hdt.* 39–40 (**IG I-2, LS 5A**), with Sedley (1988), esp. 303–4.

[30] See Ch. 6 below.

[31] I borrow this helpful phrase from Gill (2006).

and body altogether. One of the central features of a human being, the power of sensation, is a feature of a unified psychophysical entity and cannot straightforwardly be attributed to the body or the soul when considered in isolation.[32] This is so even though a special type of atom is required as part of the mixture which not only accounts for the power of sensation but also aids in giving the soul, and so the person, a cohesion and unity. The Epicurean soul, then, is not the *essential* self in the way that a Platonic soul is, but rather is just one part of a complex physical organism that helps to explain why that organism has the powers and abilities it does. We are, according to Epicureanism, embodied physical beings.

Stoic Breath

There are a number of similarities between Epicurean and Stoic thinking about the nature of human beings. Both conceive people as psychophysical unities, a combination of both body and soul. The Stoics, like the Epicureans, argue that the soul is something physical.[33] Like Epicurus, they point to interaction between body and soul as a good reason to suppose that the two are of the same nature, and they also share the Epicurean assumption that only bodies can act and be acted upon.[34] Again, like Epicurus, they see the soul as something material that is distributed throughout the body. However, because they conceive Nature as a continuum of matter, the soul that permeates an animal's body is but a fragment of a much larger soul that permeates all of Nature, namely God.

The founder of Stoicism, Zeno, identified the human soul with breath (*pneuma*). One of our sources reports his argument for this:

That thing on the occasion of whose departure from the body the living being dies is without doubt soul; but when the natural breath departs, the living being dies; therefore, the soul is natural breath.[35]

Chrysippus argued along similar lines: we live and breathe by virtue of the same thing; we breathe by virtue of breath and we live by virtue of soul; therefore breath and soul must be one and the same thing.[36]

---

[32] See e.g. Lucretius 3.334–6.
[33] Alongside Annas (1992), 37–70, note also Long (1982).
[34] See e.g. Cicero, *Acad.* 1.39 (*SVF* 1.90, LS 45A).
[35] Calcidius, *in Tim.* 220 (*SVF* 1.138, IG II-68), translated in Magee (2016), 461.
[36] See Calcidius, *in Tim.* 220 (this part in *SVF* 2.879 and LS 53G).

For the Stoics, the relationship between soul and body in a human being mirrors the relationship between God, conceived as divine breath (*pneuma*), and matter. As we saw earlier, the active, rational principle gives structure and order to Nature. The *pneuma* within an object gives it its properties, and the Stoics suggested that different properties within different objects can be explained with reference to varying levels of tension (*tonos*) of the *pneuma*.[37] At the lowest level there is 'cohesion' (*hexis*), the force that holds together lifeless objects, such as stones, logs, and the bones in our bodies. Then there is 'nature' (*phusis*), a more complex force by virtue of which living things such as plants are alive. Soul (*psuchê*) is more complex again and gives animals the powers of perception and movement. The difference between these different types of entity—mineral, vegetable, animal—is thus one of degree, not kind. The reference in the ancient sources to 'tension' (*tonos*) has been glossed by some modern commentators as an attempt to explain different levels of organizational complexity.[38] Although some have seen the Stoics as 'top-down' theorists starting with God,[39] we might alternatively see them as 'bottom-up' naturalists, explaining higher and more complex forms of life as simply the product of gradual and increasing developments within Nature.

In a human being at birth, the entire body is permeated by *pneuma*; some of that *pneuma* gives structure and cohesion to the bones, some of it gives life to insensitive parts of the body, like hair and nails, and some of it gives the powers of perception and movement, located in what early anatomists were at this period beginning to identify as the nervous system. As a human being develops and reaches maturity, some of the *pneuma* in its soul attains an even higher level of tension and gains reason (*logikê psuchê*). This is located in the ruling part of the soul (*hêgemonikon*), which Chrysippus located in the heart (echoing Aristotle),[40] although some other Stoics proposed the head.[41] In all, the soul was thought to have eight parts: the five senses, the power of reason (located in the *hêgemonikon*), the power of speech, and the power of

---

[37] For what follows see Philo, *Leg. alleg.* 2.22–3 (**LS 47P**).

[38] See e.g. Long (1982).

[39] See e.g. Sedley (1988), 297–8.

[40] See e.g. Galen, *PHP* 1.6.12; also Diog. Laert. 7.159 (**IG II-20**). For Aristotle's view see e.g. *Parv. nat.* 469a4–23.

[41] See Philodemus, *Piet.* 9,9–13, in Obbink (1996), 19–21.

reproduction.[42] One source offers a striking image of the arrangement: 'seven parts grow out of the ruling part and stretch out into the body like the tentacles of an octopus';[43] another purporting to quote Chrysippus likens it to a spider sitting at the centre of its web.[44] These tentacles of *pneuma* extend out to the sense organs and throughout the body to the skin, in order for the soul to have sensible contact with other bodies (i.e. the sense of touch). The following extended account may well be a quotation from or paraphrase of Chrysippus:

[The soul is] divided into eight parts. For it consists of the principal one and the five senses, also the substance associated with vocal sound, and the potency for sowing and procreating. Now, the parts of the soul, flowing from the seat of the heart as from a fountainhead, extend throughout the whole body and fill all its parts in every quarter with the vital breath; they regulate and control them with innumerable and diverse powers: nourishment, growth, locomotion, sensory equipment, and the impulse to action. And the soul as a whole deploys the senses, which are its functional organs, like branches extending out from the principal part or trunk, as it were, to serve as messengers of the things they sense; it for its part passes judgement, like a king, on what they have reported.[45]

To put this into context, it might be worth taking some time to consider some of the developments in anatomy that took place during this period. Three figures stand out and are worth mentioning: Praxagoras, Herophilus, and Erasistratus.[46] The first of these, Praxagoras, was from the island of Cos, famed as the home of Hippocrates and already an important centre for medicine; he was active around 300 BC. In his anatomical work he distinguished between veins and arteries but thought that only veins carried blood.[47] The arteries he thought contained air—i.e. breath (*pneuma*)—and those that he saw in corpses were indeed empty. He also thought that the arteries were in some way connected with nerves (*neura*), which consequently also contained *pneuma*. The centre of the

[42] See Galen, *PHP* 3.1.9–25 (*SVF* 2.885), who quotes Chrysippus directly. Note also Diog. Laert. 7.157 (**IG II-20**).

[43] Aetius 4.21.2 (*SVF* 2.836, **IG II-73, LS 53H**).

[44] See Calcidius, *in Tim.* 220 (*SVF* 2.879).

[45] Calcidius, *in Tim.* 220 (*SVF* 2.879, part in **LS 53G**), translated in Magee (2016), 461.

[46] In what follows I draw on the accounts in Lloyd (1973), 75–90, and Annas (1992), 20–6; see also Nutton (2013), 130–41.

[47] The ancient evidence for Praxagoras is collected and translated in Steckerl (1958), 45–107. One of the most important sources in the present context is Galen, *PHP* 1.6.13–1.8.1 (fr. 11 in Steckerl (1958), 49–53).

system is the heart, pumping both blood around the veins and *pneuma* around a system of arteries and nerves. Praxagoras identified the pneumatic system with the soul.[48] In Chrysippus's day, then, the model of a soul identified with *pneuma* centred in the heart and spread throughout the body via a system of arterial-neural tentacles was cutting-edge science based on empirical evidence, however incomplete that evidence might have been.

Praxagoras's pupil Herophilus developed the picture further. Based in Alexandria, he and his fellow scientist Erasistratus were able to undertake human dissections in a more systematic manner. Some sources even suggest that they opened up criminals who were still alive.[49] On the basis of their observations, Herophilus concluded that the arteries did contain blood, but presumed they carried *pneuma* as well. Erasistratus advanced on Praxagoras's account by distinguishing nerves from arteries and determining that the nerves were part of a system centred on the brain: 'all the nerves grow out of the brain, and on the whole the brain seems to be the source of bodily activity'.[50] He continued to think that the heart pumped *pneuma* around the arteries,[51] but drew a distinction between two different types of *pneuma*: a vital *pneuma* in the heart and arteries, and a psychic *pneuma* in the brain and nerves.[52]

During the Hellenistic period, then, we see the beginnings of real understanding of how the body works, inevitably still sketchy in many respects, but certainly making progress. A somewhat vague notion of the soul being connected with breath (because the living breathe and the dead do not) is augmented by observations from human dissections with the idea that the heart pumps this breath around the body in a series of tubes, and that this animates the body. Further dissections show that there is in fact another distinct system of tubes connected to the brain, which is also connected to the sense organs, and this looks like the most likely candidate for the ruling system of the body, and so ought to be

[48] See e.g. Athenaeus 15, 687e (fr. 30 in Steckerl (1958), 65–6), locating the soul in the heart.
[49] See Celsus, *Med.* Prooem. 23–6, printed as fr. 63a in von Staden (1989), 187, which gathers together and discusses all the ancient evidence for Herophilus, and fr. 17a in Garofalo (1988), 63–4, which does the same for Erasistratus.
[50] Erasistratus, quoted in Galen, *PHP* 7.3.10 (fr. 289 in Garofalo (1988), 170–1), and translated in Irby-Massie and Keyser (2002), 301–2.
[51] See Galen, *Ven. sect. Er.* 2 (fr. 198 in Garofalo (1988), 132), trans. in Brain (1986), 19.
[52] See Galen, *PHP* 2.8.38 (fr. 112b in Garofalo (1988), 98), with Lloyd (1973), 84.

identified with the soul. All these developments were taking place in parallel with the Stoics' attempts to describe the human being as a body animated by *pneuma* spreading through the body like a series of tentacles. Evidently there was still much to learn about the internal workings of the body, but for present purposes the important points to note are i) the Stoic account of the soul was in accord with what was then the most up-to-date scientific knowledge, and ii) that knowledge was continually being revised during this period on the basis of further observations.

Galen tells us that Chrysippus explicitly referred to Praxagoras in his own work.[53] It is hard to know if this was with deference to current empirical research, or simply as support for a pre-existing philosophical position.[54] It is interesting to note that, according to Philodemus, some later Stoics rejected Chrysippus's locating of the ruling part of the soul in the heart, and instead placed it in the brain.[55] Was this a modification of the Stoic view in the light of new empirical evidence? As empiricists, one would like to think that they would have done just that, and that Chrysippus (and indeed Aristotle) would have done the same. However, it is worth noting that Chrysippus offered independent reasons for locating the seat of the soul in the heart, for it is there he thought that we experience the emotions, especially fear, anger, distress, and excitement.[56] Voice, expressing the thoughts of the soul, also emanates from the chest, he noted.[57]

At first glance there might appear to be other problems with pushing this parallel between Stoic thinking about the soul and contemporary anatomy too far. For Praxagoras and Erasistratus, *pneuma* is something distinct within the body, contained within the arteries and nerves, and travelling back and forth from the ruling part of the soul. For the Stoics, the *pneuma* in the body is not limited to these conduits. Instead it permeates the entire body in a complete mixture, blended with it to the point of being indistinguishable, like the drop of wine in the sea.[58] There is

---

[53] See Galen, *PHP* 1.7.1 (*SVF* 2.897), fr. 11 in Steckerl (1958), 49–53.

[54] Annas (1992), 46, suggests that Chrysippus's focus on *pneuma* in place of Zeno's and Cleanthes' references to fire as the active principle reflected the influence of contemporary science, while von Staden (1989), 92–8, points to further parallels between Stoic thought and Herophilus that might suggest the influence of Hellenistic medical theory.

[55] See Philodemus, *Piet.*, 9,9–13, in Obbink (1996), 19–21.

[56] See Galen, *PHP* 3.1.25 (*SVF* 2.886, **LS** 65H).

[57] See Calcidius, *in Tim.* 220 (*SVF* 2.879).   [58] See Ch. 3 above.

no part of a human that is just body or just soul, the Stoic position implies.[59] The *pneuma* in each human being is not limited to the functions we now associate with the mind, such as perception and reasoning, for it also accounts for our simply being alive and for the cohesion of our bones. In the words of Chrysippus himself:

> The soul is *pneuma* connate with us, extending as a continuum through the whole body as long as the free-flowing breath of life is present in the body.[60]

We can perhaps get round some of these problems by being more precise with terminology. Strictly speaking, the soul (*psuchê*) is not the same as the *pneuma* that pervades the entire body; the soul is only that part of the body's *pneuma* at the appropriate level of tension.[61] The body as a whole is permeated with *pneuma* by virtue of which it coheres as a single entity and is a living organism. This *pneuma* is at the level of tension to generate cohesion (*hexis*) and life or nature (*phusis*). The soul proper is at a higher level of tension, and it is this that gives humans the powers of perception and movement. It would not be unreasonable to claim that this *pneuma* is concentrated in those parts of the body that are associated with these functions, i.e. the sense organs and nervous system. (Note that earlier we saw Erasistratus distinguish between types of *pneuma* and locate psychical *pneuma* in the brain and nerves.) *Pneuma* of an even higher degree of tension forms the ruling part of the soul (*hêgemonikon*), located in either the heart or the brain. This is part of the soul, and the part that we would now call 'mind'.

What happens when a human dies? On the Stoic account this must involve the loss of *pneuma* at levels of tension high enough to generate soul and life. Over time, as the body decays, there will no longer be enough tension even to ensure bodily cohesion. Is this simply a reduction or dissipation of tension, or does something depart the body? Although the former would seem to be the neater answer, a number of sources

---

[59] For an ancient objection based on the Stoics' own account of mixture (if the soul is completely intermixed, it loses its identity and unity) see Calcidius, *in Tim.* 221 (*SVF* 2.796), translated in Magee (2016), 465.

[60] Chrysippus, quoted in Galen, *PHP* 3.1.10 (*SVF* 2.885), translated in De Lacy (1978–84), 171.

[61] As Annas (1992) notes, the Stoics variously use the word 'soul' (*psuchê*) to refer to i) all the *pneuma* in the body, ii) the *pneuma* that is the soul proper (the eight parts outlined earlier), or iii) just the ruling part (*hêgemonikon*) of the soul.

suggest that some Stoics held that the soul actually survives the destruction of the body.[62] The reasoning behind this seems to be that the soul has attained such a high level of tension that it is much harder to destroy than the body, and so survives it. Chrysippus is reported to have said that only the souls of the wise survive the destruction of the body,[63] presumably because he held that only souls with the very highest degrees of tension would do this. It is difficult to comprehend what these disembodied souls would be like or do; according to one source, Chrysippus said they would be spherical.[64] They would last for a while, but certainly no longer than the next conflagration. Whatever they might be like, they would certainly not offer any hope of post-mortem existence. Like the Epicureans, the Stoics were committed to a form of psychophysical holism. A human being is a unified material entity comprising a material body and a material soul, neither of which can meaningfully survive without the other.

We have seen that, according to the Stoics, the human soul is simply a fragment of the divine soul permeating all of Nature. This might lead us to ask whether human consciousness is a fragment of divine consciousness. If so, that would be a startling claim to make. I do not think the Stoics are committed to claiming anything like that, because they specify different locations for the *hêgemonikon* of each person and the divine *hêgemonikon*, and the activity of thought is the product of the *hêgemonikon*, not the *psuchê* as a whole. But even so, each person's *hêgemonikon*, whether located in the head or the chest, is a part of that person's *psuchê*, and so part of the totality of *pneuma* that constitutes the divine soul, if not the divine mind.

Peripatetic Breath

The Stoics were not the only ones in this period to explain the nature of the soul with reference to *pneuma*. We find similar thoughts among some of the Peripatetics, in particular Strato. Aristotle had defined the

---

[62] See e.g. Eusebius, *Praep. evang.* 15.20.6 (*SVF* 2.809, LS 53W).
[63] See Diog. Laert. 7.157 (*SVF* 2.811, IG II-20).
[64] See *SVF* 2.815 (from a scholium in Homer). This might be explained by noting that in antiquity the sphere was held to be the most perfect form and was often associated with divine beings.

soul as the first actuality of a body potentially possessing life, and as the form of the body.[65] The soul is not a body, in the sense of being distinct from our bodies, but it is intimately bound up with our bodies. The two are inseparable, similar to the way in which an impression in wax is inseparable from the wax.[66] Aristotle also suggested that sight is the equivalent of the soul of the eye, which we might gloss as its function or activity.[67] The soul, then, for Aristotle, is not a body, but it clearly depends on and is inseparable from a body.

There has been some debate about whether the texts that we know as Aristotle's circulated during the Hellenistic period. According to Strabo, they did not, and were only rediscovered at the end of the period, although modern scholars have questioned his story.[68] What we do know is that a number of Hellenistic Peripatetics put forward quite different accounts of the soul. The third head of the Lyceum, Strato, may have identified the soul with *pneuma*: he explained the activity of the body with reference to *pneuma* extending throughout the body from a ruling part (*hêgemonikon*) which he located in the head.[69] This sounds surprisingly Stoic, but it may simply reflect his interest in the developments in medicine by Erasistratus and others that we saw earlier. It is not completely without Aristotelian precedent either, because Aristotle himself had pointed to the role of *pneuma* as the physical conduit for the soul's activities.[70] As a good naturalist, Strato—nicknamed 'the Physicist'—would of course pay close attention to developments in the empirical science of his day. No doubt Aristotle would have done exactly the same.

Another member of the Hellenistic Lyceum, Critolaus, suggested that the soul was made of ether, the fifth element after earth, air, fire, and water.[71] Aristotle had discussed ether as the element out of which heavenly bodies were made, describing it as ungenerated, indestructible,

---

[65] See Aristotle, *De an.* 2.1.   [66] Aristotle, *De an.* 2.1, 412b4–9.

[67] Aristotle, *De an.* 2.1, 412b27–413a3.

[68] See Strabo 13.1.54, with Barnes (1997).

[69] On the role of *pneuma* see e.g. Aetius 5.24.4 (fr. 128 in Wehrli (1969b), 66 in Sharples (2011)) and Tertullian, *De an.* 14.3–5 (fr. 108 in Wehrli (1969b), 59 in Sharples (2011)). On the location of the *hêgemonikon* in the head ('between the eyebrows') see Aetius 4.5.2 (fr. 119b in Wehrli (1969b), 57 in Sharples (2011)), Tertullian, *De an.* 15.4–5 (fr. 120 in Wehrli (1969b), 58 in Sharples (2011)). See further Modrak (2011).

[70] See e.g. Aristotle, *Gen. an.* 2.3, 736b30–737a8.

[71] See Tertullian, *De an.* 5.2 (fr. 17 in Wehrli (1969d), 24B in Sharples (2010)).

and divine.[72] In the wake of Critolaus, later Hellenistic sources presented Aristotle as holding a material theory of the soul, identifying it with the stuff of the heavens.[73] If that makes it sound as if Strato and Critolaus held quite different views about the soul, we should also note that Aristotle had said that the *pneuma* he connected with the soul was analogous to the fifth heavenly element.[74] Like the Stoics, we have a theory of divine breath drawing on the latest developments in anatomy and physiology. What we find in the Hellenistic Lyceum, then, is a theory of the soul quite different to the one we associate with Aristotle today, but with some foundations in other aspects of Aristotle's philosophy.

* * *

At the beginning of this chapter I suggested that 'soul' is not a very helpful translation of *psuchê*, although without a better alternative I have, like many others, continued to use it. But now that we have an outline of the Epicurean and Stoic conceptions of a person, it might be worthwhile re-describing their positions without using it.

Both schools conceive a human being as a physical entity composed of matter that is alive due to the presence of a material element within it (certain types of atoms; *pneuma*). Part of that material element by virtue of which someone is alive is also responsible for the abilities we associate with the mind, such as sensation, emotion, and thought, and both schools physically located that part in the chest. At death the matter that makes up a human being is dispersed and all of its functions cease. We are physical, embodied, mortal creatures.

---

[72] See Aristotle, *Cael.* 1.3, 270b16–25.
[73] See e.g. Cicero, *Tusc.* 1.22 (24C in Sharples (2010)). I borrow the phrase 'the stuff of the heavens' from Sharples (2010), 246.
[74] See Aristotle, *Gen. an.* 2.3, 736b37–737a1.

5

The Good

The Stoics and Epicureans were both concerned with trying to identify the goal (*telos*) of human actions—the 'that for the sake of which' we do what we do. Both agree, along with Aristotle and many other ancient philosophers, that the goal of all human action is ultimately happiness or wellbeing (*eudaimonia*). Every action aims at some good, Aristotle had claimed.[1] We might be mistaken about whether the outcome really *is* good but we at least think it will be. In Aristotle's discussion he goes on to draw a distinction between instrumental goods and intrinsic goods: some things we pursue for the sake of something else, others for their own sake. Aristotle wonders whether there might be a single highest good to which all other goods that we pursue are subordinate.[2] That is, is there a single, highest goal of all human action? If so, this would simply be 'the good'.[3] It is this highest good that Aristotle identifies as happiness or wellbeing (*eudaimonia*), namely that at which all of our actions are ultimately directed.

The great problem, of course, is that although many people will agree that happiness is ultimately the thing we really want, there is much disagreement about how to get it. In *The City of God*, Augustine reported that the first century BC Roman encyclopaedist Marcus Terentius Varro, writing at the end of the Hellenistic period, had recorded a total of 288 different philosophical accounts of what constitutes the highest good and happiness.[4] It is within this much wider debate that we can place the Stoics and Epicureans. Both schools agreed that happiness is the highest good, but they differed over what they thought would enable us to

---

[1] Aristotle, *Eth. Nic.* 1.1, 1094a1–3.   [2] Aristotle, *Eth. Nic.* 1.2, 1094a18–22.
[3] Aristotle used the contraction *tagathon* ('the good').
[4] Augustine, *Civ. Dei* 19.1. Varro (116–27 BC) had studied philosophy in Athens with Antiochus of Ascalon.

achieve that goal. In short, the Stoics suggested that virtue (*aretê*) was the key, while the Epicureans thought pleasure (*hêdonê*) was the answer.[5]

The Stoics on What is Good

The earliest extended account that we have of Stoic thinking on this topic is in Book 3 of Cicero's *On Moral Ends*.[6] This work is written as a dialogue and Cicero's account of Stoic ethics is put into the mouth of Cato the Younger, a famous Roman Stoic and defender of the Republic, who had recently chosen to commit suicide rather than accept defeat at the hands of Julius Caesar.[7]

Cato opens his exposition by introducing the Stoic theory of *oikeiôsis*, a term sometimes translated as 'appropriation'.[8] The theory is itself quite simple: 'every animal, as soon as it is born, is concerned with itself, and takes care to preserve itself'.[9] This natural instinct of self-concern leads us to prefer anything that contributes to our survival and to avoid anything that might contribute to our destruction. Our most basic ideas of what is good or bad have their origins in this instinctive concern for ourselves. We attribute positive value to things that are in accord with our own nature and negative value to those things that are not. However, as we develop into more reflective agents we start to value not just those individual things that contribute to our self-preservation, but also the frame of mind that enables us to select those things successfully and consistently. Over time, our primitive identification of things like food and shelter as being good for us is supplemented with the idea that the right frame of mind is even more vital to our wellbeing. As Cato puts it, 'through learning and reason one concludes that this is the place to find the supreme human good, that good which is to be praised and sought on

---

[5] On Hellenistic ethics see Annas (1993a); for Stoic ethics I note Inwood (1985) and Schofield (2003); for Epicurean ethics I note Mitsis (1988) and Woolf (2009).

[6] I follow Annas and Woolf (2001) in using *On Moral Ends* to translate Cicero's title *De Finibus Bonorum et Malorum*. In what follows I use Woolf's translation in that volume when quoting from *De Finibus*, very occasionally slightly modified. The central section, *Fin.* 3.16–24, is also translated in **IG II-102**. The Latin text is edited in Reynolds (1998). For a recent collection of essays on it see Annas and Betegh (2016).

[7] Cato died in 46 BC; Cicero wrote *De Finibus* in 45 BC.

[8] On this notion, see Pembroke (1971) and, at greater length, Engberg-Pedersen (1990).

[9] Cicero, *Fin.* 3.16 (**IG II-102**).

its own account'.[10] This frame of mind, which the Stoics called *homologia* (consistency, harmony), only manifests itself as a good later in our development, once we have become rational adults. However, once it has done so we see that this is the only thing that is good for its own sake. All those other things we initially counted as valuable, because they contributed in some way to our self-preservation, we now see as merely instrumentally valuable.

This might make it sound as if the Stoic account of what is good has much in common with Aristotle's. Indeed, a number of ancient critics thought just this, notably the Academic Carneades and, a bit later, Antiochus, and Cato's account of the Stoic position in *On Moral Ends* is presented as an explicit reply to the claim that the Stoics differ from Aristotle only in words rather than substantive ideas.[11] To get a better sense of both the objection and Cato's reply to it, we first need to say a bit more about the Stoic position.

Cato continues his exposition by drawing a distinction between 'appropriate actions' and 'right actions'.[12] When we act in accord with our natural instinct for self-preservation, choosing food, water, shelter, and so on, we are making 'appropriate actions'. It seems perfectly natural, normal—indeed appropriate—that we should choose these things and avoid those things that might harm us or obstruct our ability to preserve ourselves. When, later in our development, we begin to value harmony and consistency as valuable in their own right, and behave in a manner that will cultivate and preserve them, then we move into the realm of 'right actions'. These aim at the same things as 'appropriate actions', but differ from them by being expressions of a virtuous character. As virtuous actions, however, they are not merely a means to securing something external, for they are valuable in their own right. As Cato puts it, 'only wisdom is directed at itself in its entirety'.[13]

This may be a good point at which to note that it can be quite easy to slip into the trap of presenting wisdom or virtue as merely a means to a higher end, namely wellbeing or happiness (*eudaimonia*). The Stoics say that it is happiness that is the highest good—the 'that towards which all

[10] Cicero, *Fin.* 3.21 (IG II-102, LS 59D).   [11] See e.g. Cicero, *Fin.* 3.5, 3.10, 3.41.
[12] In Cicero's Latin these are *officia* and *recta*, which he uses to translate the Greek terms *kathêkonta* and *katorthômata* respectively. See *Fin.* 3.20, 24 (IG II-102, LS 59D, 64H).
[13] Cicero, *Fin.* 3.24 (IG II-102, LS 64H).

our actions are directed'—and if we want to attain that highest good, we ought to cultivate virtue. This can make it seem as if virtue is merely a steppingstone to something else. The point that Cato wants to make here is that this is not the case. Once we grasp the true nature of wisdom or virtue (he uses the terms interchangeably), we shall see their intrinsic value and pursue them for their own sakes. The Stoic claim is that only a life devoted to the pursuit of virtue for its own sake will be a genuinely good, happy life. The person who pursues virtue for the sake of the happiness it might bring is moving in the right direction, but hasn't fully grasped the nature of virtue, for when they do they will see that it is worthy of being pursued in its own right. Once we grasp our rational nature, we see that acting rationally—which the Stoics identify with acting virtuously—is simply the right thing to do. Indeed, the fully rational agent quite simply cannot act in any other way. That is why all of the Stoic sage's actions will be 'right actions'.

In the light of this, we can see that when the Stoics define the final aim or goal (*telos*) of human life to be 'to live consistently or harmoniously with Nature', the stress is on 'harmoniously' rather than 'Nature'.[14] Indeed, other sources report that Zeno's original formulation was simply 'to live harmoniously', and the addition 'with Nature' was made by Cleanthes to flesh out (but presumably not dramatically change) the original statement.[15] To live harmoniously means to live rationally, which is the same as living harmoniously with our own nature as rational beings. Given that the Stoics hold that Nature as a whole is permeated and governed by a divine rational principle, living harmoniously and rationally will also mean living harmoniously with Nature as a whole.

This focus on developing a harmonious, rational mental state leads us on to one of the central claims in Stoic ethics, namely that virtue is the only good.[16] Although we might begin by pursuing external things that contribute to our self-preservation, none of these things are in themselves good, for none of them are necessary and sufficient for happiness (*eudaimonia*).

---

[14] Cicero, *Fin.* 3.26 (**IG II-102**). In Cicero's Latin this is *congruenter naturae convenienterque vivere*, which translates the Greek phrase *to homologoumenôs têi phusei zên* (in e.g. Diog. Laert. 7.87 (**IG II-94, LS 63C**)).

[15] See Stobaeus 2,75,11–76,8 (**IG II-95, LS 63B**). However, note that Diogenes Laertius credits the expanded version to Zeno (Diog. Laert. 7.87 (**IG II-94, LS 63C**)).

[16] Cato puts it slightly differently (at *Fin.* 3.26 (**IG II-102**)) by saying that what is moral is the only good (*quod honestum sit id solum bonum*).

Only an excellent, rational mental state can secure that. This the Stoics identify with virtue, which they often associate with having a healthy mind. This idea stands behind Cicero's famous statement elsewhere that philosophy ought to be conceived as medicine for the mind (*animi medicina*).[17] Cato argues that the reason why a virtuous or moral life will also be a happy life, and indeed why it is the *only* form of life that will be a genuinely happy life, is that we can only be truly happy if we take pride (*gloria*) in what we do, and it is only when acting virtuously that we have grounds to feel such pride.[18] We can and do take pride in a wide range of things we do, but that pride will only be genuine if our achievements are the product of having behaved well. The person whose worldly success is grounded on deceitful or fraudulent behaviour ought not in all good conscience be able to take pride in their success. Indeed, as we shall see, the Stoics will place the emphasis very much on the way in which we behave when aiming at goals rather than the outcomes themselves. What really matters is not worldly success, but having behaved well when pursuing such things. Only a life marked by this sort of virtuous behaviour will be satisfying enough to count as a genuinely happy life.

One consequence of this view is that the apparently good things that we might think form part of worldly success are not actually good in themselves at all. Similarly, Cato insists that apparently very bad things are not really bad in themselves either.[19] We can admire brave or courageous behaviour in the face of physical danger and acknowledge it as virtuous. Central to that sort of virtuous behaviour is the belief that the physical danger is ultimately of no great consequence, especially when compared to the importance of acting rightly.

This point is discussed and argued for in other sources that we have for Stoicism too. In Diogenes Laertius's summary of Stoicism he reports a number of arguments for this claim, albeit in a somewhat compressed form. A number of modern scholars have noted the similarity between these arguments reported in Diogenes and a slightly more expansive discussion in one of Plato's early dialogues, the *Euthydemus*.[20] Diogenes reports the following:

---

[17] See e.g. Aristo, cited in Plutarch, *Virt. mor.* 440f (*SVF* 1.375, LS 61B). For Cicero see *Tusc.* 3.1 and the discussion that follows, which focuses on the idea that wisdom might be defined as possessing a healthy mind or soul (*animi sanitas*).

[18] Cicero, *Fin.* 3.28 (IG II-102).   [19] Cicero, *Fin.* 3.29 (IG II-102).

[20] See e.g. Long (1988), Annas (1993b), and Striker (1994).

For just as heating, not chilling, is the peculiar characteristic of what is hot, so too benefitting, not harming, is the peculiar characteristic of what is good. But wealth and health no more do benefit than they harm. Therefore wealth and health are not something good. Furthermore they say: that which can be used well and badly is not something good. But wealth and health can be used well and badly. Therefore wealth and health are not something good . . . .

'Indifferent' (adiaphora) is used in two senses: unconditionally, of things which contribute neither to happiness nor unhappiness, as is the case with wealth, reputation, health, strength, and the like. For it is possible to be happy even without these, though the manner of using them is constitutive of happiness or unhappiness.[21]

It was with arguments such as these that the Stoics developed an attitude of indifference towards external circumstances, an attitude with which they are perhaps most closely associated today. As Cato puts it in his account, the ideal person is one who 'makes light of all human vicissitudes and regards them as insignificant'.[22] However, it is important not to overstate this attitude of indifference. Zeno of Citium had been a follower of Crates the Cynic, and other early Stoics such as Chrysippus also admired aspects of Cynicism, which argued for an attitude of complete indifference to external circumstances.[23] But of course Zeno decided not simply to identify as a Cynic, and instead developed his own philosophical position. One way in which the philosophy of the earliest Stoics differed from their Cynic predecessors was in arguing that not all indifferent things are equal. This was clearly a contentious issue in the early Stoa, with Zeno's follower Aristo of Chios arguing against this new doctrine.[24] (Despite this, Aristo remained a Stoic, although he did not become head of the school. Nevertheless we are told that he was one of the most popular philosophers in Athens in his day.[25]) Some things, Zeno suggested, were preferable over others, namely those things we naturally select for the sake of our self-preservation, such as food and shelter. The Stoic, then, is indifferent to external circumstances, knowing that only virtue is necessary and sufficient for happiness, but he or she

[21] Diog. Laert. 7.103–4 (IG II-94, LS 58A-B), trans. LS.

[22] Cicero, Fin. 3.29 (IG II-102).

[23] See Goulet-Cazé (2003). For more on the Cynic background to Stoicism see Ch. 8 below.

[24] See Cicero, Fin. 3.50 (SVF 1.365, LS 58I); also Diog. Laert. 7.160 (SVF 1.351, IG II-1, LS 58G); Sextus Empiricus, Math. 11.64 (SVF 1.361, IG II-116, LS 58F). On Aristo see Porter (1996) and (in Italian) Ioppolo (1980).

[25] See e.g. Diog. Laert. 7.161 (SVF 1.333, IG II-1) and also 7.182 (SVF 1.339), which implies that he was more popular than Chrysippus as a speaker.

will still select what is in accord with Nature and avoid what is not. There is a sense in which this is what virtue is for, namely guiding us to know how best to make such choices. Cato sums up the position thus:

The supreme good is to live applying one's knowledge of the natural order, selecting what accords with Nature, and rejecting what is contrary. This is what it is to live consistently and harmoniously with Nature.[26]

Stoics Versus Peripatetics

This innovation made it possible to distinguish the Stoic position from the attitude of the Cynics, but in the process generated further problems of philosophical identity. Some ancient critics, most notably the Academic Carneades, argued that ultimately 'there was no dispute between the Stoics and the Peripatetics other than a verbal one',[27] and later, Antiochus of Ascalon would also claim the same.[28] Cicero's Cato is keen to reject such a view, insisting on a significant philosophical difference between Stoic and Peripatetic ethics.

Cato opens his defence with a question that often appeared in ancient ethical debates: can a wise person be happy even when being tortured on the rack? This image, often associated with Stoicism, was by no means unique to them. It also appears in discussions of Epicureanism and had earlier been mentioned by Aristotle, who was himself responding to previous debates. In the *Nicomachean Ethics* Aristotle wrote:

Those who say that the victim on the rack or the man who falls into great misfortunes is happy if he is good are, whether they mean it or not, talking nonsense.[29]

This is because a happy person will require certain external goods in order to live well. Aristotle himself can sometimes appear unclear about this, wanting to stress the importance of some externals while holding on to the idea that virtue alone ought to be enough.[30] His Hellenistic successor

---

[26] Cicero, *Fin.* 3.31 (IG II-102, LS 64A).

[27] Cicero, *Fin.* 3.41.

[28] See Cicero, *Fin.* 5.22 (F9 in Sedley (2012)). The long speech by Piso in *Fin.* 5 is widely held to report Antiochus's views.

[29] Aristotle, *Eth. Nic.* 7.13, 1153b19–21 (trans. Ross), perhaps referring to Plato, *Republic* 361e–362a; see also *Eth. Nic.* 1.5, 1095b32–1096a2.

[30] See e.g. Aristotle, *Eth. Nic.* 1.10, 1100b22–1101a8, where he says that it is possible to be happy (*eudaimôn*) without them (when suffering great misfortune), although not blessed (*makarios*).

Critolaus was more forthright and had no qualms in insisting that mental, bodily, and external goods are all essential for a good life.[31] For Cato, by contrast, the opposite is self-evidently true: it would be absurd to suggest that the quality of a genuinely good person's life might be affected by transient external circumstances. As he puts it, 'the wise person's life remains happy whatever the torments'.[32] For many modern readers that might sound unlikely at best, and at worst self-contradictory. Perhaps the English word 'happy' is not the best way to translate the relevant Greek and Latin terms, *eudaimôn* and *beatus*. Yet Cicero's word *beatus* has, like the English 'happy', connotations of being fortunate, and Aristotle's *eudaimôn* was clearly understood by many to have similar connotations because he explicitly argued against those who merely identified happiness with good fortune.[33] If happiness implies being fortunate, then how can one be happy when suffering great misfortune? This sounds like one of the paradoxes for which the Stoics were famous.[34]

Cicero sums up briefly the contrast between the Stoics and Peripatetics by saying that while the Stoics thought that virtue alone is necessary and sufficient for happiness, the Peripatetics held that while virtue is necessary, it is not sufficient for complete happiness, because some external or bodily goods are also required.[35] Yet as we have seen, the Stoics remained committed to the idea that some things—food, shelter, health—are worth having and that we naturally pursue them. To hold both of these views together, it was necessary for them to draw a distinction between two types of goodness. Health is something good, but not good in the same sense that virtue is good. If it were good in exactly the same sense, then it would always be better to have virtue and health than to have just virtue, but that is the claim that Stoics wanted to resist. So, they drew a distinction between what is good (*agathon*) and what has value (*axia*): virtue is the only good, but some external and bodily things, like wealth

[31] See Stobaeus 2,46,10–17 (fr. 19 in Wehrli (1969d)), but note also Cicero, *Tusc.* 5.50 (fr. 21 in Wehrli), where he is reported to have said that the goods of the soul outweigh the others combined. The relevant fragments are all translated with a commentary in Sharples (2010), 155–68. See further Sharples (2007), 627–33, and Inwood (2014), 51–72.
[32] Cicero, *Fin.* 3.42.
[33] See Aristotle, *Eth. Nic.* 7.13, 1153b21–5.
[34] See Cicero's *Paradoxa Stoicorum*, which reports a number of (non-logical) paradoxes, such as only a sage is free and every non-sage is mad.
[35] See Cicero, *Fin.* 3.43.

and health, still have value.[36] These two things are fundamentally different in kind, so that things with value cannot add or subtract from what is good. Goodness, which as we have seen is identified with virtue, right action, and living harmoniously with Nature, is not subject to cumulative enlargement: one cannot add anything to it to make it even better.[37] This claim has two consequences: the first is to downplay the importance of the external things such as wealth and health for a good life; the second is to deny that the length of one's life is significant. A virtuous life is not made any better or more virtuous if it is made longer, because virtue is simply not the sort of thing that can be quantified in that way. The virtuous person who dies at twenty is no less virtuous than the person who dies at eighty. What matters, then, is not the number of good deeds that a person might do over a lifetime (something that might in theory be quantified), but rather the possession of a particular quality. This, the Stoics claimed, was an 'all or nothing' affair: there are no degrees of virtue or wisdom, no rankings among the wise, but equally no distinctions among the non-wise, who are all equally imperfect.[38]

All these reflections on the nature of goodness, combined with the distinction between goodness and value, led the Stoics to distinguish between various kinds of 'indifferent' (adiaphoron). As we saw earlier, an indifferent is something that does not contribute to happiness or unhappiness, which for the Stoics means everything apart from virtue and its opposite, vice. We also saw that some of these indifferents—health, strength, wealth, etc.—might still be seen to have a positive value: they are things that contribute to our self-preservation, and so things that we would naturally prefer over their opposites. The Stoics called these things 'preferred indifferents' (adiaphora proêgmena) and their opposites—illness, weakness, poverty, etc.—'non-preferred indifferents' (adiaphora apoproêgmena).[39] In between, there are some indifferents about which we are genuinely indifferent, such as whether the number of hairs on our head is odd or even.[40]

---

[36] See Cicero, Fin. 3.44. Cicero uses bonum and aestimatio to translate agathon and axia respectively. For the Greek terms see e.g. Stobaeus 2,83,10–85,11 (IG II-95, LS 58D-E), which is also translated with commentary in Pomeroy (1999).

[37] See Cicero, Fin. 3.45–6.   [38] See Cicero, Fin. 3.47–8.

[39] See Cicero, Fin. 3.51.

[40] See Diog. Laert. 7.106 (IG II-94), who also gives fuller lists of the things the Stoics classed as preferred and non-preferred.

Unlike the ideal Cynic, then, who possesses virtue but has no reason to prefer one thing over another, because they are completely indifferent to the outcome of events, the ideal Stoic will use their virtue to help them pursue the preferred indifferents that they naturally desire. This led some in the Stoa (Diogenes of Babylon, Antipater) to expand the definition of the goal from 'living in accord with Nature' into 'selecting what accords with Nature and rejecting what is contrary'.[41] The problem with that definition, Carneades claimed, is that there now appear to be two goals: selecting things in accord with Nature and securing those things.[42] As we can see, the formulation is concerned only with selecting, not securing—that is, with the exercise of virtue, rather than the acquisition of preferred indifferents. Even so, Carneades seems to have pushed the point that it is a bit odd to define the goal as selecting certain things, while at the same time claiming that whether one actually attains them remains a matter of indifference.

In response to this concern, the Stoic Antipater offered the following analogy, reported by Cicero's Cato:

Take the case of one whose task it is to shoot a spear or arrow straight at some target. One's ultimate aim is to do all in one's power to shoot straight, and the same applies with our ultimate good. In this kind of example, it is to shoot straight that one must do all one can; none the less, it is to do all one can to accomplish the task that is really the ultimate aim. It is just the same with what we call the supreme good in life. To actually hit the target is, as we say, to be selected but not sought.[43]

The goal of the archer, in this analogy, is not to hit the target, but simply to shoot well. It would be imprudent to make the goal hitting the target because various other factors outside of the archer's control might intervene, such as a sudden gust of wind blowing the arrow off course. Because of these outside factors, the archer does not have complete control over whether he hits the target, but he does have complete control over how well he shoots.[44] Shooting well is thus a goal that the

[41] Cicero, *Fin.* 3.31 (**IG II-102, LS 64A**). This definition of the goal was held by Diogenes of Babylon and Antipater; see e.g. Stobaeus 2,76,9–15 (*SVF* 3.Diog.44, 3.Ant.57, **IG II-95, LS 58K**). For further discussion see Striker (1986).

[42] See Plutarch, *Comm. not.* 1070f–1072f (**LS 64C-D**), with Striker (1991). Cherniss (1976), 734–5, outlines the attribution to Carneades.

[43] Cicero, *Fin.* 3.22 (**IG II-102, LS 64F**).

[44] In the technical terminology, archery is a stochastic art. Other examples of stochastic arts often discussed in the ancient sources are medicine and navigation. See further Striker (1991) and Sellars (2003), 68–75.

archer can realistically work towards and attain. Hitting the target every time, by contrast, is an unrealistic ambition that will only lead to frustration and disappointment. Having said that, learning to shoot well usually leads to an improvement in results, even if it cannot guarantee success every time.

Something similar applies in life, Antipater is suggesting: the goal is to act well, pursuing those things that are in accord with Nature. This is something completely within the agent's control. Securing those things, on the other hand, is subject to a whole host of external factors outside of the agent's control. It would be unrealistic to expect to be consistently successful, then, and making *that* the goal would be both out of step with how the world works and counterproductive if the ultimate aim is what Zeno called a 'smooth flow of life'.[45]

* * *

As we have seen, for Cicero Stoic ethics shares something in common with Aristotelian ethics, and his reflections on this in *On Moral Ends* were probably prompted by the views of his one-time teacher Antiochus, who argued that when it came to ethics the Stoics and Peripatetics differed in words only. One of the objections raised in *On Moral Ends* against the Stoics' view effectively takes their own goal of living in accord with Nature as its point of departure.[46] If the aim is to live in accord with Nature, then surely being in a good state of physical health—itself a state in accord with Nature—is something good. The same applies to external things like food and shelter, which are natural needs and so things that we require in accord with the demands of Nature. A life that is in accord with Nature, then, will require not only a healthy, virtuous state of mind, but also a healthy body, and those external things that fulfil natural needs. Surely all three of these things ought to count as genuinely good, if one holds the Stoic *telos*.

As we saw earlier, Critolaus—one of the most important of the Hellenistic Peripatetics—argued that all three of these things were essential for a good life.[47] Consequently all three ought to be counted as

---

[45] See Diog. Laert. 7.88 (**IG II-94**, **LS 63C**).

[46] See Cicero, *Fin.* 4.72.

[47] See Stobaeus 2,46,10–17 (fr. 19 in Wehrli (1969d)). The relevant fragments are all translated with a commentary in Sharples (2010), 155–68. See further Sharples (2007), 627–33, and Inwood (2014), 51–72.

genuine goods, even if the goods of the soul outweigh the others combined.[48] The Stoics might *call* bodily health and external goods 'preferred indifferents', but that is just a quibble over terminology. The same goes for saying that they have 'value' rather than being 'good'. The fact they admit that we *naturally* pursue these things shows that the Stoics see them—or at least ought to—as parts of a life in accord with Nature. As Cicero put it, Zeno 'agrees in substance with Aristotle and the others while differing merely in words'.[49]

Panaetius on *Personae*

Later Stoics made further contributions to ethics. Once again, Cicero is our main source. In his *On Duties*, Cicero outlines a theory involving four distinct rules for living a life.[50] This is known as the four *personae* theory, and it is usually supposed that Cicero is following a now lost work by the Stoic Panaetius. There are scholarly debates about how closely Cicero follows Panaetius, and to what extent Panaetius might be deviating from the orthodox Stoic view, but putting those questions to one side, Cicero's account is on its own terms an interesting window on what might be involved in living a Stoic life.[51]

We have, Cicero says, two natures, one common and one individual. Our common nature as human beings offers one sort of guide to how to live. The fact that we are rational, social animals gives us one set of pointers to what a life in accordance with Nature might look like. In addition to this we also each have our own individual natures, the specific set of character traits that we have not chosen and that make us who we are. Some people are loud and outgoing; others shy. Some are sporty and physical; others intellectual and bookish. Some are artistic by nature; others more inclined to technical problems. None of us chose the

---

[48] See Cicero, *Tusc.* 5.50 (fr. 21 in Wehrli (1969d)).

[49] Cicero, *Fin.* 4.72.

[50] See Cicero, *Off.* 1.107–21 (part **LS 66E**). The Latin text is edited in Winterbottom (1994) and there is a detailed commentary on it in Dyck (1996); see esp. 269–95. There are two recent annotated translations, Griffin and Atkins (1991) and Walsh (2000), and in what follows I quote from the former. For further discussion see Gill (1988).

[51] For discussion of both Panaetius's orthodoxy and the extent to which Cicero draws on him in *On Duties*, see Tieleman (2007).

particular set of strengths and weaknesses that we have; they have been given to us by Nature.

Central to Cicero's account is the claim that a life in harmony with Nature ought to be sensitive to these aspects of our individual nature. It is not simply a question of following universal guidelines about being rational or virtuous; it is also about being sensitive to who we are as individuals. There is, of course, the possibility that the two might come into conflict with one another, in which case Cicero says that universal Nature comes first:

> Each person should hold on to what is his as far as it is not vicious . . . we must act in such a way that we attempt nothing contrary to universal Nature; but while conserving that, let us follow our own nature.[52]

So, while our primary commitment ought to be to universal Nature, we ought also to be true to ourselves, our unique individual natures. Living in harmony with Nature is as much about living in harmony with our own nature as it is conforming to Nature as a whole. Of course, this should not be much of a surprise, given that the former is merely a local expression of the latter.

What we need, then, is plenty of self-knowledge about who we are, what our strengths and weaknesses are, and enough self-belief to remain true to what we find, rather than trying to be like other people:

> Reflecting on such matters, everyone ought to weigh the characteristics that are his own, and to regulate them, not wanting to see how someone else's might become him; for what is most seemly for a man is the thing that is most his own. Everyone, therefore, should acquire knowledge of his own talents, and show himself a sharp judge of his own good qualities and faults.[53]

So far I have mentioned just two elements, and at the outset I said there were four. The other two, which Cicero introduces later, are chance or circumstance, and our own pursuits. Chance or circumstance refers to the aspects of situations that are out of our control. Someone might be a naturally gifted opera singer, but find themselves at home with small children unable to realize that talent. Others might by nature be gifted sportsmen, but due to injury be unable to compete anymore. Chance can throw up situations in which we are unable to remain true to our

---

[52] Cicero, *Off.* 1.110 (**LS 66E**).   [53] Cicero, *Off.* 1.113–14 (part **LS 66E**).

individual natures, although if one buys the broader Stoic view of fate, one would have to accept that these chance situations are also ultimately the product of Nature.

Our own pursuits include things like the career we choose for ourselves. Cicero says that this is one of the four elements where we actually have some choice. We decide whether to train as a doctor or a builder. Cicero suggests that this ought to involve significant deliberation. However, it is not clear just how much choice there really is, as the sort of deliberation Cicero has in mind ultimately boils down to self-examination, so that we can find out who we really are. The person well suited to become a doctor may not be well suited to the life of a builder, and *vice versa*. As Cicero puts it, 'in such deliberation all counsel ought to be referred to the individual's own nature'.[54] But we also need to take into account the chance circumstances in which we find ourselves: 'Nature carries the greatest weight in such reasoning, and after that fortune'.[55]

Central to Cicero's account, then, is the idea that we remain true to our own individual natures, to who we are. Thus self-knowledge becomes vital for a life in harmony with Nature. Once we feel secure that we know who we are, what our strengths and weaknesses are, where we fit in the world, then the only decision to be made is how best to remain true to ourselves in the circumstances in which we find ourselves. In all this Cicero is probably reporting the views of Panaetius.

Hellenistic Cynics

So far we have focused on Stoics and Peripatetics. As we have seen, the Academics Carneades, Antiochus, and Cicero disputed whether there was any great distance between Peripatetic and Stoic ethics. There was, however, a much clearer contrast between the Peripatetics and the Cynics. We met Crates the Cynic earlier, as one of Zeno's teachers, and we shall return to Diogenes the Cynic in Chapter 8. It is worth noting, though, that the Cynic tradition continued during the Hellenistic period.[56] While the works of Diogenes and Crates are lost,[57] we do have

---

[54] Cicero, *Off.* 1.119.   [55] Cicero, *Off.* 1.120.
[56] For an overview see Dudley (1937), chs 3–7.
[57] What does survive for Diogenes and Crates is gathered together in SSR V B and V H respectively.

texts by a Hellenistic Cynic, namely Teles.[58] While his *Discourses* cannot count as significant works of philosophy, they do highlight standard Cynic themes such as self-sufficiency and indifference to poverty and exile. In these works Teles relies heavily on quotations from earlier Cynics, including Diogenes, Crates, and another Hellenistic Cynic, Bion of Borysthenes; there is little evidence of innovation. Even so, the Cynics remained a living part of the philosophical scene.

On the topic of the role of external goods, Teles records an anecdote about Metrocles, a Cynic active at the very beginning of the period. Metrocles had been a student of Theophrastus in Athens and received regular food parcels from home. Even so, he felt permanently destitute due to the material expectations placed on students in the Lyceum: 'new shoes, a wool overcoat, a throng of slaves, and spacious quarters'.[59] He then left the Lyceum to study with Crates, and all his cares vanished as he adopted the far more modest way of life of the Cynics—'even without help from home he was able to feed not only himself but others too'.[60]

Teles also rallied against Epicureanism. Describing the endless pain and suffering that accompanies each stage of life—the slavery of childhood, the endless responsibilities and pressures of middle age, and the infirmity of old age—he concluded that if pleasure were the standard for a happy life, as the Epicureans claimed, then such a thing would be impossible.[61]

Epicureans on Pleasure

What did the Epicureans claim about pleasure? Cicero's book *On Moral Ends* contains a valuable account of Epicurean ethics alongside the account of Stoic ethics we considered earlier. But with Epicurus we also have the benefit of being able to read his own words, in his celebrated

[58]   These are edited in Hense (1909), reprinted with a translation in O'Neil (1977), and more recently translated in Dobbin (2012), 110–34.

[59]   Teles fr. IVa, 40,4–10 Hense (*SSR* V L 5 = V H 44; trans. Dobbin (2012), 125).

[60]   Teles fr. IVa, 40,4–10 Hense. For the entertaining story of how and why Metrocles left Theophrastus for Crates see Diog. Laert. 6.94 (*SSR* V L 1; cf. FHSG 18.13), obscured in the LCL translation but retold in Desmond (2008), 28.

[61]   See Teles fr. V, 49,3–51,4 Hense (trans. Dobbin (2012), 128–9).

Letter to Menoeceus.[62] Although it is common to describe Epicurus as a eudaimonist alongside so many other ancient philosophers, in his own account he passes over the notion of *eudaimonia* and states that it is pleasure (*hêdonê*) that is the goal of all our action.[63] He took this to be a self-evident fact, and something that we can observe in animal behaviour:

Every animal as soon as it is born seeks pleasure and rejoices in it, while shunning pain as the highest evil and avoiding it as much as possible.[64]

This is the Epicurean alternative to the Stoic claim we saw earlier that 'every animal, as soon as it is born, is concerned with itself, and takes care to preserve itself'.[65] These were known as 'cradle arguments': if you want to understand human or animal nature, look at newborns and see how they naturally behave.[66] Presumably both sides took their description to be self-evidently true.

Epicurus himself described pleasure as the *archê* and *telos* of a blessed life—its origin and its goal.[67] We might unpack that very compressed statement in the following way. Pleasure is the beginning (*archê*) of a blessed life in the sense that we have just seen: as a matter of fact people have a natural desire to pursue pleasure and to shun pain. But it is also the goal (*telos*) in that Epicurus thought that people ought to pursue pleasure if they want to achieve a blessed life. These are two slightly different types of hedonism: psychological hedonism (describing human nature) and ethical hedonism (recommending certain choices). Did Epicurus hold both types at once? Would it make sense to do so? While some commentators have argued for Epicurus holding just one type or the other,[68] his statement that pleasure is both the *archê* and the

[62] The letter is preserved within Book 10 of Diogenes Laertius (10.122–35). It has been edited and translated many times, both as part of Diogenes' work and excerpted in collections of Epicurean material (e.g. Von der Muehll (1922), 44–50; Bailey (1926), 82–93; Ar. 4). The whole letter is translated in IG I-4.
[63] See Epicurus, *Ep. Men.* 128 (IG I-4, LS 21B); cf. Cicero, *Fin.* 1.29 (IG I-21, LS 21A).
[64] Cicero, *Fin.* 1.30 (IG I-21, LS 21A); cf. Diog. Laert. 10.137 (IG I-9).
[65] Cicero, *Fin.* 3.16 (IG II-102).
[66] See further Brunschwig (1986). The Epicurean cradle argument may have come first, building on ideas from the philosopher-scientist Eudoxus (cf. Aristotle, *Eth. Nic.* 10.2, 1172b9–25).
[67] See Epicurus, *Ep. Men.* 128 (IG I-4, LS 21B).
[68] See e.g. Cooper (1999), who argues for ethical hedonism only, and Woolf (2004), who defends psychological hedonism.

telos suggests that he did indeed hold both. As we have just seen with the Epicurean 'cradle argument', Epicurus paid close attention to what people in fact pursue, namely pleasure and the avoidance of pain. He thus seems committed to a form of psychological hedonism.[69] If that is so, then why also say that people ought to pursue pleasure, if as a matter of fact they already do? There are two reasons why also being committed to ethical hedonism makes sense. The first is as a counter to others, such as the Stoics, who claim that people ought to pursue something else, such as virtue. People are by nature constituted to pursue pleasure, but sometimes they can be taken in by other views, so it is necessary to remind them that pleasure is the natural goal to which they ought to work. The second is that sometimes people might simply lose sight that by nature what they really want is pleasure. Along the way they might end up pursuing other things (money, fame, power), initially as a means to pleasure, but increasingly for their own sake. Although naturally motivated to pursue pleasure, people sometimes end up living miserably in pursuit of lesser ends. Epicurus's ethical hedonism is there to remind them what they ought to do, if indeed they want to live a blessed life.

It is worth stressing that Epicurean hedonism is not like the modern image of hedonism, or for that matter the modern sense sometimes given to the word 'epicurean' itself. Epicurus held that people as a matter of fact do and ought to pursue pleasure, but he did not equate this with excessive physical pleasures:

When we say that pleasure is the goal we do not mean the pleasures of the profligate or the pleasures of consumption, as some believe, either from ignorance or disagreement or from deliberate misinterpretation, but rather the lack of pain in the body and disturbance in the soul. For it is not drinking bouts and continuous partying and enjoying boys and women, or consuming fish and the other dainties of an extravagant table, which produce the pleasant life.[70]

Although even in antiquity the Epicureans had a reputation for decadent indulgence, it is striking that Epicurus himself explicitly disowned this from the outset. We might draw a distinction here between experiencing pleasure in the present moment and enjoying a pleasant life. Epicurus

---

[69] For further evidence, see the texts discussed in Woolf (2004).
[70] Epicurus, *Ep. Men.* 131–2 (**IG I-4, LS21B**), trans. IG.

insisted that a pleasant life might often involve passing over pleasures of the present moment, because sometimes 'things which produce certain pleasures bring troubles many times greater than the pleasures'.[71] The goal, then, was not to maximize pleasures in the present moment, but rather—as Epicurus himself said in the passage above—to attain 'lack of pain in the body and disturbance in the soul'.

In order to flesh out this distinctively moderate form of hedonism Epicurus drew a distinction between two different types of pleasure, active (*kinêtikê*) and static (*katastêmatikê*).[72] Active pleasures are those generated by a process of physical stimulation, such as eating food and other activities often associated with hedonism that Epicurus described above. A static pleasure, by contrast, is a stable state of contentment, characterized by the absence of pain, such as the state of not being hungry. This distinction formed part of Epicurus's response to, and attempt to distance himself from, the earlier hedonism of the Cyreniacs, the most famous of whom was Aristippus.[73] The Cyrenaics had claimed that pleasure is the supreme good, but the sort of pleasure they had in mind was what Epicurus would call active pleasure. The unsympathetic Cicero summed up their view by saying that the Cyrenaics view humans as 'slow and lazy sheep, fit for grazing and the pleasures of procreation'.[74] While that kind of crude hedonism focused on active pleasures,[75] Epicurus's brand of hedonism was more concerned with static pleasure. Indeed, Epicurus argued that we pursue active pleasures *in order* to reach a condition of static pleasure. So, although it is possible to enjoy the process of eating fine food, and many indeed do, the real motivation behind eating is (or should be) simply to reach the state of no longer being hungry. That condition of absence of pain is effectively the goal for Epicurus, as he made plain in the passage above.[76] In other words, for Epicurus pleasure and absence of pain amount to the same thing, and there is no neutral state in between pain and pleasure. The pleasure that

---

[71] Epicurus, *Rat. Sent.* 8 (IG I-5, LS 21D).   [72] See Cicero, *Fin.* 2.9–10 (LS 21Q).
[73] The evidence for Aristippus is gathered together in *SSR* IV A. He was an associate of Socrates and in antiquity had a reputation for a luxurious way of life. For a recent study see Lampe (2015).
[74] Cicero, *Fin.* 2.40 (*SSR* IV A 185).
[75] Epicurus explicitly wanted to distance his own doctrine from this Cyrenaic view. See e.g. Diog. Laert. 10.136–7 (IG I-9, LS 21R).
[76] See also *Ep. Men.* 128 (IG I-4, LS 21B).

Epicurus held to be essential for a blessed life is simply the static pleasure of the absence of pain.

This distinction between active and static pleasures formed the foundation for Epicurus's rejection of crude hedonism. Although active pleasures can vary in quantity, static pleasures do not. It is possible to enjoy more and more fine food when hungry, but it is not possible to become even more 'not hungry'. Static pleasures do not vary in quantity, then; they are the highest form of pleasure, but not the largest. Once one reaches a state of static pleasure, it cannot be increased in quantity by adding further active pleasures; these will only vary it.[77] So again, once one is no longer hungry there is nothing to be gained by further eating. Now of course, one might say that there is genuine pleasure to be gained from eating fine food, even when one is not hungry, but the Epicurean response to that would be to argue that such overeating is likely to bring problems in the future far greater than the immediate variation in pleasure, and so it ought to be avoided.[78] This introduced the notion of what is sometimes called 'hedonistic calculus',[79] namely weighing up immediate pleasures and pains against prospective pleasures and pains in the future.

A second distinctive way in which Epicurus distanced himself from crude hedonism was by drawing a distinction between physical and psychological pleasures. Crude versions of hedonism focus just on physical pleasures of the sort Epicurus described above. As we have seen, he rejected those in favour of the static pleasure of absence of physical pain. But he also mentioned something else, the absence of disturbance in the soul, and this takes us to the heart of Epicurus's hedonism. Alongside physical pleasures, active and static, there are also psychological pleasures, active and static. Psychological pleasures and pains often take the form of desires or fears about the prospect of future physical pleasures or pains. In that sense, physical pleasure remains foundational, upon which psychological pleasure is grounded.[80] But Epicurus suggested that

---

[77] See Epicurus, *Rat. Sent.* 18 (IG I-5, LS 21E).

[78] See Epicurus, *Rat. Sent.* 8 (IG I-5, LS 21D), quoted above.

[79] The phrase is associated with Jeremy Bentham, who was concerned with weighing up a far wider range of factors (see ch. 4 of *An Introduction to the Principles of Morals and Legislation* (first published 1789), in Bentham (1907), 29–32, but it is sometimes used in discussions of ancient hedonism.

[80] Cf. Athenaeus 12, 546f (Us. 409, IG I-130, LS 21M).

psychological pains are in fact much worse than physical ones, and can be far more debilitating. Physical pains usually fall into two types: they are either low level and ongoing, in which case we can come to tolerate them, or they are intense but short lived, in which case they will be over soon, and knowing that they will soon be gone will help us to endure them. By contrast, psychological distress can colour and consume everything, sometimes to the point of making life unbearable. Although psychological distress can come in a variety of forms, Epicurus himself was most concerned with two types, fear of the gods and fear of death, both of which he took to be far worse than mere physical pain.[81] As one of our sources puts it, 'the flesh is storm-tossed only in the present, but the soul in past, present, and future'.[82]

Combining the two distinctions made by Epicurus, we end up with four distinct types of pleasure, perhaps best represented in a table (see Table 5.1):

Table 5.1. Four distinct types of pleasure

	Active (kinetic) Pleasures	Static (katastematic) Pleasures
Physical Pleasures	Eating when hungry	Not being hungry; absence of physical pain (*aponia*)
Psychological Pleasures	Contemplating future physical pleasures or remembering past ones	Not being worried by anything; absence of psychological pain (*ataraxia*)

Whereas crude hedonism is focused on active pleasures of the body, Epicurus's version is most concerned with attaining absence of psychological pain, i.e. tranquillity (*ataraxia*). This is not to undervalue physical suffering; it is just that Epicurus thought that physical pain is much easier to manage and overcome than psychological suffering. Our basic physical needs are easily met, he suggested, so long as we keep our desires in check. People desire a wide range of external physical things that they think will contribute in some way to their wellbeing. Epicurus went

[81] On overcoming fear of the gods see the discussion of Lucretius in Ch. 3 above; on Epicurean responses to fear of death see Ch. 7 below.
[82] Diog. Laert. 10.137 (**IG I-9, LS 21R**), trans. LS.

through these and classified them under three headings: i) natural and necessary, ii) natural but unnecessary, and iii) unnatural and unnecessary.[83] The desire for food is both natural and necessary for our survival. The desire for especially fine food is, in so far as it is a desire for food, also natural, but fulfilling it is not necessary. Desires for things not prompted by natural needs are unhelpful, and are more likely to generate dissatisfaction than contribute to our wellbeing. Keeping this distinction in mind, Epicurus argued, will enable us to see how easy it is to secure what we really need to avoid physical pain. Moreover, given that much of our psychological distress is generated by concern about being able to fulfil our basic needs in the future, knowing that what is essential to our physical wellbeing is easy to obtain will also contribute to our psychological tranquillity. We in fact need very little to achieve *aponia*, and knowing that will itself bring *ataraxia*. Epicurus summed up his view thus:

The cry of the flesh: not to be hungry, not to be thirsty, not to be cold. For if someone has these things and is confident of having them in the future, he might contend even with <Zeus> for happiness.[84]

But many people fail to grasp this. Cicero's Epicurean spokesman eloquently describes their situation:

Foolish people are forgetful of past successes, and fail to enjoy present ones. They simply await success in the future, but because that is necessarily uncertain, they are consumed with anxiety and fear.[85]

Epicurean hedonism, then, is a modest affair. Pleasure is the highest good, and, as materialists, they are committed to the claim that physical pleasures, produced by the interaction of atoms, are foundational. But human life is more complex than the mere enjoyment of the senses. People are often anxious about their future prosperity, their mortality, and in some cases post-mortem punishment. The ideal Epicurean life is one in which our basic physical needs are satisfied with as little trouble as possible, removing anxiety about the future, while the study of nature removes baseless fears generated by superstition. For an Epicurean, all

---

[83] See Epicurus, *Ep. Men.* 127 (**IG** I-4, **LS** 21B).
[84] Epicurus, *Sent. Vat.* 33 (**IG** I-6, **LS** 21G), trans. IG ('<Zeus>' is an addition by the editor Hartel). See also Lucretius 5.1425–33.
[85] Cicero, *Fin.* 1.60.

one needs for a good life are barley cakes and water,[86] along with a good dose of philosophy.

Peripatetic Hedonism?

It is common in accounts of ancient ethics to present the Epicureans standing alone, the only hedonists in an intellectual landscape dominated by virtue, with Stoics, Platonists, and Aristotelians all presented as descendants of Socrates.[87] However, Cicero claimed that some of the Peripatetics, notably Hieronymus of Rhodes,[88] embraced hedonism and he often names Epicurus and Hieronymus in the same breath.[89] The evidence is meagre and what there is—not least what comes from Cicero—may be deliberately misleading. Cicero tells us that Hieronymus championed freedom from pain (*nihil dolere*) and freedom from disturbance (*vacare omni molestia*) as the goal.[90]

Did this Peripatetic embrace hedonism? If so, what might have motivated him to do so? It might have been in reaction to either Stoicism (whose rejection of pleasure may have seemed excessive) or Epicureanism (whose version of hedonism went too far), or it might simply have been an attempt to work through unresolved issues in Aristotle's own ethics.[91] Aristotle himself had insisted on the role of pleasure in a good life, not as something to be pursued directly but rather as something that would accompany virtuous activity.[92] Pleasure is not the goal of human behaviour but it is a perfectly natural by-product of the pursuit of more noble things.

If we turn to another source for Hieronymus, the picture becomes more complicated. Clement of Alexandria reports that he drew a distinction between a goal (*telos*) of living untroubled (*to aochlêtôs zên*)—echoing

---

[86] See Epicurus, *Ep. Men.* 131 (**IG I-4, LS21B**).

[87] As we have seen, there were other hedonists before the Epicureans, notably the Cyrenaics.

[88] The evidence for Hieronymus is gathered together in Wehrli (1969d) and, with translations, in White (2004a). For further discussion see White (2004b) and, on Peripatetics and pleasure more widely, Inwood (2014), 30–50. Note also White (2002).

[89] See e.g. Cicero, *Fin.* 2.32 (fr. 19 in White (2004a)), 4.49 (fr. 16c), *Tusc.* 5.87 (fr. 17), 5.118 (fr. 22).

[90] For the former see Cicero, *Fin.* 2.8 (fr. 18a in White (2004a)), 2.16 (fr. 18b), 5.14 (fr. 11), 5.73 (fr. 14); for the latter see Cicero, *Acad.* 2.131 (fr. 13a).

[91] See Inwood (2014), 47.   [92] See Aristotle, *Eth. Nic.* 10.4.

Cicero's statements—and a final good (*telikon agathon*) of happiness or wellbeing (*eudaimonia*).[93] The latter is of course the standard Aristotelian view. But the former, too, simply echoes a claim already made by Aristotle, namely that the happy (*eudaimôn*) person will not be miserable, not be changeable, and not be disturbed by the ups and downs of life.[94] Cicero's claim that Hieronymus embraced pleasure as the goal (or, at least, freedom from pain) probably reflects his own argumentative agenda in *On Moral Ends*. On balance, Hieronymus was probably not a hedonist at all, which saves him as a Peripatetic, but suggests that he was not an especially innovative thinker.[95]

Having said all that, we can also note the case of another Peripatetic, Lyco of Troas, who was a contemporary of Hieronymus (although they did not get on well together) and head of the school.[96] Although the evidence for Lyco is meagre, anecdotal stories claim that he had a taste for extravagant dining and other finer pleasures of life.[97] This reputation for decadence might indicate a shift towards hedonism, although it could equally be an unfair caricature, or perhaps his lifestyle was simply out of step with his professed philosophical views. Cicero tells us that Lyco proposed a therapy for distress by saying that discomforts of the body and unfortunate external circumstances are not evils of the soul, and so ought not to be taken too seriously.[98] That does not sound especially hedonistic and aligns with mainstream Aristotelian thinking: virtue is central, although other goods have a lesser influence.[99]

*   *   *

Having examined the important differences between the Hellenistic schools, we might conclude by noting some common ground. For both Stoics and Epicureans the ideal state does not admit of cumulative enlargement. This is true for both Stoic *aretê* (virtue) and Epicurean *ataraxia* (tranquillity). This has two consequences. Both schools reject the pursuit of material goods, for having more and more of these will

---

[93] See Clement of Alexandria, *Strom.* 2.21.127 (fr. 12 in White (2004a)).
[94] See Aristotle, *Eth. Nic.* 1.10, 1101a6–13.   [95] See further White (2004b), 400.
[96] See Diog. Laert. 5.65–8.
[97] See Athenaeus 12, 547d–548b (fr. 8 in Stork et al. (2004)).
[98] See Cicero, *Tusc.* 3.78 (fr. 9 in Stork et al. (2004)).
[99] It is noteworthy that he says that things external and things of the body are not 'evils of the soul' (*animi malis*), not that they are not evils at all. This aligns him with Critolaus, whom we discussed earlier.

make no difference to the quality of one's life. Both schools also reject concern about the length of one's life, for neither *aretê* nor *ataraxia* is increased by quantity over time. In some respects this led both schools to focus attention on the present moment (although not to the neglect of planning for the future). A life that is lived well in the here and now, whether that involves selecting natural things using virtue or selecting natural and necessary things for the sake of pleasure, is complete, and cannot be improved by ever more material possessions or extension of duration.[100] The good life in both cases is marked by the pursuit of things we need to survive, done with the right frame of mind. The Peripatetics and Cynics of the period would not dissent from this either, even if they might disagree about what we need in order to live a good life.

---

[100] For the Stoics see Cicero, *Fin.* 3.46.

6

Free Will

In the last chapter we looked at conceptions of the good, that towards which all our actions ought to be aimed, if we want to live a good life. But that presupposes that we have some choice in the matter. As we saw in Chapter 3, both Stoics and Epicureans hold broadly materialist views of Nature, in which human beings are no different in kind from any other material entity. If Nature operates in some kind of regular pattern, if one type of cause always leads to the same effect, and humans are simply parts of Nature, then is there any room to make such choices? It looks as if we shall face what we might call 'physical determinism'. There are also other forms of determinism to contend with. For instance, Socrates had insisted that no one does wrong willingly and that, if we know what the right thing to do is, we cannot but do it.[1] We might call this 'ethical determinism', in so far as it is grounded on views about what is good or bad. To these we can add what we might call 'logical determinism', a problem that Aristotle grappled with in *On Interpretation*, where he responded to the thought that the truth or non-truth of the statement 'a sea battle will happen tomorrow' might make the sea battle taking place or not inevitable.[2]

There are various ways in which one might try to respond to these different forms of determinism. Aristotle, for instance, rejected Socrates' claims about being unable to do wrong willingly—arguing that we often act against our knowledge—but that does not on its own get us to the claim that people are free to choose how they act.[3] We might not be determined by what we know, as Socrates claimed, but instead be determined by less noble causes, such as irrational desires or unconscious instincts. Critics of determinism in antiquity proposed what they

---

[1] See e.g. Plato, *Protagoras* 345d–e; *Gorgias* 509e.
[2] See Aristotle, *Int.* 9.   [3] See Aristotle, *Eth. Nic.* 7.1–10.

called the 'Lazy Argument': if future events are determined by present events, which are in turn determined by past events, then there is no point in trying to do anything, for the outcome is already decided. As we shall see, it might be possible to respond to this by showing how human actions can contribute to the outcome of events. But saying that our actions contribute to the outcome of events is not the same as saying that we could have acted other than we did.

The idea of 'free will'—that we are able to choose to act however we like and other than we actually do—has a highly contested history. When did this idea first appear in the history of philosophy? Some have credited it to Aristotle, others to Epicurus, and others to later ancient thinkers, such as the Roman Stoic Epictetus, the Aristotelian commentator Alexander of Aphrodisias, and Augustine.[4] Depending on whom one believes, the notion of 'free will' pre-dates the Hellenistic period, was born in it, or was only properly articulated sometime after it. Naturally this has considerable implications for thinking about 'free will' in Hellenistic philosophy.

It is obviously beyond the scope of this chapter to settle that debate, but it is important for us to bear in mind that a number of scholars have offered persuasive arguments for the claim that the modern notion of 'free will' simply did not exist during the Hellenistic period. During the period itself, the debate was primarily concerned with understanding what is 'up to us' (eph' hêmin). It is also interesting to note that much of the debate about the origins of 'free will' has circled around Hellenistic philosophers, whether Epicurus or later developments among the Stoics. Although the issue is far from settled, it seems safe to say that the Hellenistic period will continue to be seen as important for the development of philosophical thinking about 'free will'.

Diodorus Cronus and Chrysippus on Logical Determinism

One of the most important sources for early Stoic thinking about fate and free will is Cicero's On Fate, although only part of it has come down to

---

[4] The literature is vast but here is a selection: for Epicurus see Huby (1967) and Sedley (1977), 98–9; for Carneades see O'Keefe (2005), 9; for Epictetus see Frede (2011), 44–8; for Alexander see Bobzien (1998b); for Augustine see Dihle (1982). Note also Kahn (1988).

us. There, Cicero deals at length with the views of Chrysippus, to which we shall turn in the next section. Cicero's discussion opens by describing a dispute between Chrysippus and Diodorus Cronus, a philosopher writing around 300 BC and traditionally associated with the Megarian school of philosophy.[5] Diodorus was an accomplished logician, a lover of paradoxes, and an important Hellenistic philosopher in his own right.[6] Indeed, his importance may still be underestimated for, as one commentator has noted, 'he was active in Athens at precisely the time when Zeno, Arcesilaus, and Epicurus, the founders of the three Hellenistic schools, were arriving there and learning the ropes'.[7] In the present context he is significant for outlining what was known as the 'Master Argument' (*kurieuôn logos*), which came to be something of a classic puzzle in ancient philosophy.[8]

The argument goes like this:

These three propositions are irreconcilable in so far as any two contradict the one that is left over:

   i) that everything that has come about in the past is necessarily the case,
   ii) that the impossible cannot follow from the possible, and
   iii) that something can be possible that is not true at present nor ever will be in the future.

Recognizing this contradiction, Diodorus relied on the plausibility of the first two propositions to establish that 'nothing is possible that neither is nor ever will be the case'.[9]

---

[5] Diog. Laert. 2.111 (*SSR* II F 1) reports that Diodorus was a pupil of Apollonius Cronus, who had been a pupil of Eubulides, an important member of the Megarian school. However, as Sedley (1977), 75, argues, that does not necessarily make him a member of the Megarian school himself. In antiquity he was often referred to as a dialectician and may have been a member of a distinct 'Dialectical school', an offshoot of the Megarian school.

[6] The evidence for Diodorus is gathered together in *SSR* II F 1–33. Sedley (1977) is an important study in English; references to further work can be found in *DPhA* II 779–81.

[7] Sedley (1977), 80, who continues, 'he exercised a major formative influence on the new style of philosophy'.

[8] Cicero is the earliest source to report it (*Fat.* 12–14); it is also discussed in e.g. Epictetus, *Diss.* 2.19.1–5 (IG II-76); Plutarch, *St. rep.* 1055d–f (part IG II-83); Alexander of Aphrodisias, *in An. Pr.* 183,34–184,10; Boethius, *in Int.²* 234,10–235,9, 412,8–21. These and other texts are collected in *SSR* II F 24–31 and some are translated in LS 38. For further discussion see Bobzien (1998a), 97–122.

[9] Epictetus, *Diss.* 2.19.1 (*SSR* II F 24, IG II-76, LS 38A), trans. Hard, slightly modified. Epictetus goes on to report (2.19.5) that the Stoic Cleanthes kept a different pair of propositions (2 and 3) and Chrysippus a different pair again (presumably 1 and 3; Alexander of Aphrodisias, *in An. Pr.* 177,25–178,1 (LS 38F), confirms that Chrysippus rejected 2). Cicero, *Fat.* 14 (LS 38E), also notes disagreement between Cleanthes and Chrysippus.

It seems that Diodorus's aim was to try to understand the nature of possibility and necessity, and in particular the possibility, necessity, or otherwise of propositions. His definition of the possible as 'what either is or will be' rules out the notion of something possible that is never the case.[10] If anything is possible, on his view, then it must be the case, either now or in the future, and so there are no unrealized possibilities. His aim here was to try to understand different types of propositions rather than to propose a rigorous determinism, but nevertheless he was quickly associated with the view that all things happen out of necessity.[11] In other words, he was taken to be a proponent of what I have called 'logical determinism'. According to the first proposition, events that have already happened in the past are necessarily the case or, we might say, propositions about events in the past are necessarily true. According to the second proposition, something possible cannot follow from something impossible, because something impossible is necessarily false whereas something possible could be true or false. This appears to lead Diodorus to reject the third proposition, and so to reject the thought that there are any possible events in the future. What will not happen is not an unrealized possibility; it is an impossibility. Thus, there is in fact nothing that is merely possible that has not happened, is not happening, or will not happen; there are no unrealized possibilities. That looks like it might also lead to the thought that whatever will happen in the future is necessary, and this seems to be how the Stoics in particular understood Diodorus's position. Cicero sums up what he takes to be Diodorus's view thus:

For Diodorus says that only that is possible which either is true or will be true; that whatever will be is necessary; and that whatever will not be is impossible.[12]

Cicero then says that Chrysippus's view, in response to Diodorus, was that 'even things which will not be are possible'.[13] For example, it may be

---

[10] For his definition see Boethius, *in Int.*[2] 234,22–4 (*SSR* II F 28, **LS 38C**); see also Alexander of Aphrodisias, *in An. Pr.* 183,34–184,10 (*SSR* II F 27, **LS 38B**) and Cicero, *Fat.* 17 (*SSR* II F 25).

[11] Bobzien (1993), 75, notes that the concern may have been less with the claim that everything that happens is necessary, and more with the claim that what never happens is impossible.

[12] Cicero, *Fat.* 13 (*SSR* II F 25, *SVF* 2.954, **LS 38E**), trans. LS.

[13] Cicero, *Fat.* 13.

a fact that Socrates was put to death by the Athenians, and it may be that, given his behaviour and the attitudes of the Athenian court, this was inevitable. As a matter of fact, it could not have turned out any other way. But it is at least possible that Socrates might not have been put to death on that day in 399 and that he might have lived for another five or ten years, even though we know that he did not. That seems like a fairly natural way to think about possibility, that Diodorus rejects, but Chrysippus wants to retain. Chrysippus seems to want to say that, in such cases, the outcome is determined (by antecedent causes), but not necessary. In other words, Chrysippus is happy to accept physical determinism, but not logical determinism.

If Chrysippus rejected Diodorus's conception of possibility, with what did he replace it? Chrysippus's own definition of possibility made reference to whether something is hindered or not.[14] For Diodorus, the proposition 'I am running' expresses a possibility if I am running or will run in the future, but if I never run in the future it expresses an impossibility. For Chrysippus, by contrast, what matters is whether I am hindered from running or not. If I have sprained my ankle, but know that I shall soon recover, then it is a possibility that I shall run in the future, for I shall not be hindered from running, even if it turns out I never do run. But if I have broken my ankle in such a way that permanently disables me, then running in the future becomes an impossibility, because I am hindered from running. For Chrysippus, then, there can be propositions that are never true and yet still possible. It is possible that I shall run in the future after my sprained ankle has healed, even if I never do.

Cicero also reports that Chrysippus responded to another puzzle connected to free will, the 'Lazy Argument' (*argos logos*). This was an objection to determinism and went like this:

> If it is your fate to recover from this illness, you will recover, regardless of whether or not you call the doctor. Likewise, if it is your fate not to recover from this illness, you will not recover, regardless of whether or not you call the doctor. And one or other *is* your fate. Therefore it is pointless to call the doctor.[15]

---

[14] See e.g. Diog. Laert. 7.75 (*SVF* 2.201, **IG II-3, LS 38D**); Boethius, *in Int.*[2] 234,27–235,1 (*SVF* 2.201). Here Chrysippus was probably drawing on a third party in the debate, Philo of Megaria. For further discussion of the debate between Chrysippus and Diodorus, and the contribution of Philo, see Bobzien (1993).

[15] Cicero, *Fat.* 28–9 (**IG II-84, LS 55S**), trans. LS. See the similar account in Origen, *C. Cels.* 2.20 (*SVF* 2.957), translated in Chadwick (1953), 86.

Chrysippus rejected this, Cicero says, and responded by drawing a distinction between two types of fated event, simple (*simplicia*) and complex (*copulata*). The statement 'Socrates will die on a certain day' is simple, and does not presuppose how Socrates will die but just that he will, whereas the statement 'Laius will have a son called Oedipus' implies that Laius will have intercourse with a woman, and of course it is impossible for him to have a son without doing so. So, in the second case the event is complex, and Laius having a son and having intercourse are co-fated (*confatalia*).[16] In the case of the example used in the Lazy Argument, Chrysippus suggests that whether one recovers from the illness or not is co-fated with whether one calls the doctor. It is not obvious that this reply actually works: 'You will recover from illness' looks like a simple statement, close in form to 'Socrates will die on a certain day'; it does not seem necessarily to involve a doctor in the way that Laius having a son necessarily involves him having intercourse. After all, one might just get better on one's own. So in this particular case the example is perhaps not so well chosen. But if for the sake of argument, one assumed that calling the doctor was a required prerequisite for Socrates recovering, one still might have other concerns: my decision to call the doctor must, on Chrysippus's view, also be determined, simply by virtue of the fact that everything is determined. It may be that one's own action (calling the doctor) contributes to the final outcome (Socrates recovering), but if that action is itself fated, why make the effort to choose or not to choose to do it? Whether Chrysippus adequately responded to the Lazy Argument remains a subject of debate.[17] Either way, it is clear that he wanted to challenge logical determinism.

Chrysippus on Physical Determinism

Although Chrysippus wanted to challenge the sort of logical determinism (sometimes called 'fatalism') at work in the Master Argument and Lazy Argument, he nevertheless remained committed to physical, causal determinism.[18] Our sources report a number of statements that can be

---

[16] See Cicero, *Fat.* 30 (*SVF* 2.956, **IG II-84, LS 55S**).

[17] For a spirited critical discussion see Brennan (2005), 270–87.

[18] For a comprehensive account see Bobzien (1998a); for a briefer overview see Frede (2003).

knitted together to try to get a sense of his position. He is reported to have said that all causes are physical bodies, and these cause effects in other physical bodies.[19] Yet these causes can be contrasted with matter, which is passive, and instead are identified with the *pneuma* and the reason that pervade all things,[20] i.e. the active principle within Nature, namely God. They come together to form a chain or sequence of causes that is inviolable and inescapable.[21] This chain of causes the Stoics called 'fate' (*heimarmenê, fatum*). This is not fate in the sense of the fatalism proposed by the Lazy Argument; rather it is simply physical cause and effect. As Cicero memorably put it in his work *On Divination*, Stoic fate is not the fate of superstition, but the fate of physics.[22] Within the context of Stoic pantheism, though, this physical sequence of causes is at the same time the will of God, identified with providence (*pronoia, providentia*).[23] So we have a physical order of causes, which sounds mechanistic, but they are guided by divine reason, which does not. Either way, the order of causes is unbreakable, and the cosmos is resolutely determinist.

That might lead one to think that the Stoics denied the role of human actions in the outcome of events. Yet as we have already seen, Chrysippus wanted to insist on their contribution when replying to the Lazy Argument. In the context of physical determinism, he highlighted the way in which human actions do play their part by drawing a distinction between two types of cause, perfect and principal (*perfectae et principales*) and auxiliary and proximate (*adiuvantes et proximae*).[24] Everything does indeed take place due to antecedent causes, but not necessarily from principal causes; some things are the product of auxiliary causes. In his discussion of this in *On Fate*, Cicero quotes from Chrysippus directly:

Hence, just as the person who pushed the cylinder gave it its beginning of motion but not its capacity for rolling, likewise although the impression encountered will

---

[19] See Stobaeus 1,138,23–139,4 (*SVF* 2.336, LS 55A); Sextus Empiricus, *Math.* 9.211 (*SVF* 2.341, IG II-44, LS 55B).

[20] See Aetius 1.11.5 (*SVF* 2.340, LS 55G) and Seneca, *Ep.* 65.2 (LS 55E), although note that neither of these passages name Chrysippus in particular.

[21] See Aulus Gellius 7.2.1–3 (*SVF* 2.1000, IG II-89, LS 55K); Aetius 1.28.4 (*SVF* 2.917, IG II-79, LS 55J).

[22] See Cicero, *Div.* 1.126 (*SVF* 2.921, LS 55L).

[23] That the Stoics identified fate, God, providence, and reason is reported by various sources; see e.g. Calcidius, *in Tim.* 144 (*SVF* 2.933, LS 54U).

[24] See Cicero, *Fat.* 41 (*SVF* 2.974, IG II-90, LS 62C). For further discussion see Bobzien (1999c).

print and, as it were, emblazon its appearance on the mind, assent will be in our power. And assent, just as we said in the case of the cylinder, although prompted from outside, will thereafter move through its own force and nature. If something were brought about without an antecedent cause, it would be untrue that all things come about through fate. But if it is plausible that all events have an antecedent cause, what ground can be offered for not conceding that all things come about through fate? It is enough to understand what distinction and difference obtains between causes.[25]

This suggests a model of human action where different causes interact with one another, a mixture of what we might call internal and external causes. The cylinder rolls not solely due to the external push but also due to its own shape that makes rolling possible for it. Neither the push nor its shape is on its own enough to generate the rolling movement, but together they produce it. By analogy, Chrysippus wants to say that when we act, we do so prompted by external stimuli, but the *way* in which we respond to them is shaped by our own character, which is—like the shape of the cylinder—a vital part of the causal network generating our action. In this way, although our actions are determined, in the sense of being the product of antecedent causes, they are not forced upon us by external causes out of our control. Instead we are ourselves one of the contributing causes to our own actions. We act as we choose and not under compulsion. This view led Cicero to describe Chrysippus as holding the middle ground between those who upheld necessity and those who defended free will.[26] Or, to borrow a phrase from Alexander of Aphrodisias's discussion of the Stoic position, we might say that fate does not work against us, it works 'through us' (*di' hêmôn*).[27]

This still leaves open the question about the extent to which our characters are pre-determined. Chrysippus is presumably committed to the claim that they are the product of their own antecedent causes, whether genetic inheritance or social conditioning. Given who I am at this moment, shaped by inherited character traits, cultural values impressed upon me, and my previous experiences, it may be that I will not, and cannot, act other than I do. Yet the act is still mine, the product of me, and not forced upon me by an external chain of causes.

---

[25]   Cicero, *Fat.* 43 (IG II-90, LS 62C), trans. LS.
[26]   See Cicero, *Fat.* 39 (IG II-90, LS 62C).
[27]   See Alexander of Aphrodisias, *Fat.* 181,14 (*SVF* 2.979, LS 62G).

Epicurus Contra Democritus

Chrysippus was not the first person to reflect about physical determinism. That was probably Epicurus, who had concerns about the deterministic consequences of Democritean atomism, either as expounded by Democritus himself or by some of his later followers. Indeed, many commentators have pointed to Epicurus as the first person to think seriously about the problem of free will.[28] Democritus's version of atomism, Epicurus thought, led to a thoroughgoing physical determinism. Every event is the product of billiard ball cause and effect between atoms, removing any notion of our actions being up to us, and so our responsibility.[29] Indeed, Epicurus's principal concern about what he called 'the fate of the natural philosophers' was that it undermined the notions of praise and blame with which we all operate.[30] As he neatly put it in one of his maxims:

The man who says that all events are necessitated has no ground for criticizing the man who says that not all events are necessitated. For according to him this is itself a necessitated event.[31]

Epicurus's way out of this problem was to deny mechanistic causal determinism, by suggesting that the movements of atoms are not solely the product of antecedent causes, for if they were we would end up with a chain of fate of the sort advocated by the Stoics. He did this by proposing a doctrine of atomic swerve (*paregklisis*, *clinamen*). This notion is not mentioned in any of the surviving texts that we have from Epicurus, but it is described at length in Lucretius.[32]

---

[28] See e.g. Huby (1967); Sedley (1977), 98–9; Sharples (1991), 7.

[29] See Epicurus, *Ep. Men.* 133–4 (IG I-4, LS 20A).

[30] Epicurus, *Ep. Men.* 133–4.

[31] Epicurus, *Sent. Vat.* 40 (IG I-6, LS 20D), trans. LS. This might be taken as an attempt to show that determinism is self-refuting, or at least that the determinist who criticizes the indeterminist falls into self-refutation. In this way it parallels the Epicurean claim (see Ch. 2 above) that scepticism is self-refuting.

[32] Lucretius was probably following Epicurus's *On Nature*, which survives only in fragments on papyrus; see further Sedley (1998). Cicero attributes the doctrine to Epicurus in *Fat.* 18 and 22–3 (both IG I-15, the latter LS 20E). For further discussion see Englert (1987) and O'Keefe (2005).

Lucretius on Swerves

In *On the Nature of Things* Lucretius offers two reasons why the notion of atomic swerve is necessary. The first reason concerns the generation of objects. According to Lucretius atoms have weight and this causes them to fall straight down through the empty void. If, he suggests, they fell perfectly straight then they would never bump into one another, and so never generate the billiard ball collisions that, in turn, lead to atoms sticking together to form larger, perceptible objects. Given that such perceptible objects exist, the atoms must deviate ever so slightly from a straight path to make this possible.[33] In response to the claim that atomic collisions could be generated by heavier atoms falling onto slower-moving, lighter atoms, Lucretius says that in the void all atoms must travel at the same speed, so once again some kind of atomic swerve is necessary.[34]

The second reason that Lucretius gives concerns free will. He writes:

> Again, if movement always is connected,
> New motions coming from old in order fixed,
> If atoms never swerve and make beginning
> Of motions that can break the bonds of fate,
> And foil the infinite chain of cause and effect,
> What is the origin of this free will
> Possessed by living creatures throughout the earth?[35]

It is worth noting that Lucretius—and here he is following Epicurus—takes the existence of freedom of the will (*libera voluntas*) as a given. Our own subjective experience of making choices presents us with a self-evident truth, and rather than see the potential determinism of atomism challenge that subjective experience, he would rather modify the physical theory to bring it into line with what we think we already know. This makes him and Epicurus far less radical thinkers than Democritus, whose approach has been compared to modern-day eliminative materialism.[36] Lucretius continues:

> Whence comes, I say, this will-power wrested from the fates
> Whereby we each proceed where pleasure leads,

---

[33] See Lucretius 2.216–24 (**IG I-28, LS 11H**).
[34] See Lucretius 2.225–50 (**IG I-28, LS 11H**).
[35] Lucretius 2.251–6 (**IG I-28, LS 20F**; in the Latin this sentence continues until line 260, but Melville adds a break here).
[36] See O'Keefe (2005), 9.

Swerving our course at no fixed time or place
But where the bidding of our hearts directs?
For beyond doubt the power of the will
Originates these things and gives them birth
And from the will movements flow through the limbs.[37]

Our actions, then, are the product of our own will (*voluntas*). They originate with us and are not determined by some external force, whether 'fate' or an 'infinite chain of cause and effect'. Lucretius continues with a couple of examples: there is a difference, he says, between choosing to move forwards and being pushed forwards by someone else. If I decide to walk, then the movement originates with me, but if someone else pushes me, then the movement has its source external to me. Our will is the source of those movements that originate internally, within us. It is worth noting that this distinction between internal and external sources of movement does not touch directly the traditional debate about 'free will'. As we saw in the case of Chrysippus's cylinder, it is possible to account for people's ownership of their actions without denying physical determinism. My decision to walk may well come from within, but that decision might be the product of a whole range of antecedent causes.

The final part of Lucretius's account is the most complex. He says that the same thing applies to atoms, namely that as well as being pushed about by other atoms, they also have their own internal source of movement.[38] This seems to imply that the atoms are in some sense alive, self-moving entities rather than merely passive, inert billiard balls. He then says that this internal source of movement in atoms is the source of our own internal movement: we are self-moving because the atoms that constitute us are self-moving.[39] This looks like an argument against the claim that the most characteristic features of living creatures are emergent properties. Indeed, he seems to reject such a view in the next line: 'since nothing ever can be produced from nothing'.[40] So, the ability we have as agents to move ourselves, and not merely be pushed around by external causes, is underwritten by the fact that each individual atom has this internal power to swerve that is itself undetermined and distinct from the movements it has that are generated by either its weight or impacts from other atoms. The argument seems to go

---

[37] Lucretius 2.257–62 (IG I-28, LS 20F).
[38] Lucretius 2.285 (IG I-28, LS 20F).
[39] See Lucretius 2.286 (IG I-28, LS 20F).
[40] Lucretius 2.287 (IG I-28, LS 20F).

like this: we have the power to initiate our own movement; that power could not exist if it did not already exist in atoms; therefore atoms have the power to initiate their own movement. This is clearly not an argument *for* free will; if anything, it is an argument *from* the self-evident fact of free will, which is simply taken as a given. Yet we must again be cautious about using the phrase 'free will' here. Lucretius is primarily taking about autonomous action, caused from within,[41] and his word *voluntas* may be better understood as 'impulse' than 'will'.[42] Whether that action is 'free' remains an open question. Indeed, if we took Lucretius to be talking about the sort of conscious deliberation we associate with freedom of choice, his account would start to sound very odd, for he would effectively be saying that atoms must have that power of choice too.

Later in the poem Lucretius briefly discusses the nature of human action.[43] As in the passage we have just considered, he reflects on how it is we have the power to move our bodies. What is interesting about this later discussion is that he does not mention atomic swerve at all; instead he says that our actions are prompted by perceptions and images we have, and these atomic impacts prompt us to action. Indeed, he is explicit that our actions are not random or unexpected events, completely uncaused. There is nothing in this passage to suggest that we ought to identify random uncaused movements of atoms with acts of free will, as one traditional line of interpretation has often supposed.[44] But if that is the case, then what is the role of the swerve in relation to the freedom of human actions?

The role played by atomic swerve is to underwrite the idea of self-caused movement. We are not merely passive lumps of matter who only move due to external forces pushing us or internal features of ourselves over which we have no control; we can also cause ourselves to move. If we can do that, then so must the atoms out of which we are made.

---

[41] O'Keefe (2005), 11–18, outlines four different interpretations of the Epicurean account of freedom. My own view is closest to what O'Keefe calls the 'internal cause interpretation', which he attributes to Furley (1967) and Bobzien (2000).

[42] See O'Keefe (2005), 19, who, following Annas (1992), 176, suggests that the Latin *voluntas* might translate the Greek *hormê*, which is usually translated into English as 'impulse'.

[43] See Lucretius 4.877–96, esp. 881–5 (LS 14E).

[44] See the discussions in Bailey (1928), 435, and O'Keefe (2005), 44.

A thoroughly deterministic theory of Nature—such as the atomism of Democritus—will not do for Epicurus and Lucretius because it fails to do justice to this self-evident fact. In this sense, the idea of atomic swerve is merely a way of saying that deterministic atomism will not do as an explanation of the world as we actually experience it. For the Epicureans, atomism is supposed to explain naturalistically what we already know, not challenge our experiences by pointing to some deeper, hidden truth.

Atomic swerve is also discussed briefly by Cicero in *On Moral Ends*, where he compares Epicurus's physical theory with that of Democritus.[45] Cicero's highly critical view is that everything plausible in Epicurean atomism has simply been taken from Democritus, while the few innovations that Epicurus introduced just make the theory worse.[46] The idea of atomic swerve is one such innovation that Cicero finds absurd. He takes it to be an uncaused cause, something impossible:

The swerve itself is an arbitrary invention—he says that the atom swerves without a cause, when the most unprincipled move that any physicist can make is to adduce effects without causes.[47]

Cicero's focus here is on the first of Lucretius's reasons for positing the swerve, that is, to overcome the problem of atoms all falling downwards and never colliding with one another. He makes no mention here of this being important for human freedom. In *On Fate*, Cicero mentions the doctrine again, in equally critical terms.[48] This time he presents it as Epicurus's attempt to avoid the necessity of fate and to preserve voluntary movements of the mind. Yet it is merely the product of wishful thinking, not serious argument, Cicero says.[49] This sort of criticism does seem to miss the point that we saw Lucretius make earlier. The argument in favour of atomic swerve is concerned with 'saving the phenomena'. The only reason to posit it is to ensure that atomic theory does not contradict our familiar experience of being self-moving agents. From the perspective of the scientific theory, it might look like an arbitrary addition, but from the perspective of our everyday experience, it is an essential modification in order to keep the theory in line with what we already know.

---

[45] See Cicero, *Fin.* 1.17–21, esp. 1.19–20 (IG I-14).
[46] See Cicero, *Fin.* 1.21.   [47] Cicero, *Fin.* 1.19 (IG I-14), trans. Woolf.
[48] See Cicero, *Fat.* 46–8; cf. 18, 22–3 (all in IG I-15).
[49] See Cicero, *Fat.* 47 (IG I-15).

The important point in the present context, though, is that all of this remains neutral with regard to the traditional problem of free will. Epicurus wanted to insist that our actions do indeed come from us, but he did not tackle the sorts of issues that Chrysippus tried to address with his cylinder analogy. Chrysippus too wanted to attribute actions to individuals, and not merely to see them as being pushed about by external forces, but his response as we have seen was quite different.

Other commentators have understood the Epicurean swerve quite differently. Some have identified it with free acts of the will, while others have seen it as opening a gap whereby human choices alter the movements of atoms.[50] The problem with these interpretations, it seems to me, is that they attribute to Epicurus an absurd view. In the early eighteenth century Leibniz wrote:

> It is comical that a man like Epicurus, after having discarded the gods and all incorporeal substances, could have supposed that the will, which he himself takes as composed of atoms, could have had control over the atoms, and diverted them from their path, without its being possible for one to say how.[51]

Leibniz is surely right to find this amusing. Equally absurd is the idea that Epicurus thought that completely random and unpredictable movements of atoms might form a credible basis for free human actions. If freedom is simply the product of unexpected atomic swerves, then people are no longer self-determined but rather merely the puppets of chance.[52] That seems no better than the determinism that the doctrine is supposed to avoid. So for these reasons it is more plausible, I think, to see the doctrine as a modification of Democritean atomism simply designed to 'save the phenomena'.[53]

Carneades' Distinctions

When thinking about questions regarding free will and determinism in the Hellenistic period, the first figures who usually come to mind are those we have just considered: Chrysippus with his compatibilism and Epicurus with his swerve. Yet there was another Hellenistic philosopher

---

[50] For a survey of the various interpretations see O'Keefe (2005), 11–18.
[51] Leibniz, *Essais de Théodicée* (first published 1710), § 321, trans. in Leibniz (1951), 320.
[52] See Bailey (1928), 435, whom I paraphrase here, and O'Keefe (2005), 44.
[53] For a similar line of argument, see Wendlandt and Baltzly (2004).

whom commentators have pointed to as having made important contributions on this topic: Carneades.

Earlier we drew a distinction between logical determinism (the sort of thing propounded by the Master Argument) and physical or causal determinism. It is not always clear in the sources whether philosophers during the Hellenistic period fully appreciated that distinction and this has led to some confusion, perhaps by the Hellenistic philosophers themselves, and sometimes among commentators trying to reconstruct their arguments. It has been suggested that Carneades was the first person properly to grasp the difference between these two types of determinism.[54] Indeed, he appears to have distinguished between three types: logical, physical or causal, and epistemic determinism.[55] The latter is the idea that, if it were possible, foreknowledge of future events would make them inevitable. Debates about fate before Carneades had tended to connect epistemic determinism with logical determinism, as in the case of Aristotle's sea battle. Carneades rejected that connection, instead arguing that the only form of epistemic determinism possible would be connected to physical determinism, and would require knowledge of all the relevant antecedent causes. Such knowledge is more or less impossible, and certainly so for anything less than an omniscient divine being. Meanwhile, logical determinism, separated from epistemic determinism, becomes innocuous and simply a matter of the tenses of truth statements.

Carneades has also been credited with being the first person to argue for free will in the modern sense of the term, drawing on Epicurus and pitching himself against Chrysippus.[56] However, this may simply have been part of a sceptical strategy against Stoic determinism, designed to generate suspension of judgement, and not an expression of Carneades' own views. According to Cicero, Carneades argued that Epicurus did not need to posit atomic swerve to account for free human actions.[57] To do that was simply to fall into the determinist trap, by assuming that all human actions require external antecedent causes. Instead, Carneades argued, it is not necessary to look for external causes of voluntary movements of the mind, for they have their own power and do not require any further cause. At the same time, he argued against Stoic

---

[54] Sedley (1977), 96.   [55] See Cicero, *Fat.* 31–3 (IG II-84, LS 70G).
[56] See O'Keefe (2005), 153–62.   [57] See Cicero, *Fat.* 23–5 (IG I-15, LS 20E).

causal determinism and, like Epicurus, appealed to our experience of things being in our own power:

If all things come about through antecedent causes, all things come about through interconnexion in a natural chain. If that is so, all things are the product of necessity. If that is true, nothing is in our power. But there *is* something in our power. But if all things come about through fate, all things come about through antecedent causes. Therefore it is not the case that whatever happens happens through fate.[58]

It looks, then, as if Carneades argued against causal determinism and in favour of free will, and at the same time disarmed the threat seemingly posed by logical determinism. Yet it is worth stressing that this was probably part of a dialectical strategy against Stoic determinism, rather than an expression of Carneades' own views. Either way, it is clear that he made significant contributions to the debates about these issues. We are primarily dependent on Cicero's report of Carneades' views in a text that is itself fragmentary, but even so, Carneades' importance shines through.

Cicero's Contribution

Throughout this chapter we have drawn on material recorded in Cicero's *On Fate*, which stands as the most important extant text dealing with this topic. Anyone interested in these issues should read it in its entirety.[59] But what of Cicero's own views on this thorny topic? As a follower of the sceptical Academy we might expect him, like Carneades, to suspend judgement on such a complex issue. Towards the beginning of *On Fate* Cicero re-affirms his Academic affiliation and has his interlocutor Hirtius say, 'since your discussions at Tusculum show that you have adopted this Academic practice of arguing against something proposed, I would like, if you don't mind, to propose something on which I can hear you'.[60] There is then a break in the text, and what follows is his sustained polemic against Stoic determinism, along with swipes against the Epicurean position. Cicero rejects the physical determinism of the Stoics and, like Carneades, is unconcerned by logical determinism, seeing the

---

[58] See Cicero, *Fat.* 31 (**IG II-84, LS 70G**), trans. LS, my emphasis.
[59] There is a LCL edition with translation, now dated. For a more recent complete translation, with useful notes, see Sharples (1991).
[60] Cicero, *Fat.* 4, trans. Sharples.

arguments about necessity, possibility, and impossibility as merely arguments about the meaning of terms.[61] Questions concerning the truth of propositions about the future are quite distinct from concerns about causal determinism, Cicero suggests. In many respects, then, Cicero seems close to his Academic predecessor Carneades. That leaves us with the same question we had earlier: is this a sincere defence of free will or is it merely part of an Academic argument? In fact, there are a number of possible motivations:

  i) a rejection of all existing positions (Stoic and Epicurean) as absurd;

 ii) a rejection of determinism in particular in order to defend free will;

iii) an argument against determinism in order to counter-balance it and so generate suspension of judgement;

iv) an argument against a thesis proposed (by Hirtius), simply for the sake of display.

It is difficult to be sure about which of these motivations or combination of them guided Cicero, especially given the fragmentary nature of the text as it has come down to us. One recent commentator has suggested that 'Cicero's overall position in the work is relatively clear. He seeks to defend the idea that humans have free will'.[62] That is certainly plausible, and is supported by the facts that Cicero speaks in his own voice and the text is an exposition of just one view rather than a dialogue between views, but it is also undercut by the explicit statement of affiliation to the Academy at the beginning of the work. Yet it often seems that Cicero's commitment to Roman common sense trumps his fascination with the sceptical approach of the Academy. Indeed, his own attempt to reconcile these two tendencies within him led him to endorse Philo's more moderate brand of scepticism, which acknowledged certain views as plausible, without claiming them to be true. It may be that here Cicero's own view is that free will is far more plausible than the determinist alternative.

---

[61] See Cicero, *Fat.* 20 (IG I-15).   [62] Woolf (2015), 86.

7

Finitude

In the last two chapters we have considered a number of topics connected to ethics and human action. We have done so in a fairly theoretical way, examining the theories put forward by Stoics, Epicureans, and others, and the arguments for them. However, at a number of points so far I have suggested that for many Hellenistic thinkers philosophy was something more than simply the presentation of philosophical theories; it was also a source of guidance and advice on how to live. We shall come back to that idea in more detail in the final chapter. In this chapter we shall focus on topics that build upon the material we have discussed in the preceding chapters and that impact directly on how we think about our lives and our place within Nature. In particular we shall consider a handful of topics that engage with the notion of human finitude.

The physical theories of both the Epicureans and the Stoics highlight human finitude. For Epicurus humans are merely momentary and chance aggregations of atoms within an infinite void. We have no special place within the Epicurean cosmos, which is indifferent to our existence. At the same time, humans are often haunted by anxiety about their own death. For the Stoics, we are but tiny parts of a much larger whole. Although it is reported that Chrysippus said that some elements of the natural world were designed for our benefit,[1] the general thrust of Stoicism is to insist that we ought to conform ourselves to Nature rather than expect it to accommodate us. Fate, for the Stoics, is a force to which we should submit, not that we have any choice in the matter. The sceptical tradition also highlights human finitude in a different way, doubting our ability truly to understand the workings of the world in which we live. Peripatetics also highlighted human limitations in their

---

[1] See e.g. Plutarch, *St. rep.* 1044d (*SVF* 2.1163, LS 54O).

reflections on the extent to which humans can be completely self-sufficient. In each case we are reminded of our physical or intellectual limitations. In this chapter, then, we shall explore these issues further, cutting across the usual divisions between physics, epistemology, and ethics.

Cleanthes on Fate

Stoic reflections on human finitude focus on the role of fate. This became a central preoccupation for the later Roman Stoics writing after the Hellenistic period. Both Seneca and Epictetus quote from Cleanthes on this topic and we are fortunate to have a slightly longer text by Cleanthes as well, the *Hymn to Zeus*, preserved by the anthologist Stobaeus.[2] Although only a couple of pages long, Cleanthes' *Hymn* is the longest surviving text by a Stoic of the Hellenistic period, and so for that reason alone deserves our attention. First, some brief comments on Cleanthes' remarks about Zeus, before turning to his statement on fate.

Cleanthes' *Hymn* opens by describing Zeus as immortal, all-powerful, and the ruler of Nature. The 'whole universe', Cleanthes writes, addressing Zeus directly, 'obeys you wherever you lead'.[3] Zeus, he says, directs the universal reason that permeates all things, creating an 'ever-existing rational order for everything'.[4] Many people fail to grasp God's universal law and, although they desire a good life, they pursue the wrong things. These misguided people are said to be outside the control of all-powerful Zeus.[5] (Another source tells us that Cleanthes distinguished between fate and providence; presumably these bad people fall outside the scope of Zeus's providence but remain subject to fate.[6]) Zeus's universal reason, then, does not quite govern everything after all.[7] Towards the end, Cleanthes entreats God to 'deliver human beings from their destructive ignorance'.[8]

---

[2] The *Hymn to Zeus* is in Stobaeus 1,25,3–1,27,4 (*SVF* 1.537). It has been translated many times, including in **IG II-21** and **LS 54I**. See Thom (2005) for a new edition of the text, with a translation and detailed commentary. In what follows I rely on his edition and translation, citing his line numbers.

[3] Cleanthes, *Hymn*, lines 7–8.   [4] Cleanthes, *Hymn*, lines 12–13 and 21.

[5] Cleanthes, *Hymn*, lines 15–17.

[6] See Calcidius, *in Tim.* 144 (*SVF* 1.551, **LS 54U**).

[7] See further Bobzien (1998a), 347.   [8] Cleanthes, *Hymn*, line 33.

When read within the wider context of Stoic physics and theology, Cleanthes' *Hymn* can seem deeply problematic. It describes Zeus in terms familiar from traditional Greek religion as the highest of the immortals and the wielder of the thunderbolt. It also presents Zeus as a force outside of Nature, rather than one within it or identical to it. Thus Zeus is described as *directing* the rational principle within Nature, when we might expect Zeus to be presented as *being* that rational principle. It asks Zeus to deliver the non-wise from their ignorance but, within the wider context of Stoic philosophy, it is difficult to comprehend how such a thing would be expected to work.

Cleanthes is widely considered to be the most religious of the early Stoics, separating theology off from physics.[9] His *Hymn* raises some wider questions about Stoic attitudes towards religion. Some have taken it as part of a larger shift, in which the Hellenistic philosophical schools come close to becoming religious movements, with sets of beliefs and devoted followers.[10] But what of wider Stoic attitudes towards religion? How seriously ought we to take these prayers to Zeus? Let me offer two potentially competing images.

One image would present the Stoics as thoroughgoing materialists, explaining the order within Nature as the product of a physical force, *pneuma*, informed by the contemporary scientific studies of Praxagoras and Erasistratus.[11] Although they often referred to a single God, which they identified with Nature, and to the gods of traditional Greek religion, their sliding between these two simply highlights their lack of concern with such issues. Indeed, the Stoics were noted for offering allegorical interpretations of the traditional gods, explaining them away in terms of physical processes. A famous example of this is Chrysippus's interpretation of an image of Zeus and his wife Hera entwined with one another as a representation of the active principle in Nature inserting the *spermatikos logos* into the passive principle, matter.[12] Diogenes Laertius tells us that it appeared in a book devoted to natural philosophy and was intended as a defence of physics.[13] On this view, the Stoics had little time for religion.

---

[9] See e.g. Algra (2003), 153; Thom (2005), 5.
[10] This view has been held widely; see e.g. Sedley (1989), 97; Thom (2005), vii.
[11] See Ch. 4 above.   [12] See e.g. Origen, *C. Cels.* 4.48 (*SVF* 2.1074).
[13] See Diog. Laert. 7.187–8 (*SVF* 2.1071, **IG** II-1).

An alternative image would present the Stoics as deeply religious thinkers. They are insistent that Nature is a living being (*zôion*), rational (*logikon*), animate (*empsuchon*), and intelligent (*noeron*).[14] They offer a whole series of formal philosophical arguments recorded in Cicero's *On the Nature of the Gods* about why we ought to identify Nature with God.[15] And, of course, they write devotional texts such as Cleanthes' *Hymn to Zeus*. Although they might allegorically explain away the traditional Greek pantheon of gods, their commitment to the idea that Nature is itself an intelligent, divine being is beyond doubt. On this view, the Stoics are deeply religious and to live in accord with Nature is ultimately to live in accord with the will of God.

It would probably be a mistake to try to push the contrast between these two images very far. The Stoics can hold both that Nature is a divine being *and* that the best way to understand this living being is through the study of physics. The real problem arises, though, when the Stoics use very personalistic language about God that presents him/her/it as an entity distinct from Nature. When Cleanthes appeals to God in the *Hymn*, he seems to be forgetting that we are ourselves part of the Stoic God, and that the *pneuma* that constitutes our soul is itself a fragment of the divine soul permeating Nature. Is this merely a literary device—a nod to traditional Greek hymns—or is it intended as a serious contribution to Stoic theology?

Perhaps the solution is to be found by remembering that the Stoics held that the divine soul permeating Nature has a ruling part (*hêgemonikon*) with a specific location, just as the human soul has a central location where the mind resides. Cleanthes is reported to have located this divine mind in the sun.[16] While our souls are fragments of the divine soul, our minds are not (on this account) fragments of the divine mind. God's intelligence is distinct from ours and so it is not so inconsistent to discuss God as if something distinct from ourselves.

One of the central themes of the *Hymn* is the all-powerful nature of Zeus. This is picked up in the shorter text attributed to Cleanthes by

---

[14] See Diog. Laert. 7.142 (**IG II-20**).   [15] See Ch. 3 above.
[16] See Diog. Laert. 7.139 (**IG II-20**). Chrysippus and Posidonius are reported to have located the divine mind in the heaven (Diog. Laert. 7.139), but the point I make here applies either way.

Seneca and Epictetus, the *Prayer to Zeus*.[17] Just four lines of Greek text survive:[18]

> Lead me, O Zeus, and you O Fate,
> to whatever place you have assigned me;
> I shall follow without reluctance, and if I am not willing to,
> because I have become a bad man, nevertheless I will follow.[19]

In the last chapter we saw Chrysippus argue against the Lazy Argument, insisting that even in a determinist world human actions play their part in contributing to the outcome of events. Fate does not work against us; it works through us. Here, however, we see his immediate predecessor and teacher Cleanthes presenting fate as an overpowering force external to us, to which we shall succumb either willingly or unwillingly. Indeed, a potential fifth line of the text, surviving only in Latin, reads: 'Fate leads the willing, and pulls the unwilling'.[20]

As in the *Hymn to Zeus*, Cleanthes here uses personalistic language about Zeus, which again might simply reflect the literary conventions surrounding hymns. God and fate, which other Stoic sources identify as one and the same thing,[21] are here distinguished from one another. This might reflect that, according to another source, Cleanthes (unlike his successor Chrysippus) is said to have distinguished between providence and fate, claiming that while everything that comes from providence is fated, not everything that is fated comes from providence.[22] If that is correct, then there are two distinct powers controlling our destiny, although it seems clear that Zeus takes precedence. Either way, our place within the world has already been determined by a greater force, and the only choice left to us is whether to embrace that destiny or to fight against it, for it will come to pass no matter what. Cleanthes

---

[17] See Seneca, *Ep.* 107.11 and Epictetus, *Ench.* 53 (both *SVF* 1.527, the latter **IG II-22, LS 62B**).

[18] Seneca translated Cleanthes' text into Latin (*Ep.* 107.11) and his version has a fifth line at the end. It is not clear whether this is also by Cleanthes or an addition by Seneca. Augustine would later quote Seneca's version (*Civ. Dei* 5.8), attributing it all to Seneca himself.

[19] Cleanthes, quoted in Epictetus, *Ench.* 53 (*SVF* 1.527; **IG II-22, LS 62B**), trans. IG. For commentary see Bobzien (1998a), 346–9.

[20] Seneca, *Ep.* 107.11 (*SVF* 1.527).

[21] See e.g. Alexander of Aphrodisias, *Fat.* 203,12–14 (*SVF* 2.928); Augustine, *Civ. Dei* 5.8 (*SVF* 2.932).

[22] See Calcidius, *in Tim.* 144 (*SVF* 1.551, 2.933), translated in Magee (2016).

presents the person who struggles against fate as a bad person, and although we do not get a reason why, it is clear that he thought that embracing what happens is an important part of leading a good life. The reason may be a simple theological one: the person who resists the will of God is impious. Equally, it seems clear that a 'life in accord with Nature' will be incompatible with an attitude that continually resists what Nature brings to pass. In sum, we might say that what happens to us is out of our control, but our view of what happens to us remains within our choice.[23] The view that we take—either acceptance or struggle—will of course have a significant impact on whether we reach the Stoic goal of 'a smooth flow of life'.[24]

The view we find in Cleanthes' *Prayer* is echoed in another text, although this time the view is attributed to Zeno and Chrysippus:

When a dog is tied to a cart, if it wants to follow it is pulled and follows, making its spontaneous act coincide with necessity, but if it does not want to follow it will be compelled in any case. So it is with men too: even if they do not want to, they will be compelled in any case to follow what is destined.[25]

Once again, the contrast is between embracing or struggling against what will, of necessity, come to pass. It is not making a contribution to theoretical debates about determinism, but rather is about one's attitude towards what happens. As finite beings, some things are simply out of our control, and it is up to us whether we accept that or fight against it.

Preparing for Future Evils

These Stoic reflections on the nature of necessity or fate were designed in part to lessen the blow of seemingly unpleasant events. The person who grasps the necessity of such events, not to mention their place within a providentially ordered Nature, can console themselves in the face of apparent adversity. For a Stoic sage, this sort of adversity is of course only ever apparent, for it is merely within the realm of 'indifferents'.

---

[23] This distinction became central to the philosophy of the later Stoic Epictetus, which perhaps explains why he chose to quote this passage.

[24] Diog. Laert. 7.88 (IG II-94, LS 63C).

[25] Hippolytus, *Haer.* 1.21 (*SVF* 2.975, **LS 62A**), trans. LS. For commentary see Bobzien (1998a), 351–7, who, however, questions whether it really reports the view of Zeno or Chrysippus.

According to Cicero, Cleanthes held that the task of consolation is 'to teach the sufferer that what happened is not an evil at all'.[26] Even so, the Stoics were well aware that for most people a wide range of external events can seem deeply unpleasant, and one way in which they tried to help people was to encourage the practice of contemplating future evils (*praemeditatio futurorum malorum*).[27]

Later Stoics such as Seneca, writing after the Hellenistic period, made great use of this idea, but Cicero tells us that Chrysippus also proposed the contemplation of future evils.[28] Other Hellenistic philosophers also engaged with the idea, while Epicurus and Carneades both argued against its usefulness. Carneades argued against Chrysippus,[29] while Epicurus was probably responding to the earlier Cyrenaics, who also adopted this practice.[30]

The idea is that one mentally rehearse potentially unpleasant events that might happen in the future, in order to prepare oneself better to cope with them, should they come to pass. In some cases, the event in question definitely will happen (friends and relatives must at some point die); in other cases, the event might never happen (such as a prolonged, painful illness). In either case, the suggestion goes, mentally rehearsing such events in advance can help us to cope with them, if or when they happen. Cicero reports that Chrysippus held the view that 'what is unforeseen strikes us with greater force' than what we have already rehearsed in our minds.[31]

Unfortunately we do not know much more about how the Stoics explained the effectiveness of this practice or how they used it. Cicero tells us that the Cyrenaics claimed that this sort of preparedness was an antidote to distress, for distress is *only* produced by misfortunes that are not foreseen or anticipated.[32] Cicero doubts the claim that unexpected-ness is the sole cause of distress, but accepts the more modest one that

---

[26] Cicero, *Tusc.* 3.76 (*SVF* 1.576). This and subsequent translations come from Graver (2002). Cicero goes on to note, 3.77 (*SVF* 1.577), that this approach is directed at the sage, who does not need consolation.

[27] Cicero, *Tusc.* 3.29. Cicero discusses this topic at length in Book 3 of the *Tusculan Disputations* and is our main source of information.

[28] Cicero, *Tusc.* 3.52 (*SVF* 3.417). On Cicero's use of Chrysippus's book *On Emotion* in the *Tusculan Disputations* see Graver (2002), 203–14.

[29] Cicero, *Tusc.* 3.59.   [30] Cicero, *Tusc.* 3.32 (Us. 444).

[31] Cicero, *Tusc.* 3.52 (*SVF* 3.417).   [32] Cicero, *Tusc.* 3.28 (*SSR* IV A 208).

'things that are considered bad are worse when unforeseen'.[33] This brings him close to Chrysippus's view.

As with so many other things, the Academic Carneades took issue with Chrysippus on this, claiming that reflecting on unpleasant events will do nothing to relieve distress. On the contrary, being continually reminded that we shall die along with all our loved ones is only likely to cause us to grieve even more at the human condition.[34]

Epicurus was also sceptical about the benefits of reflecting on future evils. There is little to be gained, he suggested, from rehearsing misfortunes that are not yet present and in fact may never happen.[35] On the basis of his hedonistic principles, pre-rehearsing a potential future evil will simply multiply the pain, for one will experience the anticipation of the physical pain as well as the physical pain itself. Why torture oneself imagining the horrors of a painful illness when such a thing might not even happen? The contemplation of future evils, then, is simply a recipe for permanent anxiety, Epicurus suggested. Much better instead to remember past pleasures or anticipate future ones.

Epicureans on Death

Although Epicurus might have been sceptical about the value of some therapeutic practices, he remained committed to the general idea that philosophy might offer some kind of therapy for human suffering. The later Epicurean Philodemus summarized the central principles of Epicurean philosophy in his 'fourfold cure' (*tetrapharmakos*): 'don't fear God, don't worry about death; what is good is easy to get, and what is terrible is easy to endure'.[36] Epicurus was especially concerned about anxiety generated by fear of divine punishment and by fear of death, both of which he took to be common forms of psychological distress. His physical theory functions as a response to the first of these, denying the existence of any kind of divine intervention in the workings of Nature, but what about fear of death?

---

[33] Cicero, *Tusc.* 3.30; see also 3.59.   [34] Cicero, *Tusc.* 3.59–60.
[35] See Cicero, *Tusc.* 3.32–3 (Us. 444).
[36] Philodemus, *Adv. Soph.* (*PHerc* 1005), in LS 25J.

Epicurus's argument that 'death is nothing to us' is one of the most celebrated parts of his philosophy.[37] The central ideas are set out in his *Letter to Menoeceus*, where he makes a number of inter-related points.[38] First, he says that 'all good and evil come from sensation, but death is the absence of sensation', so death is neither good nor evil. The dead have no sensations and so experience neither pleasure nor pain. Of course, this is an unhelpful way of putting it, for there are no *dead* people, and this way of thinking is precisely part of the problem. We are tempted to ask questions such as, 'what will happen to me when I am dead?', not fully grasping the fact that I will never *be* dead, because after my death I will no longer exist. There will be no 'me' to whom things will happen after my death. Our anxiety about death is generated in part by the difficulty of grasping our own future non-existence. If death is non-existence, then, by definition, we shall never experience it, and so have nothing to fear from it.

Knowing this, he suggests, ought to make life more pleasant, and he gives us a reason why: there can be nothing terrible in life for someone who grasps that there is nothing terrible in not living. The worst thing that can happen to someone while they are alive is that they die or get killed. Apart from the physical pain involved, which Epicurus will of course acknowledge as genuinely evil, fear of things like poverty, hunger, or violence ultimately boil down to the fear that these things taken to extremes might kill us. Once we realize that the worst possible outcome is in fact not evil in itself, indeed it is nothing at all, then our fear of all those things will also be reduced.

Epicurus seems to be suggesting that once we grasp this central claim, our fear will all but disappear, but on his own terms we still have good reasons to fear the physical pain that comes with, say, hunger or violence, even if we are no longer disturbed by the prospect of death. But it is worth remembering that Epicurus thinks psychological pain is significantly worse than physical pain, and he offers other 'remedies' for coping with physical suffering.[39] Indeed, as he continues, his focus is squarely on

---

[37] For discussions see e.g. Furley (1986), Nussbaum (1994), 192–238, and Warren (2004a).

[38] See *Ep. Men.* 124–7 (IG I-4, LS 24A). All of my references to Epicurus in what follows are to statements in this passage, unless otherwise noted.

[39] In particular he suggests that physical pain is either mild or short, and so, either way, easy to bear. See *Rat. Sent.* 4 (IG I-5, LS 21C) and *Ep. Men.* 133 (IG I-4).

the psychological pain of the expectation of death, and he wants to show that if we can grasp the idea that 'death is nothing to us', then we shall see that fearing something of no concern to us is absurd. As he puts it, 'that which while present causes no distress causes unnecessary pain when merely anticipated'.[40]

If one were to accept this claim that death ought to be of no concern to us, would one become indifferent to one's own survival? It looks as if our fear of death leads us to do many things that contribute to our continued existence. Epicurus responds to this kind of concern by saying that the wise person will neither deprecate living nor fear death,[41] and they will certainly reject the view, repeated a number of times in antiquity, that it would have been better never to have been born.[42] Although he does not say this explicitly, Epicurus's view, in line with his ethics, seems to be that the bare fact of existence is neither good nor bad in itself, and its value is determined by the pleasures and pains that it contains. Equally, death is neither good nor bad in itself, and that might lead one to conclude that there is little to choose between life and death. But Epicurus is quite insistent that pleasure can always be found in life, whether simple pleasures in the here and now or remembering past pleasures, and both these things are, he suggests, always readily accessible.

Epicurus's remarks on death are very brief, the equivalent of just a couple of modern paragraphs. Lucretius gives us a little more, although again only a handful of paragraphs when translated into English prose, but he does add a series of further points.[43] His first point is that there is a symmetry between the period of non-existence before we were born and that of non-existence after our death. We are not overly concerned by the fact there was once a period of time during which we did not exist, and so equally there is no reason to be concerned about the fact that there will again be a time when we do not exist. I am not particularly concerned by

---

[40] *Ep. Men.* 125 (**IG** I-4, **LS** 24A), trans. IG.

[41] Part of the text where this statement occurs is a supplement proposed by Usener (1887) and generally accepted by editors.

[42] Epicurus cites Theognis, which is echoed in a passage in Sophocles (*Oedipus Coloneus* 1224-7) and in the so-called 'wisdom of Silenus', reported by Aristotle in a now lost work (the *Eudemus*) quoted by Plutarch, *Cons. ad Apoll.* 115b-e (Aristotle fr. 44 Rose³, in Ross (1955), 18).

[43] See Lucretius 3.830–911 (**LS** 24E). In what follows I shall mention four points that Lucretius makes in this passage: i) symmetry (832–42), ii) separation (843–6), iii) continuity (847–60), and iv) non-existence (861–901).

the fact that I did not exist in 1500 AD, and I am equally unconcerned that I shall not exist in 2500 AD. However, critics have argued that we are rightly far more concerned about our non-existence in the very near future, not least for all of the very real opportunities that are taken away from a life cut short.[44] Most of us would be quite concerned to learn that we might not exist next week.

Lucretius then considers different forms of post-mortem existence. What if the mind continued to exist with the power of sensation after the death of the body? Even if that were the case, it should still be of no concern to us, because we are a conjunction of mind and body, and so whatever survived would not be 'us'.[45] Although he does not elaborate on this, the point fits with other Epicurean claims, in particular that all good and evil depend on sensation, and that sensation depends on the body. It is far from clear what, if anything, a disembodied mind or spirit (*anima*) would experience when separated from the sense organs of the body. Whatever such an existence might look like, it would be nothing like the embodied existence with which we are familiar. Without sensation, dependent as that is on the body, the highly unlikely prospect of consciousness after death would be devoid of physical pleasure and pain, and so neither good nor evil.

A quite different form of post-mortem existence would be the physical reconstitution of our bodies after a period of dissolution: a physical resurrection.[46] Even this, Lucretius suggests, ought to be of no concern to us, for this future copy of ourselves would no longer be 'us', because it would have no recollection of being 'us'. The lack of continuous memories would undermine any claim to identity. If the prospect of these future doppelgangers sounds somewhat unnerving, Lucretius adds that such duplicates may have already existed: given limitless time, there is no reason not to suppose that the atoms that form our bodies now did not come together in the same arrangement at some point in the past. Lucretius raises this possibility to make the point that we would feel no

---

[44] See Nagel (1979), 1–10. For further discussion see Warren (2004a), 57–108.

[45] Lucretius uses the word *anima* (soul, life) rather than *animus* (soul, mind), but I render this as 'mind' here. LS translate it as 'spirit'.

[46] Lucretius tackles these different forms of post-mortem existence not to specify the conditions for personal identity, but instead to undermine different forms of fear of death.

concern about these doubles from the past, so equally we should have no concern for any double that might exist in the future.[47]

Most anxiety about death, however, derives from failing to grasp fully the fact that we shall no longer exist. As Lucretius puts it, 'if there is going to be unhappiness and suffering, the person must also himself exist at the same time'.[48] Yet many of the fears people have about death implicitly suppose that they will still be present to suffer in some way. If someone imagines their dead body not being accorded proper respect, or their not being able to look after their children in the future, they are often assuming that some part of them will be around to observe these things taking place. The unhappiness stems from imagining oneself as an observer of the rest of the world continuing after one's death. The point Lucretius makes is that this simply will not be the case. We might imagine various hypothetical situations here and now, dreaming up worst-case scenarios that feed our anxiety, but in reality we shall never be able to experience any of these things.

The topic of death continued to preoccupy later Epicureans. While Epicurus and Lucretius each devoted the equivalent of just a few paragraphs to it, Philodemus wrote an entire treatise, in at least four books. A papyrus recovered from Herculaneum preserves part of Book 4 of his *On Death*, in which he discusses from an Epicurean perspective a whole range of human concerns related to fear of death, such as dying without having had children, dying far from one's homeland, dying in bed rather than on the battlefield (a common modern fear, similar in kind, might be dying in hospital rather than at home), and being forgotten after one's death.[49]

Perhaps the most significant of the topics that Philodemus addresses (in the relatively small fragment of the treatise that survives) is the importance of the length of one's life. One might accept the central Epicurean claim that there is nothing to fear from death, for it is simply non-existence, and so neither good nor evil, yet still be concerned about the length of one's life. Surely it is better to live to eighty years old rather

---

[47] The Stoics were committed to the existence of such past and future doubles via their doctrine of cyclical recurrence, which has led to debates about personal identity: am I the *same* person as the copy of me in other cosmic cycles?

[48] Lucretius 3.862–3 (LS 24E).

[49] See Henry (2009) for an edition of the text with facing translation. For a discussion, see Sanders (2011).

than die at forty, or even twenty. One might not be concerned about death itself, but one might still be very concerned about missing out on a whole range of opportunities in life that death takes away.[50] We still have good reasons, then, to be anxious about death.

Philodemus responded to this sort of objection by arguing that what matters is the quality rather than quantity of life. A long life that is wretched is no blessing at all, so claiming that a long life is better than a short one is too simplistic.[51] For the especially foolish, Philodemus harshly comments, it may be better all round if they die young. But one might still come back with the thought that, for a good person, a longer life will be preferable to one cut short. To this Philodemus alludes to the Epicurean distinction between active and static pleasures: for the person who has achieved static pleasure, life is complete in the present moment, and no further amount of anticipated future active pleasure can increase it.[52] Indeed, life as it is lived is always only in the present moment; a longer life is not more pleasurable than a shorter one because pleasure is not increased by duration. For someone anxious not about death itself, but about the length of their life, the Epicureans think their theory of pleasure can offer the necessary therapeutic consolation.

Philodemus picks up this idea again at the end of his treatise (that is, at the end of Book 4, which may or may not have been the last book of the whole work), where he suggests that we ought always to be prepared for death.[53] It would be foolish, he says, to be shocked or surprised by the prospect of an imminent death, given that we all know we are mortal creatures destined to die. It would be equally foolish to devote excessive energy to planning our future years well in advance. Instead, Philodemus counsels that we ought to live in the present moment, grateful for what we have in the here and now, with no great expectations for the future. We ought to live each day as it comes, and be completely unsurprised when death appears to be upon us.[54] This implicitly suggests that we

---

[50] Nagel (1979), 1–10, argued for an asymmetry between non-existence before birth and after death as an objection against Lucretius. Here we can see that this concern had already been raised in the Hellenistic period.

[51] See Philodemus, *Mort.* col. 12,2–13,28 (translated in Henry (2009), 27–31).

[52] See e.g. Epicurus, *Rat. Sent.* 19 (IG I-5, LS 24C). On Epicurean pleasure see above, Ch. 5.

[53] See Philodemus, *Mort.* col. 37,18–39,25 (translated in Henry (2009), 87–93).

[54] See esp. *Mort.* col. 38,14–25 (translated in Henry (2009) 88–9).

ought to take up some form of regular reflection on our own mortality, in order to remind us of this basic fact about human existence. It is worth noting, however, that such reflections on the fact of our future non-existence would be quite different from the premeditation of future evils that Epicurus rejected.[55] For, as we have seen, non-existence is no evil.

Academics on the Limits of Human Knowledge

Although on the face of it less concerned with these sorts of existential issues, the sceptically minded Academics also stressed human finitude. Arcesilaus's turn to scepticism may have been, in part, inspired by the example of Pyrrho.[56] But, as the heir to Plato's Academy, he also claimed to be continuing a tradition of thought inaugurated by Socrates, and recorded in the Platonic dialogues. Socrates had famously claimed that all that he knew was that he knew nothing. This, at least, is how Arcesilaus understood him.[57] However, Socrates' own statements on this in Plato's *Apology* are not quite so strong, saying only that he was aware of not knowing anything.[58] Either way, Arcesilaus insisted that nothing can be known, not even *that* one knows nothing.[59] His philosophical project, then, was less concerned with what he could or could not know, and more with the claims to knowledge made by others.

Arcesilaus positioned himself as a follower of Socratic-Platonic practice by taking up Socrates' dialectical method of arguing against others on their own terms.[60] The procedure is purely destructive, as we can see in many of the early Platonic dialogues. The arrogant interlocutor who thinks he knows something is shown that, in fact, he knows far less than he supposed. For Socrates, this may have been a depressing and disappointing process in his quest for knowledge about how to live well, but for Arcesilaus it seems to have become a deliberate procedure aimed at generating suspension of judgement (*epochê*) in himself and others—not out of a negative dogmatic view that knowledge is impossible, but more from a sense, borne out by experience, that knowledge is something extremely hard to come by. The sceptical Academics, then, along with

---

[55] See Cicero, *Tusc.* 3.32.   [56] See Sedley (1983).   [57] See Cicero, *Acad.* 1.45.
[58] See e.g. Plato, *Apology* 21b. I owe this point to Annas (1994), 310.
[59] See again Cicero, *Acad.* 1.45. This passage is quoted and discussed in Ch. 2 above.
[60] See e.g. Cicero, *Fin.* 2.2 (IG III-16, LS 68J).

other sceptics of the period, made the limitations of human knowledge the central preoccupation of their philosophical activity.

Peripatetics on the Limits of Self-Sufficiency

We also find Peripatetics of the period stressing human finitude and the ways in which human happiness can be dependent on fortune. Aristotle had suggested that a good life requires not merely virtuous activity but also some external goods. Yet his considered position is not entirely clear. In the *Nicomachean Ethics*, he argued that although some externals are required for a truly happy life, their absence was not fatal; one could be happy (*eudaimôn*) without them when suffering great misfortune, although not blessed (*makarios*).[61] In his *Eudemian Ethics*, he considered further the role of good fortune in human life, admitting that some people do very well in life despite lacking any kind of understanding.[62]

Perhaps reflecting on these accounts, Theophrastus took a slightly different view, emphasizing the role of fortune in human life, and so the contingency of human happiness. Misfortune, torture, exile, and child-lessness can all make life genuinely miserable, he claimed.[63] That thought was developed further by Critolaus's account of three types of goods (mental, bodily, external), all of which he argued are required for a good life.[64] In both cases these ethical claims reflect an attempt to understand human beings within the context of Nature, as finite embodied beings with real physical needs. Any dispassionate study of human beings, as just one type of animal among many, will surely show that a lot more than merely an excellent mental state will be required for them to flourish. Perhaps one consequence, then, of the Hellenistic Lyceum's focus on the study of physics was an increased appreciation of humans as merely parts of Nature, limited in power, whose wellbeing is thus inevitably subject to the whims of fortune.

---

[61] See e.g. Aristotle, *Eth. Nic.* 1.9, 1099b27–8, on the role of externals, and 1.10, 1100b22–1101a8, on the role of misfortune.

[62] See Aristotle, *Eth. Eud.* 8.2.

[63] See Cicero, *Tusc.* 5.24 (FHSG 493); also *Fin.* 5.12 (FHSG 498), with Inwood (2014), 34–6.

[64] See e.g. Stobaeus 2,46,10–17 (fr. 19 in Wehrli (1969d), 18I in Sharples (2010)); cf. Sharples (2007), 628, with the discussion in Ch. 5 above.

Despite arguing that a good life requires external goods, Theophrastus's claim that those goods are ultimately out of our control led him to suggest that we should focus our attention on improving our internal mental state. If, for instance, gaining both an education and money are essential for a good life, but the latter is beyond our control, then we ought to concentrate our efforts on the former. He wrote:

Of all men the educated man alone is neither a stranger in foreign places nor lacking in friends, when the members of his household and relatives are lost. Rather he is a citizen in every state and able to disdain without fear the hard accidents of fortune. But he, who thinks himself to be fortified not by the defences of education but those of good luck, makes his way by slippery paths and is brought to ruin by a life which is not stable but infirm.[65]

Education makes us a citizen of the whole world, a thought that leads us neatly on to our next topic: politics.

---

[65] Vitruvius, De arch. 6 pr. 2 (FHSG 491), trans. FHSG. This may or may not be a direct quotation from Theophrastus (via Latin).

8

Community

In ancient philosophy, Plato and Aristotle stand out as the preeminent political philosophers, in the sense that they were deeply concerned about the form and function of the city-state or *polis*. By contrast, philosophers in the Hellenistic period seem at first glance to have much less to say. Traditional narratives of ancient philosophy put this down to the transformation of the ancient world in the wake of Alexander the Great. Subsumed by centralized Empires, the Greek city-states were no longer autonomous self-governing entities in which citizens might have a say (the prime example being Athens during its democratic phase), but now merely provinces centrally governed by rulers often far away. No wonder, so the traditional story goes, that philosophers in the Hellenistic period paid little attention to questions in political philosophy, a subject that must now have seemed irrelevant.

Even so, philosophers in this period remained deeply concerned about how human beings might best live together.[1] While less concerned about the mechanics of political organization, unsurprisingly questions about what an ideal human community might look like did not just go away. In this chapter, we shall consider some examples of Hellenistic thinking about human communities, both utopian and highly practical. But before we turn to them directly, it might be helpful to say something about a philosopher contemporary with Alexander the Great, and so active just before the Hellenistic period proper: Diogenes of Sinope, the Cynic.

Diogenes was no doubt a colourful character, so colourful that it can be hard to know how best to take the numerous anecdotes that purport

---

[1] The studies by various hands in Laks and Schofield (1995) illustrate the range of thinking about politics in the Hellenistic period. There are also a number of relevant chapters in Rowe and Schofield (2000), esp. chs 22–4.

to record events from his life. It would be nice to accept all of them as true, but he was probably the sort of person around whom legends easily grew. One of the anecdotes that survives describes a confrontation between Diogenes and Alexander.[2] When Diogenes was idly basking in the sun one day beside a road, Alexander and his troops marched past. When Alexander was level with Diogenes he greeted him, saying he could grant him anything; what would he like? Diogenes responded, 'for you to get out of my light!'. To this Alexander is said to have commented, 'If I were not Alexander I would wish to be Diogenes'.[3] Whether or not this encounter took place, it reminds us that Diogenes was a contemporary of Alexander, a first-hand witness to the political transformation of the ancient world initiated by Aristotle's most famous pupil. It is within this context that Diogenes is reported to have described himself on some other occasion as a *kosmopolitês*, a cosmopolitan or citizen of the cosmos, rather than a citizen of any particular city.[4] There are two ways in which we might understand this declaration. It might be i) a purely negative claim, refusing to identify as a citizen of any particular city-state, or it might be ii) a more positive statement expressing an active allegiance to the world as a whole. If it is a positive statement, it might, in turn, be understood in two distinct ways: iia) affirming a global community of all humankind, or iib) expressing a commitment to follow the natural laws of the cosmos, rather than the arbitrary laws of any human community. With only limited evidence, it is hard to know for sure what Diogenes intended.

As I have already noted, traditional narratives attribute this new cosmopolitan attitude to the decline in the political importance of the individual city-state. However, Diogenes never lived to see this, as he died around the same time as Alexander, and it is also worth noting that similar cosmopolitan attitudes are credited to Socrates and a number of Socratic philosophers, such as Aristippus, all predating the rise of the

---

[2] See Plutarch, *Alex.* 14.1–3 (*SSR* V B 32), parts of which are repeated in Diog. Laert. 6.38, 6.32; Cicero, *Tusc.* 5.92 (*SSR* V B 33). In the following lines I paraphrase the passage. For further anecdotes that bring Diogenes and Alexander together see the texts gathered in *SSR* V B 31–49.

[3] This line is repeated in a number of sources; see e.g. Plutarch, *De Alex. fort.* 331e–f (*SSR* V B 31).

[4] See Diog. Laert. 6.63 (*SSR* V B 355).

Hellenistic kingdoms in the wake of Alexander.[5] It is difficult to know how reliable such evidence is, but it hints at the thought that ancient cosmopolitanism was not merely a theoretical echo of Hellenistic political events. Although Diogenes himself falls outside the Hellenistic period proper, his views on this topic form important background when approaching the early Stoics.

Stoic Cosmopolitanism

The founder of Stoicism, Zeno, began his philosophical journey as a pupil of Crates the Cynic, himself a onetime pupil of Diogenes. Crates embraced Diogenes' cosmopolitan attitude in his life and over time accumulated an equally entertaining collection of anecdotes. Some sources suggest that it was during his time with Crates, or not long after, that Zeno wrote his first work of philosophy, the *Republic*.[6]

The surviving evidence for the *Republic* is relatively thin, but the longest passage describing its contents, written by Plutarch, points to a cosmopolitan attitude probably inherited from the Cynics:

The much admired *Republic* of Zeno, the founder of the Stoic sect, is aimed at this one main point, that our household arrangements should not be based on cities or parishes, each one marked out by its own legal system, but we should regard all humans as our fellow citizens and local residents, and there should be one way of life and order, like that of a herd grazing together and nurtured by a common pasture. Zeno wrote this, picturing as it were a dream or image of a philosopher's well-regulated society.[7]

Other evidence for the *Republic* fleshes out what this ideal cosmopolitan community would look like: no money, law courts, or temples; open sexual relationships, with men and women wearing the same sort of clothes.[8] In

---

[5] For Socrates see Cicero, *Tusc.* 5.108 (*SSR* I C 492); for Aristippus see Xenophon, *Mem.* 2.1.13 (*SSR* IV A 163).

[6] See Diog. Laert. 7.4 (*SVF* 1.2, **IG II-1**). It may be that this claim was made up by later Stoics, scandalized by some of the ideas in the *Republic*, and trying to distance themselves from it by dismissing it as a youthful and immature work. See further Schofield (1991), 3–21.

[7] Plutarch, *De Alex. fort.* 329a–b (**LS 67A**).

[8] See esp. Diog. Laert. 7.32–3 (**IG II-1, LS 67B**). The evidence for the *Republic* is gathered together and translated in Sellars (2007), 25–9.

short, it rejects almost all elements of conventional social life, and seems to propose a global anarchistic 'hippy' community.[9]

How was this supposed to work? Could a community without any kind of law really be viable? Did Zeno seriously propose such a thing? The evidence we have for the *Republic* offers three ways that we might respond to these questions. First, a number of passages refer to the 'citizens' of this ideal community as wise or virtuous.[10] While some commentators have taken this to mean that Zeno proposed a ruling class of philosophers, possessing full citizenship and distinct from the rest of the population, it seems more likely that Zeno was imagining an ideal situation in which everyone is virtuous and wise. For a community of perfectly rational Stoic sages who always act virtuously, traditional laws would indeed become superfluous. Second, one of the passages we have says that the security of this ideal community will be underwritten by Eros, the god of friendship.[11] Social relationships will be harmonious because of friendship between citizens rather than legislation, an idea that we shall return to when we look at Epicurus. We are also told that only the virtuous can be true friends, again suggesting that everyone in this ideal community will be wise.[12] Third, and finally, we need to return to the description of Zeno's cosmopolitan vision quoted above. In Plutarch's description of the *Republic*, he states that all human beings should be regarded as fellow citizens, all living according to a common way of life, like a herd 'grazing together and nurtured by a common pasture'. The word translated here as pasture is *nomos*, which can also mean 'law', so we might alternatively translate the final part as 'nurtured by a common law'. For a Stoic, this common law will be the divine reason permeating all of Nature, not the man-made laws of any particular political body.

That last point was made by a later Stoic, Diogenes of Babylon, during the course of his famous visit to Rome in 155 BC as one of three Athenian ambassadors. His fellow ambassador Carneades quipped that Diogenes did not think that Rome was a real city at all.[13] The Romans present were both insulted and baffled that anyone could think such a thing. This was

[9] Indeed, writers on anarchist political thought have claimed him for their own; see e.g. Marshall (1992), 69–71.

[10] See e.g. Diog. Laert. 7.33 (IG II-1, LS 67B), 7.121, 7.129, 7.131 (all IG II-94).

[11] See Athenaeus 13, 561c (*SVF* 1.263, LS 67D).   [12] Diog. Laert. 7.33.

[13] Cicero, *Acad.* 2.137 (*SVF* 3 Diog. 9). On this and the idea of the cosmos as a city more widely see Obbink (1999).

yet another of the so-called 'Stoic paradoxes', in which the Stoics subverted the usual understanding of words, some of which are reported and discussed in Cicero's *Paradoxes of the Stoics*. How did Diogenes justify such a claim? The Stoics are reported to have defined a city (*polis*) as a community of virtuous people united under a common law. A quick glance at existing political communities, then or now, soon shows that such a community does not exist, and probably never has.[14] In the words of Diogenes of Babylon himself, 'among the non-wise (*aphronôn*) there exists no city nor any law'.[15] This is a strong claim given how few people, if any, the Stoics think have managed to attain wisdom.

The Stoic political ideal, then, is unconcerned with the man-made laws of political communities, whether it be the Athenian *polis* or the Roman Republic. Instead, it involves living in accordance with the law of Nature. For a Stoic, the *only* thing regulated by a properly rational law is Nature itself, the cosmos. Although writing after the Hellenistic period, the later Stoic Seneca captured the thought well:

Let us take hold of the fact that there are two communities—the one, which is great and truly common, embracing gods and men, in which we look neither to this corner nor to that, but measure the boundaries of our citizenship by the sun; the other, the one to which we have been assigned by the accident of our birth.[16]

This is all well and good, but how do we go about trying to create something the Stoics would acknowledge as a *real* community? How might we try to improve existing political communities? The Stoic response to both questions would be simply to encourage as many people as possible to cultivate virtue. Virtuous people who understand and embrace the rational order of Nature will recognize one another as kindred spirits and fellow citizens of the cosmos, following the same law, whether they live near one another or far apart. They will be members of a shared community of the wise, one that does not need legislation or law courts, and regard one another as friends. For the Stoics, this will be a *real* city, a cosmic city, even if its citizens might be scattered across the world.[17] Of course, the ultimate ideal would be for

---

[14] See e.g. Clement of Alexandria, *Strom.* 4.26 (*SVF* 3.327).
[15] This comes from Philodemus, *Rhet.* 2,211 (*SVF* 3 Diog. 117), following the reconstruction of the papyrus text in Obbink and Vander Waerdt (1991).
[16] Seneca, *De otio* 4.1 (**LS 67K**).
[17] For further discussion of the Stoic cosmic city see Vogt (2008).

everyone to become a member of this cosmic city of the wise, but the Stoics were under no illusions about how unlikely that would be to happen. In the meantime, in imperfect political communities, largely populated by the non-wise, the best one can hope for is to increase the number of wise people within it, one by one.

Stoic Political Role Play

Chrysippus appears to have followed in the same vein as Zeno in his work *On the Republic*, which may have been a commentary on Zeno's *Republic*.[18] But Chrysippus wrote another work relevant to politics that would prove to be far more influential. Later, especially under the Roman Empire, the Stoics had a reputation for being active participants in politics rather than utopian idealists, and this tradition appears to have begun with another work by Chrysippus called *On Ways of Life*. In that work, Chrysippus outlined the various different roles in everyday life that a wise person might take on, including associating with kings and earning a living by making money.[19] The implication is that the Stoic wise person will have no problem in participating in the usual affairs of conventional social life: they will marry, have children, engage in politics, and take various other social roles. However, they will remember that these are merely roles and not ends in themselves. Nevertheless, these roles offer numerous opportunities to exercise virtue. Writing later, Cicero summed up this more moderate Stoic view thus:

It is consistent with human nature for the wise person to want to take part in the business of government, and, in living by nature, to take a spouse and to wish to have children. . . . Some Stoics say that the Cynics' philosophy and way of life is suitable for the wise person, should circumstances arise conducive to its practice. But others rule this out altogether.[20]

Cicero's final remark suggests an ongoing debate within the Stoa about the extent of its affinity with Cynicism. Chrysippus's contemporary and fellow Stoic Aristo is said to have compared a wise person to an actor who takes on whatever roles fate assigns to him,[21] presumably including

---

[18]   For a list of fragments and brief discussion see Sellars (2007), 18.
[19]   See Diog. Laert. 7.188–9 (*SVF* 3.685, IG II-1).
[20]   Cicero, *Fin.* 3.68 (part LS 57F), trans. Woolf.
[21]   See Diog. Laert. 7.160 (*SVF* 1.351, IG II-1, LS 58G).

roles in conventional politics. This same idea can be found among the Hellenistic Cynics, notably Bion and Teles, so perhaps this more engaged Stoic attitude towards politics also had a Cynic pedigree.[22]

Epicurus on Justice

The traditional view is that, like the Stoics, the Epicureans also had little interest in politics. Epicurus is reported to have said that 'the purest security is that which comes from a quiet life and withdrawal from the many'.[23] This quietist and isolationist attitude is neatly summed up in the Epicurean motto 'live unnoticed'.[24] Despite this limited interest in participating in traditional politics, Epicurus devoted considerable thought to questions that we would now think of as part of political philosophy. In particular he was interested in questions about the nature of justice.

A number of the texts we have suggest that Epicurus saw justice as the product of mutual agreements between people, and so we might think of him as a precursor to later social contract theory:

Justice was not a thing in its own right, but [exists] in mutual dealings in whatever places there [is] a pact about neither harming one another nor being harmed.[25]

Thus he insists that in the animal world, for instance, there is no such thing as justice, for they are unable to enter into those sorts of mutual agreements. By extension, there can be no justice between humans and animals. The same goes for primitive societies that are unwilling or unable to make such agreements.[26] (In his lengthy and fascinating account of the development of human civilization, Lucretius describes two types or phases of such agreement: primitive mutual alliances among inarticulate people wanting to avoid violence, and much later a formal social contract based on written laws.[27]) However, Epicurus does seem to want to hold on to the idea that it is possible to judge laws generated by such mutual agreements

---

[22] See esp. Teles fr. VI, 52,2–54,4 Hense (translated in Dobbin (2012), 129–30).

[23] Epicurus, *Rat. Sent.* 14 (IG I-5), trans. IG.

[24] On this Epicurean maxim (cf. Us. 551) see the treatise by Plutarch, *Is 'Live Unknown' a Wise Precept?* (*De lat. viv.*), and the extended study in Roskam (2007).

[25] Epicurus, *Rat. Sent.* 33 (IG I-5, LS 22A), trans. IG.

[26] See Epicurus, *Rat. Sent.* 32 (IG I-5, LS 22A); note also Lucretius 5.958–9 (LS 22J).

[27] See Lucretius 5.1019–20 (LS 22K), where he describes this as friendship (*amicities*), and 5.1143–7 (LS 22L), where he refers to the creation of laws (*leges*). Another Epicurean account of social contract attributed to Epicurus's successor Hermarchus can be found in

as just or unjust. A just law, Epicurus says, is one that embodies the principle 'neither to harm one another nor be harmed'.[28] Implicitly, then, there is a distinction between what we might call conventional justice and natural justice. Although justice is the product of convention, it also has an objective foundation, namely the need for protection from harm. Any system of law that fails to deliver protection from harm for its participants has failed to fulfil its purpose. Epicurus writes:

if someone passes a law and it does not turn out to be in accord with what is useful in mutual associations, this no longer possesses the nature of justice.[29]

Further, laws that were once just, because they did contribute to mutual protection from harm, can become unjust if circumstances change and they no longer achieve this goal:

if objective circumstances do change and the same things which had been just turn out to be no longer useful, then those things were just as long as they were useful for the mutual associations of fellow citizens; but later, when they were not useful, they were no longer just.[30]

All conventional justice, then, is arbitrary in so far as it is the product of mutual agreement, but there is nevertheless an underlying principle— what Epicurus calls 'the justice of nature'—that enables us to assess those conventions and to amend them as and when necessary.[31]

Epicurus goes on to give us two reasons why one ought to obey the laws of conventional justice, both grounded in his hedonism. The first is that if those laws do prevent people from harming one another then we ought not to undermine them, because we would ourselves like to avoid harm. As we have already seen, for Epicurus physical pain is a very real harm,[32] so this is a good hedonist reason why one ought to support and obey a system of law designed to minimize physical harm to both ourselves and others.

The second reason is slightly different, but again based on hedonist principles. Epicurus says we ought to obey the law, even if we think we

Porphyry, *Abst.* 1.7–12 (LS 22M-N), translated with helpful notes in Clark (2000), 33–6 with 126–9.

[28] Epicurus, *Rat. Sent.* 31 (IG I-5, LS 22A), trans. IG.

[29] Epicurus, *Rat. Sent.* 37 (IG I-5, LS 22B), trans. IG.

[30] Epicurus, *Rat. Sent.* 38 (IG I-5), trans. IG.

[31] For the phrase 'the justice of nature' (*to tês phuseôs dikaion*), see *Rat. Sent.* 31 (IG I-5, LS 22A).

[32] See Ch. 5 above.

can break it while avoiding detection, because the fear of punishment will be a form of psychological distress antithetical to the Epicurean ideal of *ataraxia*. He writes:

> It is impossible for someone who secretly does something which men agreed [not to do] in order to avoid harming one another or being harmed to be confident that he will escape detection, even if in current circumstances he escapes detection ten thousand times. For until his death it will be uncertain whether he will continue to escape detection.[33]

This is a second reason, then, to obey the law: to avoid the constant anxiety generated by the fear of being found out. It is worth noting here that Epicurus is giving a reason for obeying the law in a community where the laws do work towards avoiding harm, but the reason would work equally well when faced with unjust laws that fail to do that. Indeed, in an unjust regime there might, for a hedonist, be even more reason to obey the law, given that punishments for disobedience may be much harsher. This is one aspect of 'living unnoticed' that may cause some concern. Indeed, elsewhere Epicurus says:

> Injustice is not a bad thing in its own right, but [only] because of the fear produced by the suspicion that one will not escape the notice of those assigned to punish such actions.[34]

This passage might be taken to suggest that Epicurus prioritized this second reason over the first, and that he had little interest in encouraging people to follow conventional justice for the greater good of reducing overall harm. Injustice—even injustice in the face of fair and reasonable laws—is not a bad thing in its own right. There is little sense here of acting for the greater good of the community. The focus is squarely on reducing one's own physical and psychological pain. Although one might have some concerns about such an attitude, it is entirely consistent with his ethics. There is just one reason, according to Epicurus, to be just:

> The just life is most free from disturbance, but the unjust life is full of the greatest disturbance.[35]

---

[33] Epicurus, *Rat. Sent.* 35 (IG I-5, LS 22A), trans. IG; see also *Sent. Vat.* 7 (IG I-6) and 70 (IG I-6, LS 22D), and compare with Lucretius 5.1154–60 (part LS 22L).

[34] Epicurus, *Rat. Sent.* 34 (IG I-5, LS 22A), trans. IG.

[35] Epicurus, *Rat. Sent.* 17 (IG I-5, LS 22B), trans. IG.

It may be that the focus on the second reason outlined above simply reflected doubts about the effectiveness of existing systems of justice. If existing political communities were completely effective in their systems of justice—i.e. had fair and equitable laws that consistently protected people from harm—then there would be no need or good grounds for anyone to break the law. In such an ideal society, the first reason would be reason enough to justify obeying the law. But in imperfect communities, where the law does not quite reach that standard, there may be many occasions where reasonable people may well think it justified to break the law. It is to people in that situation that the second reason is addressed, and it is possible that Epicurus thought that that was the situation that most people find themselves in. After all, no political community is perfect.

Epicurean Friendship

All this might seem somewhat negative. Epicurus does not have much that is positive to say about existing political communities, and he encourages obedience simply for the sake of self-interest. There is little in the way of constructive political philosophy here or any sense of a desire to try to change things for the better. Far better to live a life of quiet obedience than lust for political power, said Lucretius.[36] Even so, Epicurus did have a serious interest in how one might build a positive human community. The foundation for this, he thought, was not the implicit fear of harm that underpins the mutual agreements that create conventional justice, but something altogether more attractive: friendship.

Friendship for Epicurus is something that is choice-worthy for its own sake, though he suggested that, like justice, it has its origins in mutual benefit.[37] A true friend is someone that one can rely on in time of need; that is part of what it means to be a friend. That practical help is of course very important when it is needed, but Epicurus suggested that what is just as valuable, if not more so, is the *knowledge* that we can rely on them in time of need. In his own words, 'we do not need utility from our friends so much as we need confidence concerning that utility'.[38] Knowing that we have a support network of friends that we can rely on can

---

[36] Lucretius 5.1129–30 (LS 22L).   [37] See Epicurus, *Sent. Vat.* 23 (IG I-6, LS 22F).
[38] Epicurus, *Sent. Vat.* 34 (IG I-6, LS 22F).

significantly reduce our anxiety about the future, and so having friends directly contributes to our mental tranquillity or untroubledness (*ataraxia*). However, the balance between friendship and utility must be just right. A friend who is constantly asking for assistance, and seems only interested in the relationship for what they can get out of it, is not a very good friend. Equally the friend who never asks for anything, and seems indifferent to offering mutual support, is not a very good friend either. A true friend offers and is open to receiving support in times of need, but does not see the relationship as merely a series of exchanges or an insurance policy. As Epicurus himself put it:

> The constant friend is neither he who always searches for utility, nor he who never links [friendship to utility]. For the former makes gratitude a matter for commercial transaction, while the latter kills off good hope for the future.[39]

We can put these theoretical reflections about the nature of friendship into a very practical context by remembering that Epicurus founded a community of people in a garden, just outside the city walls of Athens. This was a private community of friends, brought together by a shared desire to live a life shaped by Epicurean values. As a community of friends, the members would have presumably given each other support of just the kind Epicurus described. Although the Epicureans are known for promoting a very simple form of life, focused on securing only those things that are natural and necessary,[40] even that life will be improved by the knowledge that there are others close at hand to whom one can turn in times of need.

Epicurus's account of friendship, then, offers a different model for thinking about how people might live together in a community. In contrast to what we might call a community grounded in justice, created by a mutual agreement (or social contract), and ultimately based on fear of being harmed, a community grounded in friendship is one based on mutual affection and support. While that sounds like a far more attractive foundation for a political community, its great limitation is that it requires all of the members to be friends. The group will need to be self-selecting and there will be a limit to how big it can become. Epicurus's Garden offers a model for this, but I doubt that even he thought it could be translated to the entire city of Athens just outside the Garden's walls,

---

[39] Epicurus, *Sent. Vat.* 39 (IG I-6, LS 22F), trans. IG.   [40] See Ch. 5 above.

which by later Roman standards, let alone modern ones, was itself a relatively small political community.

Despite some important differences, Epicurus shares with the Stoic Zeno a utopian image of an ideal community populated by philosophically minded individuals who care and respect for one another, based on their philosophical commitments and a sense of friendship, rather than from obedience to legislation. In both cases, what we end up with is an idealistic form of anarchism, and in both cases it seems likely that they were well aware of their utopianism. Back in the world of real politics, we see a sharper difference between the two schools, with the Stoics prepared to engage in civic life and the Epicureans accepting quiet obedience to the law, whatever it may be.

Among later Epicureans, Lucretius broadly follows Epicurus's injunction to remain aloof from politics. He adopts what is sometimes referred to as a 'view from above' in order to belittle the practical and political concerns of ordinary people:

> But nothing sweeter is than this: to dwell
> In quiet halls and lofty sanctuaries
> Well fortified by doctrines of the wise,
> And look thence down on others wandering
> And seeking all astray the path of life—
> The clash of intellects, the fight for honours,
> The lust for wealth, the efforts night and day
> With toil and sweat to scale the heights of power.
> O wretched minds of men! O hearts so blind![41]

In contrast to this indifference, though, Lucretius's contemporary and fellow Epicurean Philodemus devoted an entire treatise to the ideal political leader, called *On the Good King according to Homer*.[42] In this work Philodemus drew on examples of political rule from Homeric poetry that might inspire his patron Piso. Although elsewhere Philodemus did warn against the risks of getting involved in politics,[43] here his concern was to

---

[41] Lucretius 2.7–14 (**LS 21W**). Part of this passage is echoed at 3.59–64, where Lucretius attributes the lust for political power to fear of death. For discussion of political themes in Lucretius (including these passages) see Fowler (1989).

[42] This work, *De bono rege secundum Homerum* (*PHerc* 1507), is edited in Dorandi (1982) and translated into English and discussed in Asmis (1991). For further discussion see Gigante (1995), 63–78, and Fish (2011).

[43] See Dorandi (1982), 30; Gigante (1995), 69.

encourage those who did get involved to be the best leaders they could be. We might try to connect this with wider Epicurean doctrine by noting that Epicurus had suggested that the gods offer a model for an ideal human life, serene and untroubled, and so here Philodemus looked to Homeric representations of the gods for models of ideal rulers.[44] He presented the Homeric good ruler as someone who hates both war and the lovers of war, and appears to have done his best to present the Homeric gods as harmonious and peaceful.[45] However, Epicurus distanced his image of the gods from the traditional Homeric images, so there is a limit to how far such a line might be pushed. If the work is somewhat anomalous among other Epicurean texts, this perhaps simply reflects the complex political situation in which Philodemus was writing, supported by a patron who happened to be the father-in-law of Julius Caesar.

Cicero's Political Theory

Much of what we have encountered thus far has been largely indifferent towards practical problems associated with running a political community. Writing at the very end of the Hellenistic period, and more or less contemporary with Lucretius and Philodemus, Cicero produced two works of political philosophy that were closely engaged with the political problems of his day in Rome. These are his *Republic* and *Laws*, both of which take some inspiration from Plato's two works of the same names, although as we shall see they were also shaped by ideas deriving from the Hellenistic schools.[46]

The *Republic* as we now have it, the bulk of which was recovered as a palimpsest in the early nineteenth century,[47] is incomplete. The part that survives is most concerned with the nature of political constitutions, but further sections now largely lost discussed justice, education, and the ideal statesman. The opening preface, of which we only have a part, argues

---

[44] See Gigante (1995), 70.

[45] See Philodemus, *Hom.* cols 27–9 Dorandi, translated in Asmis (1991), 31.

[46] Both texts are edited in Powell (2006) and translated in Rudd (1998), which contains a helpful introduction and notes by Powell. For an overview of both works see Woolf (2015), 93–124.

[47] It was recovered by Angelo Mai and first printed in 1822. The only extended part of the text known before then was the 'Dream of Scipio' from Book 6, which circulated with a commentary by the Neoplatonist Macrobius, written in the fifth century AD.

forcefully against Epicurean disengagement from politics.[48] Cicero is adamant that the philosopher ought to play their part in politics, reflecting both natural human sociability and the expertise that the philosopher is able to bring to bear on what Cicero considered the most pressing problems of his day. His position, then, is more Stoic than Epicurean, insisting that virtue is preferable to pleasure and that virtue is 'entirely a matter of practice',[49] which is to say that it is an activity rather than merely a body of knowledge. As we shall see, there are other Stoic elements in both of Cicero's political works, although the points he makes here are equally compatible with Aristotelianism. It is worth noting that some scholars have suggested that, at this point in his intellectual career, Cicero renounced the moderate scepticism of Philo in favour of the philosophy of Antiochus, who drew heavily on both Stoic and Aristotelian ideas, and tried to downplay the distance between them.[50] On these points, at least, Cicero seems fairly insistent that virtue trumps pleasure as the appropriate goal for human action, and that humans are by nature social animals. The subsequent discussion of different constitutions does try to come to a final conclusion, which also counts against the idea that its author was a committed sceptic. Yet the way in which that discussion is presented draws on a number of sceptical practices, with a final compromise position being reached precisely because none of the opening options are convincing by themselves. The debate is presented as a dialogue between people already dead, creating a distance between the arguments presented and what Cicero himself may or may not have believed. In short, we may have to suspend judgement (no pun intended) on the extent of Cicero's commitment to scepticism in these works. Instead, let us focus on some of the arguments offered about the nature of the ideal constitution.

Unlike the abstract and seemingly utopian reflections of the Stoics and Epicureans, Cicero is concerned with the ideal constitution for a real political community, in particular Rome. Should Rome be governed by an aristocratic elite or by a more populist form of democracy? Or should it revert to its previous state of monarchy? All these were extremely live issues in the Rome of Cicero's day, before, during, and after the time at which he wrote the *Republic*. One of the central characters in the dialogue, Scipio Africanus (who had been a close associate of the Stoic

---

[48] See Cicero, *Rep.* 1.1–12.   [49] Cicero, *Rep.* 1.2.
[50] See e.g. Glucker (1988) and the reply in Görler (1995).

Panaetius), outlines what he takes to be the three most basic forms of constitution: monarchy, aristocracy, and democracy.[51] These are three different ways in which a republic or state (*res publica*) might be governed. A republic, says Scipio, is a gathering together of people 'brought together by legal consent and community of interest'.[52] That reference to common interest might make one think that he has some kind of social contract in mind, of the sort we saw discussed by Epicurus, but he goes on to say explicitly that this gathering together is not the product of weakness but rather an expression of an 'innate desire on the part of human beings to form communities'.[53] The state, including the state of Rome, is a natural, and one might say almost inevitable, product of human sociability. However, 'state' may not be the best word to use here, for it implies something over and above the community, whereas Cicero's Scipio is referring to the community of people itself.[54]

Political communities may be inevitable, but the form they take remains an open question. Any community of people, if it is to last, will need to have some kind of decision-making process, and those decisions can be made either by one person alone, a few people, or everyone together.[55] Those three possibilities lead to the three forms of government already mentioned: monarchy, aristocracy, and democracy. Scipio argues that each of these forms of government has its virtues and vices. With monarchy, the general population have too little a voice; the same applies with aristocracy, which can too easily become focused on the interests of a privileged class. Democracy overcomes that fault, but fails by assuming that everyone's voice ought to count equally, regardless of ability.[56] All three forms share the fault that they are inherently unstable and can easily slide into degenerate versions of themselves.[57] For example, an ideal monarchy is ruled by a just king who acts on behalf of, and in the interests of, the population as a whole, but if they become unjust or lose sight of on whose behalf they rule, the monarchy immediately switches to tyranny.[58] In such a situation, 'nothing belongs to the public, and the public itself belongs to one man'.[59] The same goes for an

[51] See Cicero, *Rep.* 1.42.
[52] Cicero, *Rep.* 1.39. On Cicero's definition of *res publica* see Schofield (1995).
[53] Cicero, *Rep.* 1.39.   [54] See further Schofield (1995).
[55] See Cicero, *Rep.* 1.41–2.
[56] See Cicero, *Rep.* 1.43.   [57] See Cicero, *Rep.* 1.65–8.
[58] See Cicero, *Rep.* 1.65.   [59] Cicero, *Rep.* 3.43 (slightly paraphrased).

aristocracy that can degenerate into oligarchy, and democracy that can descend into mob rule. In each case, the difference between the three forms of government and their corrupted counterparts is that the former are just and they act on behalf of the community. A proper republic, a *res publica*, is literally a 'public thing', something that belongs to the population as a whole, and whose leaders—whether they are one, few, or all—act on behalf of, and for the sake of, everyone. Such a community is marked by justice, social agreement, and partnership.[60]

Scipio goes on to offer a lengthy account of how each of these forms of constitution can change into one of the others, in part to highlight their inherent instability. This sets things up for his conclusion that the most preferable arrangement is a mixed constitution embodying elements of all three forms.[61] (Of the three pure forms, he places monarchy above the other two, but will not champion it as the best option due to how easily it can slide into tyranny, the worst of all forms of government.) All this forms a theoretical background for a historical account of the Roman constitution that discusses Rome's monarchy and Republic in the light of these distinctions.[62] Cicero's aim, we presume, is to show the way in which philosophical reflection about possible forms of government might inform one's understanding of Roman politics past and present. Indeed, at a number of points Cicero is explicit that while theoretical reflection is valuable and enjoyable in its own right, it is all the more significant when put to work in the service of practical problems such as how to run a country.[63]

Cicero's accounts of both the different types of constitution and the political history of Rome probably drew on earlier and very similar accounts made by the historian Polybius, who was an associate of the historical Scipio. Polybius discussed these three forms of government and their three counterparts, and he also suggested that a mixed constitution is best.[64] He suggested that the origin of political community was in fact human weakness, the view that Cicero's Scipio explicitly rejects, although he does add that it ought to be seen as an entirely natural and

---

[60] See Cicero, *Rep.* 3.43.   [61] See e.g. Cicero, *Rep.* 1.45, 1.54, 1.69.

[62] This is in Book 2 of the *Republic*.

[63] Comments to this effect appear throughout the *Republic*; especially noteworthy is the lengthy discussion at the beginning of Book 1 about the value of studying celestial phenomena.

[64] Polybius 6.3–10. On Polybius as political theorist see Hahm (1995).

inevitable development.[65] Cicero alludes to conversations that the historical Scipio may have had with Polybius and the Stoic Panaetius on these topics, and Polybius implies that he is also drawing on the work of others.[66] Perhaps Panaetius stands behind the accounts of both Cicero and Polybius, and so here we have an echo of his political philosophy.[67]

There are further echoes of Stoicism later in the work. As we have seen, one of the distinguishing features that separates the three pure forms of government from their deviant counterparts is justice: a genuine *res publica* is just. But what is justice? In Book 3 of the *Republic* Cicero tackles this question but, as with the rest of the work, what has come down to us is only fragmentary. He opens by presenting some arguments against justice, which his character Philus attributes to the Academic Carneades. These possibly draw on an (in)famous speech that Carneades made during the embassy of Greek philosophers to Rome in 155 BC (the same one during which the Stoic Diogenes of Babylon denied that Rome was a true city). At that event, Carneades is reported to have argued in favour of justice one day and then against it the next, to the outrage of his Roman audience.[68] Of course, Carneades' goal was to argue for both sides and so push his listeners towards scepticism, but here that framework of sceptical argument is put to one side, and Carneades is more or less presented as a straightforward enemy of justice.[69] In particular, he is said to have argued that there is no such thing as natural law, something made plain by the ways in which different communities construct their own arbitrary laws, based on local customs.[70]

Cicero responds to this in the dialogue by having his character Laelius insist that there is in fact a single common law above all human laws, which he defines in explicitly Stoic terms as 'right reason in harmony

[65] Compare Polybius 6.5.7 with Cicero, *Rep.* 1.39.
[66] See Cicero, *Rep.* 1.34 (**LS 67T**) and Polybius 6.3.
[67] Diog. Laert. 7.131 (*SVF* 3.700, **IG II-94**, **LS 67U**) reports that Stoics held that the best form of constitution would be mixed, but without specifying which Stoics. Erskine (1990), 73, suggests that the doctrine was Panaetius's and, 194–5, that Panaetius's thought stands behind Cicero's discussion. This seems plausible, but far from certain given that we have no direct evidence for Panaetius's views on this topic.
[68] See Lactantius, *Div. inst.* 5.14.3–5 (**LS 68M**) with Plutarch, *Cat. Mai.* 22.
[69] See e.g. *Rep.* 3.8 but note that some of the following text is lost and so the original text might have given a different impression.
[70] See Cicero, *Rep.* 3.15, 3.18; cf. Lactantius, *Div. inst.* 5.16-2-3.

with Nature' (*recta ratio naturae congruens*).[71] This is unchanging and eternal, and applies to all humankind at all times. Once again, the account in the *Republic* is only fragmentary but thankfully Cicero develops this theme further in his other work of political philosophy, the *Laws*. But before we leave behind the *Republic*, we might note that the extended 'Dream of Scipio' from Book 6 has Scipio imagine himself viewing the whole universe from a cosmic perspective (as we saw Lucretius do earlier), looking down on the Roman empire and seeing only a dot on the surface of the Earth.[72] The point of this is not entirely clear, but it might be taken to be downplaying the human laws of particular countries in favour of the natural law that embraces everything.

The notion of a single, universal natural law is discussed further in the *Laws*. Like the *Republic*, the *Laws* was modelled in part on Plato's work of the same name.[73] In both of these works, Cicero takes up the Platonic idea that it is the philosopher or sage who is most suited to govern the country, because they have access to the appropriate knowledge. In Plato's *Republic* it is the philosophers who have knowledge of the Good; in Cicero it is the sage who has knowledge of, and lives according to, natural law. The image of a sage living in accordance with the law of Nature comes from Stoicism, and the way in which Cicero blends Platonic and Stoic themes here has, as we have noted, led some to suggest that in these works Cicero was closer to the syncretism of Antiochus than the moderate scepticism of Philo.

The aim of the work as a whole is to discuss the nature of civil law.[74] Cicero's main target in the book is the Epicurean view we considered earlier, which claims that justice is simply the product of an agreement between people. Instead, Cicero wants to place human law on a firmer footing. Speaking in his own voice—Cicero is himself a character in this dialogue—he says that the foundation of civil law is to be found in 'universal justice and law' (*universus ius ac lex*), which in turn 'has to be deduced from the nature of man'.[75] He goes on to define universal law as:

---

[71] Cicero, *Rep.* 3.33 (*SVF* 3.325, LS 67S). Note also *Rep.* 1.27 where a contrast is drawn between the citizen who lives according to civil law and the wise person who lives according to natural law.

[72] See Cicero, *Rep.* 6.16. I use 'empire' with a lowercase 'e'; this was both written and dramatically set before the imperial period.

[73] See Cicero, *Leg.* 1.15.

[74] See Cicero, *Leg.* 1.13–14.   [75] Cicero, *Leg.* 1.17.

the highest reason, inherent in nature, which enjoins what ought to be done and forbids the opposite. When that reason is fully formed and completed in the human mind, it, too, is law. So they think that law, whose function is to enjoin right action and to forbid wrong-doing, is wisdom.[76]

This is a Stoic definition of law.[77] Law is something inherent within Nature, the right reason that pervades Nature that is identified with God, and it defines the Stoic sage, who lives in accordance with this divine and natural law. The sage does not 'follow' this law as if obeying a set of commands; instead he is simply in harmony with it by virtue of his wisdom. A life in harmony with Nature is equally a life in harmony with this natural law.

Cicero asks his Epicurean friend Atticus to accept for the sake of the argument that Nature is governed by divine forces ('the immortal gods'). Implicitly Cicero is doing the same himself if, at this point, he remained committed to the sceptical Academy.[78] Both the Epicurean and the sceptic, then, suspend their doubts while a broadly Platonic-Stoic view is developed. The argument that Cicero develops goes like this:[79] human beings were created by 'the supreme God' (*supremus deus*) as the only animals endowed with reason. As such they share something with God, with whom they are in a 'primordial partnership' (*prima societas*). Not only do they share reason with God, they also share law, defined as 'right reason' (*recta ratio*). Thus humans are 'partners with the gods in law' and so, so to speak, members of a shared political community. This leads Cicero to say that 'this whole universe must be thought of as a single community shared by gods and men'.[80]

As we can see, Cicero vacillates between referring to a single creator God and gods. Whether this is an uneasy compromise between a Platonic-Stoic philosophical conception of God and the traditional pagan

---

[76] Cicero, *Leg.* 1.18–19 (*SVF* 3.315), trans. Rudd.

[77] Compare with Cicero, *Nat. D.* 1.36. The Stoics probably inherited it from Heraclitus; cf. Sextus Empiricus, *Math.* 7.133 (DK 22B2).

[78] Alternatively this might again be taken as evidence that during this period Cicero was closer to Antiochus than Philo. A little later, at *Leg.* 1.38, Cicero lists members of the Old Academy, Peripatetics, and Stoics together as all agreeing with the view he is putting forward, which might be read as Cicero advocating a version of Antiochus's syncretism. See also *Leg.* 1.53–5.

[79] What follows comes from Cicero, *Leg.* 1.22–3, with translations taken from Rudd (1998).

[80] Compare this with Seneca, *De otio* 4.1 (**LS 67K**), quoted above.

pantheon of gods or, instead, a hint at a more complex theological hierarchy involving a supreme God and a series of lesser gods is hard to say.[81] Immediately afterwards, Cicero muddies the water further by crediting Nature with organizing the world in a way suitable for humans and equipping them with the skills and abilities they need.[82] Although at first glance this sounds very Stoic, and might lead one to think that Cicero is identifying God with Nature, in fact he draws a distinction between the two, suggesting that while God created humans (i.e. their rational souls), Nature is responsible for their bodies and the natural environment in which they live.

In the present context, however, Cicero is concerned simply to make one point, namely that 'we are born for justice, and that what is just is based, not on opinion, but on nature'.[83] His attempt to ground justice in nature is based on the claim that ultimately human beings are more alike than they are different. The things that unite us are greater than the things that separate us. One definition applies to all human beings, and that is that we are all rational creatures. There is, he writes, 'no essential difference within mankind' and 'nor is there any member of any nation who cannot attain moral excellence by using nature as his guide'.[84] Cicero's point, then, is to say that if justice involves treating everyone equally and fairly, then grasping the idea that humans are ultimately the same in nature, and ought to be thought of as members of a single global community, will enable us to underwrite justice as a perfectly natural attitude.[85] Cicero is arguing in favour of natural justice grounded on cosmopolitanism and a universal human nature.

This is all in stark contrast to the Epicurean account of justice we considered earlier. Cicero is quite clear about his objections to the Epicurean view:

If justice is a matter of obeying the written laws and customs of particular communities, and if, as our opponents allege, everything is to be measured by self-interest, then a person will ignore and break the laws when he can, if he

---

[81] See Ch. 3 above. Later Stoics such as Seneca and Epictetus often fall into the same habit, sliding without comment between 'God' and 'gods'. Rather than see this as an inconsistency, or an awkward compromise between monotheism and polytheism, it might reflect henotheism, i.e. belief in a single god without denying the existence of other deities.

[82] See Cicero, *Leg.* 1.25–7.   [83] Cicero, *Leg.* 1.28.

[84] Cicero, *Leg.* 1.30.   [85] See Cicero, *Leg.* 1.33–5.

thinks it will be to his own advantage. That is why justice is completely non-existent if it is not derived from nature, and if that kind of justice which is established to serve self-interest is wrecked by that same self-interest. And that is why every virtue is abolished if nature is not going to support justice.[86]

So, civil law must be grounded on natural law, and not some form of social contract. A system of justice based on self-interested parties coming together will be arbitrary and insecure, Cicero thinks. By contrast, a system built upon the reason within Nature—identified with the intelligence of God—can have no firmer footing.[87]

After laying this foundation, Cicero goes on in the remainder of the *Laws* (or what we have of it; it also survives incomplete) to discuss specific civil laws within political communities. Here his concern is with the practicalities of legislation within the Roman Republic. This is essential for human flourishing, he thinks. Although natural law might be of far higher standing than civil law, the latter remains necessary. In Book 1 we are reminded that we are ultimately citizens of the cosmos, but in Book 2 we are also reminded that we owe a commitment to our country, which 'should have first place in our affections'.[88] Cicero has no desire to end up in the more or less anarchist position of the early Stoics and Cynics, who imagine a sage living according to the law of Nature without regard to existing political communities. He is not an advocate of that sort of cosmopolitanism. Natural law is not a replacement for civil law, but instead is (or ought to be) its foundation and source of authority. In all this, Cicero wants to be able to point to an objective criterion against which the civil laws drafted by people may be judged. As a legislator himself, he sees this as a concrete, real-world problem that needs to be addressed. Perhaps that is why in these two works of political philosophy—the *Republic* and the *Laws*—he drops Academic speculation about the possibility of knowledge in favour of a more emphatic theory about the origin of justice, drawing on Plato, the Stoics, and perhaps also Antiochus.

* * *

The Hellenistic period formally ends with the collapse of the last of the Hellenistic kingdoms founded in the wake of Alexander, Ptolemaic

---

[86] Cicero, *Leg.* 1.42–3 (trans. Rudd).   [87] See Cicero, *Leg.* 2.8.
[88] Cicero, *Leg.* 2.5.

Egypt. The events that brought that about also led to the collapse of the Roman Republic and the beginnings the Roman Empire under Octavian Augustus. Cicero was embroiled in all of this, in fact far too embroiled for his own good, and his attempts to save the Republic cost him his life. His reflections on ideal constitutions and civil law would be of little consequence under the new regime. Even so, they make an important contribution to Hellenistic political philosophy.

9

What Was Hellenistic Philosophy?

The French scholar Pierre Hadot championed the idea that in antiquity philosophy was not merely a theoretical enterprise but also—indeed, above all else—the pursuit of a certain way of life.[1] One studied with the Stoics or the Epicureans not merely to learn about the nature of knowledge or the physical world, but primarily to live a Stoic or an Epicurean life.[2] Unlike much of contemporary philosophy that tends to model itself on the sciences, on this account the ancient philosophical schools shared something in common with religious communities, with groups of like-minded people coming together to live communally according to a shared set of principles. According to Hadot, during the Middle Ages this aspect of ancient philosophy was taken over by Christianity and philosophy became the impersonal intellectual activity with which we are familiar today.

This image of ancient philosophy as a way of life has inspired many people, but it has also attracted a number of criticisms. One criticism that has been made is that it is a mistake to make the universal claim that *all* ancient philosophers conceived philosophy in this way. Some may have, to be sure, but others probably did not.[3] Just as they do today, different philosophers may have had different understandings about the nature of what they were doing. In an era long before academic specialization, in which the boundaries between what we now think of as distinct subjects were far from clear-cut, this should come as no great surprise. So instead

---

[1] See Hadot (1995) and (2002).
[2] For Hadot's accounts of Stoicism and Epicureanism see Hadot (2002), 91–145.
[3] See Cooper (2012).

it has been suggested that we should think of *some* ancient philosophical schools as each offering a different way of life, but not all.[4]

Of all the periods in the history of ancient philosophy, the Hellenistic period is often thought to be the one for which the image of philosophy as a way of life fits best.[5] On the face of it, this seems like a reasonable claim, and both the Epicureans and Stoics offered clear conceptions of what an ideal life would look like and attracted adherents to those ways of life. But some of the Stoics had a very wide range of intellectual interests, ranging from astronomy to grammar, and it is not immediately obvious how these might contribute to an enterprise conceived *primarily* as cultivating a specific way of life.[6] What about some of the other philosophers active in the Hellenistic period? The Peripatetics seem to have had little interest in this sort of approach to philosophy. And what about the sceptical Academics? On the one hand, they might be seen as committed followers of Socrates' practice of continual questioning, embracing his view that this was ultimately directed towards transforming one's life; on the other, they might be seen as narrowly concerned with technical questions in epistemology, with no great thoughts about the practical implications of their arguments. The Pyrrhonians, by contrast, might seem more firmly committed to this idea of philosophy as a way of life to the extent that their ultimate goal was tranquillity.

In this chapter I want to explore these ideas further, for despite the dangers of making too-wide generalizations, or trying to force ancient evidence into a preconceived model, this idea of philosophy as a way of life does seem to capture something important about how much of ancient philosophy differs from much of contemporary philosophy in its ambitions. The origins of this idea are usually credited to Socrates, and it seems to have been embraced by a number of the Socratic schools that developed after his death.[7] But it is in the Hellenistic period that this approach to philosophy really seems to come to the fore.[8] Any account of Hellenistic philosophy that restricted itself solely to a report of the

---

[4] See again Cooper (2012).   [5] See e.g. Nussbaum (1994).

[6] Such pursuits might fit if the Stoics were proposing a way of life devoted to intellectual inquiry, akin to Socrates' life of continual questioning or Aristotle's image of a contemplative life.

[7] See Hadot (2002), ch. 3; Cooper (2012), ch. 2.

[8] See Dihle (1986), 186, and Dihle (1990), who argues that the Hellenistic idea of philosophy as an *ars vitae et moriendi* was inspired by the *exemplum Socratis*.

central ideas and arguments of the various schools would, I think, miss something important about the philosophy of the period.

Philosophy as Medicine

A common theme in accounts of philosophy as a way of life is the idea that philosophy is a form of medicine and, in particular, medicine or therapy for the mind.[9] If the task of philosophy is to learn how to live well, and the way in which we live is determined (or at least heavily shaped) by our thoughts, feelings, and attitudes, then the principal task becomes one of working on those inner mental items. Socrates was one of the first philosophers to articulate this idea with his reflections on taking care of the soul. In the *Apology* Plato has Socrates chide his fellow citizens for paying great attention to their possessions, bodies, and reputation, but very little attention to their souls.[10] Although Socrates claims to know nothing, in his quest to learn how to live well he seems at least to be sure that the key will reside in the soul, rather than with the sorts of external things on which other people focus their attention.[11] Thus he presents philosophy as an art concerned with taking care of the soul, analogous to the way in which medicine is an art that takes care of the body.[12] Just as there are experts in medicine, so too are there in philosophy, he suggests.[13]

A number of Hellenistic philosophers repeat similar thoughts, although not necessarily under the influence of Socrates. The Stoics probably were influenced by Socrates, as were the Academics, although the Stoics may have also been drawing on earlier Pythagorean influences as well.[14] The Pyrrhonians may have been indirectly influenced by Socrates, via the Academics, but their appeal to the historical Pyrrho, whose philosophy was influenced by his encounter with Indian sages, adds a further

---

[9] See esp. Nussbaum (1994).
[10] See Plato, *Apology* 29d–30b.
[11] For Socrates' concern about living well see Plato, *Apology* 21c–22e.
[12] See e.g. Plato, *Alcibiades I* 128a–129a, where the analogy is with gymnastics as the art that takes care of the body, and *Gorgias* 464c, where gymnastics and medicine, both arts concerning the body, are contrasted with arts concerning the soul.
[13] This is the implicit conclusion at Plato, *Apology* 25a–b.
[14] See Thom (2001).

dimension.[15] The Epicureans, by contrast, seem not to have been influenced by Socrates at all, instead drawing on ideas articulated by their atomist predecessor Democritus, who had also drawn an analogy between philosophy and medicine.[16] But, in different ways, all these schools embrace the idea that philosophy has a therapeutic benefit for the soul. This is not (or at least not only) in the modern sense that philosophy aims to clear away muddled thinking, but rather in the sense that philosophy removes mental disturbances that hamper an individual's ability to live well.

To what extent, though, can *all* philosophy be seen as therapeutic in this way? As we have seen, the Epicureans and Stoics discussed a wide range of topics, and while some of these might look like they quite easily contribute to a project of therapy for disturbances of the soul, others, at first glance at least, do not. To explore this and some of the other questions that have already been raised, we must turn to the individual schools and see what they have to say.

Epicurean Therapy

In his *Letter to Menoeceus* Epicurus is explicit that he thinks the study of philosophy leads to 'the health of the soul' (*to psuchên hugiainon*).[17] This he identifies with happiness (*eudaimonia*), or at least suggests it is necessary for happiness, but either way it is philosophy that produces both a healthy soul and happiness.[18] He then goes on to recount a number of Epicurean ideas we have already discussed about the gods, death, and pleasure, suggesting that these are all essential for living well (*kalôs zên*).[19] For Epicurus, as we have seen, living well involves enjoying pleasures and avoiding pains, but it is psychological pleasure and pain that is most

---

[15] See Diog. Laert. 9.61 (IG III-22, LS 1A), with Flintoff (1980), Bett (2000), 169–78, and further discussion in the Appendix.

[16] See Democritus as quoted by Clement of Alexandria, *Instr.* 1.6.2 (DK 68B31): 'Medicine heals diseases of the body, wisdom frees the soul from passions'. Democritus is usually classified as a 'Presocratic', but was in fact a contemporary of Socrates. Diogenes Laertius says that some claim Democritus visited the gymnosophists in India (9.35), that he knew of Socrates (9.36), and that he was an admirer of the Pythagoreans (9.38) and wrote a book on Pythagoras. For further discussion of the Democritean background to Epicurean *ataraxia*, see Warren (2002).

[17] Epicurus, *Ep. Men.* 122 (IG I-4, LS 25A).

[18] Epicurus, *Ep. Men.* 122.   [19] Epicurus, *Ep. Men.* 123 (IG I-4).

important for a happy life. Given that Epicurus denies that there is any intermediate state between pleasure and pain, psychological pleasure is identified with the absence of psychological pain. Thus a central theme throughout Epicurus's philosophy is how to overcome psychological pain or distress, such as fear of the gods or fear of death. If, through philosophical therapy of the soul, we can overcome these forms of psychological distress, then we shall be able to live well.

With this aim in mind, Epicurus repeatedly justifies the study of natural philosophy by stressing the way in which it contributes to therapy for psychological distress. In his *Letter to Herodotus* Epicurus says that the study of nature brings calm to his life (*malista eggalênizôn tôi biôi*).[20] He also says that our blessedness (*to makarion*) depends on those things that natural philosophy examines, in particular meteorological events:[21]

For, if we attend to these things, we will give a correct and complete causal account of the source of our disturbance and fear, and [so] dissolve them, by accounting for the causes of meteorological and other phenomena which we are constantly exposed to and which terrify other men most severely.[22]

It is by investigating the causes of the weather that we shall see that these are merely natural phenomena, and not the product of divine intervention reflecting displeasure at human actions. Only by knowing the real causes of things can we reject superstitions that feed on and generate psychological anxieties. Thus the study of the weather is an essential part of philosophy aimed at the health of the soul, and Epicurus is explicit that the reason why we study it is for its contribution to this wider therapeutic project:

Were we not upset by the worries that celestial phenomena and death might matter to us, and also by failure to appreciate the limits of pains and desires, we would have no need for natural philosophy.[23]

The same point is made by Lucretius, who is explicit at the beginning of Book 1 of *On the Nature of Things* that everything that follows in his poem is aimed at alleviating mental suffering or 'terror of the mind' (*terrorem animi*) generated by superstition (*religio*).[24] Superstition leads

[20] Epicurus, *Ep. Hdt.* 37 (IG I-2).   [21] Epicurus, *Ep. Hdt.* 78 (IG I-2).
[22] Epicurus, *Ep. Hdt.* 82 (IG I-2), trans. IG.
[23] Epicurus, *Rat. Sent.* 11 (IG I-5, LS 25B), trans. LS.
[24] See Lucretius 1.146–58. See further Erler (1997) on the role of physics in Epicurean therapy.

both to fear and to immoral behaviour, so the naturalistic explanations that he offers have a practical, therapeutic goal. Even the seemingly abstract Parmenidean metaphysical principle that nothing ever comes from nothing contributes to this therapeutic project:

> We start then from her first great principle
> That nothing ever by divine power comes from nothing.
> For sure fear holds so much the minds of men
> Because they see many things happen in earth and sky
> Of which they can by no means see the causes,
> And think them to be done by power divine.
> So when we have seen that nothing can be created
> From nothing, we shall at once discern more clearly
> The object of our search, both the source from which each thing
> Can be created, and the manner in which
> Things come into being without the aid of gods.[25]

It is noteworthy that Lucretius reminds his readers of this therapeutic task immediately before launching into his discussion of atomist metaphysics, which might strike some as the least practically relevant part of the book. It turns out, however, to be foundational for his philosophical project of purging the mind of terror of the gods, so that one might enjoy a life of mental tranquillity. The openings of the subsequent books of *On the Nature of Things* contain similar reminders: only reason can help us overcome fear and anxiety; such fears will only take flight once we have uncovered the true nature of things; the cure is presented as poetry to sugar-coat the medicine; philosophy purges the mind of the impediments to tranquillity.[26] Equally important, though, is his insistence that it is *only* via a true understanding of Nature that such therapy is possible.[27] Only physics can save us.

Lucretius's contemporary Philodemus also stressed this therapeutic model of philosophy. We have already seen his contribution to the Epicurean project of giving arguments to help overcome the fear of death,[28] and he also wrote about therapy for anger.[29] He is also remembered for four

---

[25] Lucretius 1.149–58 (trans. Melville), following the revised line order at 1.155–8 adopted by modern editors.

[26] See Lucretius 2.53–4 (LS 21W), 3.14–16, 4.10–25, and 5.1–21 respectively.

[27] See Lucretius 1.146–8, repeated verbatim at 2.59–61 (LS 21W), 3.91–3, and 6.39–41.

[28] See Ch. 7 above.

[29] For a thorough examination of therapeutic themes in Philodemus see Tsouna (2007).

short lines of Greek text known as the 'fourfold cure' (*tetrapharmakos*) which neatly summarize the central therapeutic claims of Epicurean philosophy: 'don't fear God, don't worry about death; what is good is easy to get, and what is terrible is easy to endure'.[30] As we have seen, fear of God and fear of death are, claim the Epicureans, the most common forms of anxiety. Fear of future pain is another common concern, addressed in Philodemus's third and fourth points. Philosophy for all the Epicureans was something medicinal.

Stoic Remedies

The Stoics, unlike the Epicureans, do seem to have taken inspiration from Socrates when thinking about the nature of philosophy.[31] This probably came both directly from reading Socratic dialogues by Plato and other authors, and also indirectly via the Cynics and others.[32] Zeno is reported to have read Xenophon's accounts of Socrates and he also studied with Polemo in the Academy.[33] According to Diogenes Laertius,

Polemo used to say that we should exercise ourselves with things and not with mere logical speculations, which leave us, like a man who has got by heart some paltry handbook on harmony but never practised, able, indeed, to win admiration for skill in asking questions, but utterly at variance with ourselves in the ordering of our lives.[34]

Influenced by Polemo, not to mention his first mentor Crates the Cynic, it should come as no surprise if Zeno's own philosophy also shared this distinctively practical orientation.

Like Socrates, the Stoics drew analogies between philosophy and various arts and crafts, leading them to describe philosophy as the art of living.[35] This they conceived, again following Socrates, as an art that

---

[30] Philodemus, *Adv. Soph.* (*PHerc* 1005), in **LS 25J**.

[31] For a fuller discussion of Stoic ideas about the nature of philosophy see Sellars (2003).

[32] Zeno studied in the Academy under Polemo, was inspired to study philosophy after reading Xenophon's account of Socrates in the *Memorabilia*, and was a disciple of Crates the Cynic. See Diog. Laert. 7.2–3 (**IG II-1**).

[33] See Diog. Laert. 7.2 (**IG II-1**).

[34] Diog. Laert. 4.18. On Polemo's approach to philosophy and his influence on Zeno see Dillon (2003), 159–77.

[35] See e.g. Sextus Empiricus, *Math.* 11.170. On the Stoic idea of philosophy as an art of living see Sellars (2003).

heals the soul analogous to the way in which medicine heals the body. The Stoic Chrysippus said:

> It is not true that whereas there is an art, called medicine, concerned with the diseased body, there is no art concerned with the diseased soul, or that the latter should be inferior to the former in the theory and treatment of individual cases.[36]

This latter art is, of course, philosophy, and Chrysippus described the philosopher as 'the physician of the soul'.[37] While the Epicureans were most concerned about fear of things such as the gods and death, the Stoics were primarily concerned about the disruptive impact of emotions or passions (*pathê*) on an individual's ability to live well.[38] Thus Stoic therapeutic strategies focused on how to cope with and avoid emotions.

One of the fullest accounts of the Stoic approach to emotions we have is in Cicero's *Tusculan Disputations*.[39] Cicero reports that Chrysippus spent much time examining the similarities between illnesses of the soul and those of the body.[40] It has been suggested that Cicero's account draws heavily on Chrysippus's now lost book *Therapeutics*, which may have been just one book in a larger work, *On Emotions*.[41] (There has been some debate about whether Chrysippus's account differed from his predecessor Zeno,[42] but here we shall focus on Cicero's account, drawing mainly on Chrysippus.)

The Stoics claimed that all the different emotions we experience may be reduced to four main categories, each category reflecting an origin in a

---

[36]   Galen, *PHP* 5.2.22 (De Lacy (1978–84), 298).

[37]   Galen, *PHP* 5.2.23 (De Lacy (1978–84), 298).

[38]   The Greek *pathê* and Latin *passio* are often translated as 'emotion'. That is not ideal because the English word is somewhat vague and certainly broader than what the Stoics had in mind. Traditionally these terms were translated as 'passion', in many ways preferable, although Tieleman (2003), 15–16, notes that for some this word might be too closely associated with ideas of sexual desire. Tieleman, following Frede (1986), opts for 'affection'. I have decided, with some reservations, to stick with 'emotion' here.

[39]   See esp. *Tusc.* 4.11–33. The Latin text is in Pohlenz (1918) and is translated and discussed in Graver (2002). It is examined in relation to the other evidence for Chrysippus's account of the emotions in Tieleman (2003), 288–320.

[40]   See *Tusc.* 4.23.

[41]   See e.g. Dougan and Henry (1905–34), ii, xxx–xlvii. For a thorough study of Chrysippus's lost *On Emotions* see Tieleman (2003).

[42]   Compare e.g. Sorabji (2000), 55, and Tieleman (2003), 8. There has also been much debate about whether the later Stoic Posidonius disagreed with Chrysippus. One of our principal sources, Galen, claims he did but some scholars have begun to doubt him. See e.g. Cooper (1998), Gill (1998), and Tieleman (2003), 198–287, with dissent in Sorabji (1998) and (2000), 93–108.

specific type of belief.[43] Thus, the emotion of 'gladness' is the product of a belief in a present good, 'desire' is the product of a belief in a future good, 'fear' is the product of a belief in a future evil, and 'distress' the product of a belief in a present evil (see Table 9.1):[44]

Table 9.1. Summary of Stoic categories for emotions

	Present	Future
Good	Gladness, pleasure (*hêdonê, laetitia*) (belief in a present good)	Desire, appetite (*epithumia, libido*) (belief in a future good)
Evil	Distress, pain (*lupê, aegritudo*) (belief in a present evil)	Fear (*phobos, metus*) (belief in a future evil)

Following Socrates, the Stoics held that people naturally pursue what they think is good, and avoid what they think is evil, so these beliefs not only generate these emotions but also determine how we act. The Stoics went on to claim that these beliefs were ultimately the product of judgements we make, and in particular value judgements about whether something is good or evil. Thus the emotion of fear is the product of judging that something terrible is going to happen in the future. Once the judgement has been made, the emotion is generated, which if unchecked can run out of control and take on a life of its own. In particular the turbulence of emotions can become habitual, leading to a generalized state of inconsistency and agitation.[45]

Cleanthes thought he could offer therapy for emotions such as grief by challenging the value judgements that underpinned them.[46] His successor Chrysippus appears to have doubted this, primarily because it is difficult to reason with someone when they are in the midst of emotional turmoil. Instead, he seems to have offered two different types of therapy for the emotions. The first type was immediate help for emotional disturbance, and Chrysippus is reported to have claimed that he could help anyone currently suffering emotional turmoil, even people with little interest in Stoic philosophy. In a passage saved for us by Origen, we find Chrysippus prepared to offer emotional therapy to Peripatetics

---

[43] See Cicero, *Tusc.* 4.16 for lists of different emotions under each category.
[44] See Cicero, *Tusc.* 3.24–5; 4.11–14; cf. Stobaeus 2,88,8–90,6 (**IG II-95, LS 65A**).
[45] See Cicero, *Tusc.* 4.24.   [46] See Cicero, *Tusc.* 3.76.

and Epicureans in the grip of an emotion, even though he knows they may be unlikely to accept any Stoic premises.[47] However, the first type of therapy does not involve that sort of philosophical argument, again because someone in the grip of a powerful emotion is unlikely to listen to reason.[48] Chrysippus writes:

The man who is troubled by passion should not worry about the doctrine which has gained possession of his mind at the moment when the passions are at their height, lest somehow he should be concerned at the wrong moment with the refutation of the doctrines that have gained possession of his soul, and possibility of cure is lost.[49]

Instead, says Chrysippus, they ought to be offered therapy consistent with the beliefs that they already hold:

if pleasure is an ultimate value, men should try to heal their passions assuming this to be correct; and supposing that there are three kinds of good, it is just as true to say that people who are entangled with their passions ought to be delivered from them by following this principle.[50]

Precisely what forms this first type of therapy took, we do not know, but Cicero suggests that the focus may have been on offering arguments about the inappropriateness of an excessive emotional response.[51] One can also imagine the sorts of visualization techniques described by later Roman Stoics, such as adopting a 'view from above'.[52] All of these things might offer immediate respite for someone in the midst of an emotional crisis, whether they share Chrysippus's own philosophical views or not.

The second type of therapy for the emotions is quite different. This is aimed at avoiding emotions altogether, and involves a philosophical analysis of the judgements that generate the beliefs that create the

[47] See Origen, *C. Cels.* 8.51, 1.64 (both *SVF* 3.474). These texts have been interpreted in a number of different ways. Nussbaum (1994), 318, and Sorabji (2000), 2, 178, take them to mean that Stoic therapeutics need not depend on Stoic philosophy at all (or at least not the theory of value), while Inwood (1985), 153, Donini (1995), and Tieleman (2003), 166–70, take the line I follow here, namely that there must be two different types of therapy on offer.

[48] Here Chrysippus seems to be advancing on the view of his predecessor Cleanthes; see Cicero, *Tusc.* 3.76.

[49] Origen, *C. Cels.* 8.51 (*SVF* 3.474); trans. Chadwick (1953), 489–90.

[50] Origen, *C. Cels.* 1.64 (*SVF* 3.474); trans. Chadwick (1953), 59.

[51] See Cicero, *Tusc.* 3.76 and the discussion in Tieleman (2003), 166–70.

[52] See e.g. Marcus Aurelius 7.47, with discussion in Hadot (1995), 238–50. The idea was already current in the Hellenistic period and can be seen in Lucretius 2.7–14 (**LS 21W**) and Cicero's 'Dream of Scipio' (a fragment from Book 6 of his *Republic*). See Ch. 8 above.

emotions in the first place. As Chrysippus notes, this sort of analysis can hardly be done when someone is in the grip of an emotion, and must wait until the immediate disturbance has passed. This second type of therapy, unlike the first, draws explicitly on central claims in Stoic philosophy, most notably their theory of value and their psychology, and potentially much of their physics and theology as well. Once the emotionally disturbed Peripatetic or Epicurean has calmed down, Chrysippus will try to show them with philosophical arguments that the real cause of their emotional disturbance was the mistaken values that they hold, and that the only way to avoid suffering such emotions in the future is to adopt the Stoic theory of value. This second type of explicitly philosophical therapy will ultimately help only those who are prepared to accept some of the central claims of Stoic philosophy.

The first type of therapy has aptly been called 'first aid',[53] while the second has been compared with modern cognitive psychotherapy.[54] In the present context, what is most relevant is the fact that this study of the emotions involved not just a theoretical account of how they were thought to arise, but also a series of practical remedies under the heading of 'therapeutics', which may have been presented separately for a wider audience.[55] In all this, Chrysippus draws on medical terminology and makes extensive use of the analogy between philosophy and medicine.[56]

The Stoics developed this therapeutic approach to the emotions within a broader conception of philosophy as an art of living (*technê peri ton bion*).[57] Central to this way of thinking about philosophy seems to have been an attempt to combine a concern with a wide range of abstract philosophical issues within a broadly therapeutic understanding of the purpose of philosophy. Once again, medicine offered itself as a helpful model. This is not only because they wanted to present philosophy as an art that heals the soul analogous to the way in which medicine heals the body, but also because medicine subsumes the study of complex theoretical material within a thoroughly practical activity aimed at transforming people's lives for the better.

---

[53] See Inwood (1985), 300.   [54] See e.g. Sorabji (2000), 2.
[55] See Galen, *PHP* 5.7.52, but with reservations in Tieleman (2003), 140–2.
[56] See Galen, *PHP* 5.2.22, quoted above, and Cicero, *Tusc.* 4.23.
[57] See further Sellars (2003). All of the surviving references to an 'art of living' in both Greek and Latin sources are connected in some way to Stoicism; see Sellars (2003), 5 n. 27.

The Stoics, then, thought that philosophy was an art concerned with how to live well, a medicine for the mind analogous to medicine for the body. Like the art of physical medicine, it involves both complex theory and a series of practices designed to put those theories into practice. Ultimately these practices are aimed at curing the soul of harmful and irrational emotions, which the Stoics see as the greatest impediment to living well. The aim of philosophy, then, is a practical one, just as it is for the doctor, who learns complex medical theories, not simply for the sake of learning, but for the sake of curing his patients. In the case of the philosopher, the patient is above all himself, and each student of philosophy must become their own doctor. As Arius Didymus puts it in his epitome of Stoic ethics:

It is not the person who eagerly listens to and makes note of what is spoken by the philosophers who is ready for philosophizing, but the person who is ready to transfer the prescriptions of philosophy to his deeds and to live in accord with them.[58]

The Stoics were also interested in questions of bodily health and physical regime alongside matters purely mental. Chrysippus praised a plain and simple diet, and warned against the perils of drunkenness.[59] This idea that care of the soul and care of the body are closely intertwined should come as no surprise, given the way in which the Stoics conceived the relationship between soul and body. It also serves to underline the practical orientation of Stoic philosophy as a whole.

Although it is clear that the Epicureans saw their philosophy as therapeutic in intent, and that the Stoics were concerned with the therapy of emotions, some commentators have remained sceptical about the claim that the Stoics conceived philosophy as such in these sorts of terms. The Stoics were interested in a much wider range of intellectual topics, from astronomy to grammar, and there is little in the evidence that survives to suggest that they defended their interest in these things with reference to their contribution to a therapeutic project.

[58] Arius Didymus, in Stobaeus 2,104,17–22 (IG II-95), printed and translated in Pomeroy (1999), 80–3.

[59] See e.g. Plutarch, St. rep. 1044b (SVF 3.706) and Diog. Laert. 7.127 (SVF 3.237, IG II-94, LS 61I) with helpful discussion in Tieleman (2003), 162–6. Later Roman Stoics, such as Musonius Rufus, also stressed the importance of physical training alongside mental training. These sorts of concerns in Stoicism were probably inherited from the Cynics.

But we might just say that there was no need to, for these are valuable pursuits in their own right.[60] They also devoted considerable energies to highly technical parts of philosophy with no immediate practical application, such as the study of logical paradoxes. Chrysippus was famed in antiquity, as he is now, as a logician, probably the most important ancient logician after Aristotle. In his work *Philosophical Lives for Sale*, the later satirist Lucian presents him as a logic-chopping obscurantist rather than a healer of souls.[61]

Perhaps we ought not to see these as opposed alternatives. When the Stoics presented philosophy as therapy for the soul, they thought that it could cure the soul of certain illnesses or diseases. What were these diseases? We might naturally think of out-of-control emotions, such as anger, but, as we have seen, strictly speaking the Stoics did not claim to be able to cure these: the person in the grip of anger cannot be reasoned with, so philosophy can offer little help. The sufferer must simply wait for the emotion to subside in its own due course. What philosophy can do is help to make sure that further emotions are not generated, and it does this by paying close attention to the judgements that generate beliefs, which in turn cause emotions. The central therapeutic task, then, is paying attention to one's judgements—value judgements, epistemological judgements, and logical judgements. While some of Chrysippus's fine-grained logical analysis of hypothetical syllogisms might seem of little immediate practical benefit,[62] it is in fact essential to the process of learning how to make correct judgements. His interest in paradoxes might equally reflect a desire to expose inconsistent and contradictory thoughts.[63] Logic is about learning how to think straight; it is a remedy for confused, illogical thinking. For the Stoics, a confused, illogical mind can hardly embody the reason and consistency that they suggest mark the life of the sage. In short, the healthy mind that the Stoics aim for and think their philosophy can cultivate is not some vague 'good feeling about one's life'; the healthy mind is rigorously logical and

---

[60] Only if the Stoics i) conceived these interests as parts of philosophy and ii) saw philosophy as fundamentally therapeutic would this be an issue.

[61] See Lucian, *Vit. auct.* 21–5 (part LS 37L). In fact, Lucian's character Chrysippus does claim that the study of logic is necessary for living well, but this is part of the parody.

[62] A charge made by Williams (1994) in a review of Nussbaum (1994).

[63] I owe this thought to Johanna Schmitt.

rational, and the study of logic is thus an essential part of their practical philosophical project.

Pyrrhonian Cures

The Pyrrhonians also embraced the language of therapy when describing their philosophical activity:

Sceptics are philanthropic and wish to cure by argument, as far as they can, the conceit and rashness of the Dogmatists. Just as doctors for bodily afflictions have remedies which differ in potency... so Sceptics propound arguments which differ in strength.[64]

This summary of the Pyrrhonian view was written much later by Sextus Empiricus and, as we saw in a previous chapter, recent scholarship has highlighted the differences between Sextus, the Hellenistic reviver of Pyrrhonism Aenesidemus, and Pyrrho himself.[65] According to Sextus's version of Pyrrhonism, this 'cure by argument' involves finding objections to an individual's dogmatic beliefs that will lead them into a state of doubt by generating a balance between opposed arguments. This leads to suspension of judgement (*epochê*) by the now confused individual. The important point in Sextus's version is that the individual does not choose to suspend judgement; rather, they find themselves simply unable to commit when faced with these competing reasons. Sextus goes on to suggest that this state of suspended judgement will, in turn, generate a state of tranquillity (*ataraxia*). Once again, this is not something the individual can choose directly; it simply happens. The dissatisfied individual, earnestly striving for a happy life, who turns to philosophy in search of guidance, will only attain peace of mind as if by accident, when they give up the quest in a state of utter confusion. Pyrrhonism, in Sextus's version, cures us of our mental disturbances by offering arguments designed to generate the confusion necessary to generate tranquillity.

The broad outlines of Sextus's version agree with what we know about Aenesidemus's position.[66] He too suggested that tranquillity would

---

[64] Sextus Empiricus, *Pyr.* 3.280 (**IG III-28**), trans. Annas and Barnes (1994).

[65] See e.g. Bett (2000).

[66] The surviving evidence is gathered together and translated, with commentary, in Polito (2014). The extent to which Aenesidemus and Sextus agree has been subject to debate; see e.g. Woodruff (1988) and Schofield (2007), with Polito (2014), 168–72.

inevitably follow from suspension of judgement.[67] He also claimed that someone who, like him, 'philosophizes after the fashion of Pyrrho', will be happy, this happiness being the product of his suspension of judgement.[68] It is tempting to assume that part of the motivation for Aenesidemus's turn to Pyrrho as a figurehead for his own brand of scepticism was an admiration for Pyrrho himself, whose reputation rested primarily on his way of life.[69]

Pyrrho is said to have learned his philosophy of suspension of judgement (*epochê*) from the gymnosophists he encountered in India, living a life shaped by this new attitude.[70] Diogenes Laertius presents an image of a philosopher who refused to accept the evidence of his own senses and only avoided constant mishaps by being guided around by his friends.[71] That frankly absurd image is presumably informed by ancient polemics against the plausibility of Pyrrhonism as a way of life,[72] polemics that were likely made precisely because Pyrrhonism presented itself as such. Other anecdotes present the image of someone not indifferent to the evidence of their own senses, but rather someone calm and serene, sometimes retreating into solitude, indifferent to immediate events that might upset his tranquillity (*ataraxia*).[73]

Philosophers who did not share Pyrrho's philosophical outlook also admired his way of life, including Epicurus and the Stoic Posidonius.[74] Indeed, Pyrrhonians, Epicureans, and Stoics were all on common ground in proposing that an ideal life would be marked by tranquillity, and that philosophy was the way to attain it. At this level it was often easy for philosophers of competing schools to admire one another and to share

---

[67] This seems to be implicit in Diog. Laert. 9.107 (B21B in Polito (2014), **IG III-22**, **LS 71A**). See also Diog. Laert. 9.78–9 (B16 Polito, **IG III-22**, part **LS 71B**).

[68] See Photius, *Bibl.* 212, 169b18–31 (B1 in Polito (2014), **IG III-25**, **LS 71C**).

[69] For some doubts on this see Polito (2014), 5–6, discussed further below.

[70] See Diog. Laert. 9.61 (DC 1A, **IG III-22**, **LS 1A**). See the Appendix for more on his trip to India.

[71] See Diog. Laert. 9.61 with discussion in Bett (2000), 63–70. For a Pyrrhonian response to this image of their philosophy see Diog. Laert. 9.104–5 (**IG III-22**, **LS 1H**).

[72] Diogenes reports that his account comes from a work by Antigonus of Carystus.

[73] See Diog. Laert. 9.63–8 (**IG III-22**, part **LS 1B-C**).

[74] See Diog. Laert. 9.64 (DC 28, **IG III-22**, **LS 1B**) and 9.68 (DC 17A, EK F287, **IG III-22**) respectively. Diogenes places Pyrrho in a succession that runs from Democritus to Epicurus. See further Warren (2002).

anecdotes for the purpose of philosophical instruction. Posidonius reported the following:

> When his [Pyrrho's] fellow-passengers in a storm were showing the strain, he remained calm and stiffened the spirit by pointing to a piglet in the boat continuing to feed, and said that the wise man ought to be in such a settled, unperturbed state.[75]

A later writer, Theodosius, claimed that because Pyrrho literally did not believe anything, it was impossible to become a Pyrrhonian at the level of doctrine; the only meaningful sense in which someone might follow Pyrrho was to emulate his way of life.[76]

The extent to which Aenesidemus admired Pyrrho's way of life has been the subject of debate. On one view, his revived Pyrrhonism was primarily concerned with epistemological theory and he had little interest in anecdotes concerning Pyrrho's way of life.[77] Only the early followers of Pyrrho, such as Timon, paid attention to such things. That may be right to a point, but it leaves unanswered the question why Aenesidemus chose to name his new philosophical position after Pyrrho, if not out of admiration for the man himself. That is a question it may be impossible to answer.[78] In the present context, though, it seems safe to say that both early and later Pyrrhonism were marked by distinctively practical outlooks, offering respectively an image of an ideal life of tranquillity and therapy for mistaken beliefs that would also lead to tranquillity.

Academic Therapy

Later Pyrrhonism probably developed in response to debates within the Academy in the first century BC. One of the motivations for this was the feeling that the later Academy had lost its way and had drifted too far from its more radical beginnings. In this sense, the Pyrrhonists might be seen not only to be followers of Pyrrho, but also the true heirs of

---

[75] Diog. Laert. 9.68 (DC 17A, EK F287, **IG III-22**), trans. Kidd (1999).

[76] See Diog. Laert. 9.70 (DC 41).

[77] See Polito (2014), 5–6, drawing on Polito (2007).

[78] It is also bound up with a number of other difficult questions, including: was Aenesidemus a disaffected member of the Academy? If so, did he want to return to the scepticism of Arcesilaus? Did Arcesilaus admire Pyrrho? Was Pyrrho really a sceptic? For further discussion see Bett (2000), 214–22.

Arcesilaus.[79] One question we might ask is whether the Pyrrhonists thought that their broadly therapeutic conception of philosophy reflected the original spirit of the sceptical Academy. It is difficult to answer this question directly, due to lack of evidence,[80] but we do have evidence for later Academics who did think that philosophy had a therapeutic function, in particular Philo. According to the later doxographer Stobaeus, Philo drew an analogy between philosophy and medicine, claiming that a philosopher is like a doctor:

Just as it is the function of the doctor, then, first to persuade the sick person to accept his therapy, and secondly to undermine the arguments of those urging him against treatment, so it is also for the philosopher.[81]

Philosophical arguments, then, are for the sake of therapy. The passage above refers to the first stage of philosophical therapy, which Philo calls 'protreptic', and which exhorts people to a life of virtue. After this comes the second stage, 'therapeutic', during which the philosopher offers cures for diseases of the soul, namely false beliefs. This involves putting forward arguments that will undermine false beliefs, and others that will generate correct beliefs concerning goods and evils. The third stage is concerned with the goal of the whole process, namely happiness, which is analogous to the goal in medicine, health. This involves offering guidance on how to live in a way that will maintain one's newly restored mental health, addressing questions such as whether one should marry or engage in politics. This final stage, which we might call 'preservative', may well be Philo's original contribution, insisting that philosophical therapy is not a one-off cure, but rather something that must be practised throughout one's life.[82]

---

[79] See e.g. Diog. Laert. 4.32–3 (IG III-1, LS 68E), Numenius in Eusebius, *Praep. evang.* 14.6.4–6 (LS 68F), Sextus Empiricus, *Pyr.* 1.232–4 (IG III-27, LS 68I), and the discussion in Ch. 2 above.

[80] Although there seems to be no evidence to suggest Arcesilaus adopted a therapeutic model, there is ancient discussion of his way of life. While Cicero praises Arcesilaus for acting consistently with his philosophy (*Acad.* 1.45 (IG III-19, LS 68A)), the Stoic Cleanthes is reported to have ridiculed him for not living in accordance with his beliefs (Diog. Laert. 7.171 (IG II-1, LS 69C)), instead relying in daily life on what seems reasonable.

[81] Stobaeus 2,39,20–41,25 (this extract 2,40,1–4), printed and translated as Philo test. 32 in Brittain (2001), 364–6. For a helpful discussion see Schofield (2002).

[82] See Schofield (2002), 98–9, who notes that this point was also made later by the Roman Stoic Musonius Rufus (fr. 36 Hense, from Plutarch, *De cohib. ira* 453d–e).

Is this distinctively Academic? It is not obviously sceptical in outlook, and, as we have already seen, Philo's own philosophy may have moved away from the stronger forms of scepticism of the earlier Academy. But it is a broadly Socratic outlook, and the Academy throughout its history claimed to be the true heirs not only of Plato but also of Socrates.[83]

This therapeutic image of philosophy is discussed at length by Philo's most famous pupil, Cicero, in the *Tusculan Disputations*. This work discusses philosophical therapy for a range of impediments to a happy life, including fear of death, dealing with pain, and overcoming sorrow.[84] In his own survey of his philosophical writings, Cicero describes the concluding book of the *Tusculan Disputations* as shedding 'the brightest light on the entire field of philosophy'.[85] This might suggest that Cicero thought that the sort of philosophical therapy outlined in the *Tusculan Disputations* was indeed the ultimate task of philosophy.

Peripatetics Out of Step?

So far it looks as if all of the major philosophical movements of the Hellenistic period conceived philosophy in ways that share enough in common that they might fall under a common banner, such as Hadot's 'philosophy as a way of life'. This looks true for the Epicureans, Stoics, and various brands of sceptics. But what about the fourth school of the period, the Lyceum? At first glance it looks as if the Hellenistic Peripatetics might be an important exception. The traditional view of the Lyceum of this period presents Theophrastus and his successors as devoted Aristotelians, following their school's founder in both their range of interests and their methods. Thus Theophrastus wrote his own treatise on metaphysics, and extended Aristotle's biological works into the realm of botany. Subsequent Peripatetics pursued interests in scientific topics and rhetoric, occasionally getting drawn into philosophical debates with their contemporaries in other schools, but for the most part continuing the Aristotelian

---

[83] On Philo's Socratic outlook (and its influence on Cicero) see Schofield (2002), esp. 96, where he suggests that Philo is simply rewriting 'the Socratic conception of philosophy in the language of the favoured Hellenistic metaphor of therapy'.

[84] See Cicero's own summary at *Div.* 2.2.   [85] Cicero, *Div.* 2.2.

way of doing things, unperturbed by wider developments. Indeed, this apparent lack of interest in the wider changes taking place in philosophy has been cited as one of the reasons why the Lyceum slowly declined in importance during this period.[86]

How much of this is true? Were the Peripatetics out of step? Are they an important exception to the general approach to philosophy we have been considering? If we turn to the surviving evidence for Theophrastus's successor at the Lyceum, Strato of Lampsacus, we find little to challenge the picture just sketched. The bulk of the information we have deals with topics in physics, psychology, and zoology, and very little deals with ethics.[87] One source describes him as a practitioner of *phusiologia*, the study of nature,[88] while a whole range of ancient writers refer to him as a *pusikos*, a naturalist or physicist.[89] One of his pupils, Aristarchus, went on to propose a heliocentric model of the solar system almost 2,000 years before Copernicus.[90] We do have a list of titles of books written by Strato that includes works called *On Happiness* (*Peri Eudaimonias*) and *On Ways of Life* (*Peri Biôn*),[91] but the latter might simply be descriptions of different ways of life on the model of Theophrastus's *Characters*. There is no evidence of any attempt to offer a definition of philosophy, either as therapy for the soul or as anything else.

It seems, then, that Hellenistic Peripatetics remained more or less faithful to Aristotle's way of doing things.[92] Aristotle gives his account of philosophy in the *Metaphysics*, where he presents it as a search for knowledge, which he divides into three types: practical, productive, and theoretical.[93] Theoretical knowledge is prioritized over the practical and

---

[86] For an ancient account of its decline, see Cicero, *Fin.* 5.9–14, esp. 5.13, who is, it should be noted, not a neutral source and here principally concerned with contributions to ethics.

[87] Cicero also notes Strato's lack of interest in ethics; see *Fin.* 5.13 (fr. 12 in Wehrli (1969b), 8A in Sharples (2011)).

[88] See Galen, *Hist. Phil.* 3, in Diels (1879), 601,1–2 (fr. 7 in Wehrli (1969b), 3 in Sharples (2011)).

[89] See e.g. Diog. Laert. 5.58 (fr. 1 in Sharples (2011)), with numerous further examples in frr. 10, 11, 35, 45A, 45B, 54, 60, 61, 63B, 75 in Sharples (2011).

[90] See Heath (1913), 299–316, for discussion and references to the ancient sources.

[91] See Diog. Laert. 5.59 (fr. 1 in Sharples (2011)).

[92] White (2004b), arguing in favour of a continued interest in ethics among Hellenistic Peripatetics, highlights the ways in which they remained broadly faithful to Aristotle's approach.

[93] Aristotle, *Metaph.* 6.1, 1025b24–8.

productive, as it includes first philosophy, which deals with what is unchanging.[94] This sort of knowledge, the subject of metaphysics, is the paradigm for Aristotle's understanding of philosophy. While he might eulogize a life devoted to theoretical contemplation in his ethics,[95] that seems to be a corollary to his commitment to first philosophy, rather than evidence for the claim that he thought philosophy was primarily a way of life. Although proponents of the idea that ancient philosophy was a way of life have tried to show that Aristotle shares this approach,[96] it looks as if his approach to philosophy is quite different from that of, say, Socrates.[97]

This kind of variety of approaches and commitments is only to be expected, and we might point to a number of other periods in the history of philosophy where those who self-identified as philosophers did not all agree on what they thought philosophy was. This is all the more to be expected in the Hellenistic period, during which there were significant developments in the way in which people understood and approached a wide range of intellectual inquiry. Indeed, it may well be that these wider developments contributed to the Hellenistic emphasis on the idea that philosophy is fundamentally a guide to life. Before trying to flesh out that claim, it may be useful to say something about these wider intellectual developments. As we shall see, this is where the Hellenistic followers of Aristotle really left their mark.

From Athens to Alexandria

If at the beginning of the Hellenistic period Athens was the predominant centre of philosophical activity, by the end the picture was far more complex. This was due not only to the rise of other centres of activity but also to the rise of other intellectual disciplines. To put it simplistically, if before the Hellenistic period almost all intellectual inquiry fell under the heading of 'philosophy', by the end there were a whole range of new labels with which to classify thinkers and their increasingly specialized areas of interest. The historical story is a complex one, made all the more difficult to reconstruct due to the inevitably fragmentary evidence, and it

---

[94]   Aristotle, *Metaph.* 6.1, 1026a22–3.   [95]   See Aristotle, *Eth. Nic.* 10.6–8.
[96]   See Hadot (2002), 77–90, and Cooper (2012), 70–143.
[97]   On the difference between Socrates and Aristotle see Sellars (2003), 33–6.

will not be possible to do it justice here. Even so, a brief outline may help to put into wider context the ways in which philosophy was conceived in the period. In particular I want to focus on developments in Alexandria.

During the Hellenistic period the library and museum at Alexandria became one of the most important centres of intellectual inquiry in the ancient world.[98] It was founded by the first King Ptolemy around 300 BC and, according to some accounts, severely damaged by Julius Caesar in 48–47 BC.[99] It is not clear how much, if any, of the library was destroyed then, and Alexandria remained an important centre of intellectual activity throughout late antiquity, but the golden age of Alexandria sits firmly within the Hellenistic period. Its early years were marked by close connections with the Lyceum in Athens. The library's founder, Ptolemy I Soter, invited Theophrastus to come to Alexandria without success, but did manage to persuade his pupil Demetrius of Phaleron to come and to act as his adviser. According to one source, Demetrius was 'head of the king's library'.[100] Demetrius had a wide range of intellectual interests, as can be seen from the surviving list of his works in Diogenes Laertius.[101] These included politics, rhetoric, and poetry. He is reported to have assisted Ptolemy II Philadelphus in bringing books from all over the ancient Mediterranean world to Alexandria;[102] he is also credited with organizing and supervising the translation of the Hebrew Bible into Greek, producing the text we now know as the Septuagint.[103] Demetrius was not the only Peripatetic to visit Alexandria; Strato also made the trip. If Demetrius brought with him Peripatetic interests in rhetoric and poetry, Strato 'the physicist' emphasized another aspect of the intellectual interests of the Lyceum.[104] There is a widely held view, dating back to Cicero, that the Hellenistic Lyceum went through a period of decline and made little impact compared to the other Hellenistic schools in

---

[98] For general accounts see Sandys (1903), 105–43, Fraser (1972), i, 305–35, and Casson (2001), 31–47. The other great library of the period, at Pergamum, also deserves mention in an account of Hellenistic philosophy because it was home to a number of Stoic philosophers, including Crates of Mallos and Athenodorus of Tarsus; see Sandys (1903), 144–64, and Pfeiffer (1968), 234–51.

[99] See Plutarch, *Caes.* 49.3, and Dio Cassius 42.38.2.

[100] See Aristeas, *Ep. ad Philoc.* 9 (fr. 66 in Wehrli (1968a), 59 in Stork et al. (2000)).

[101] See the life in Diog. Laert. 5.75–85 (text 1 in Stork et al. (2000)).

[102] See texts 58A–B in Stork et al. (2000).   [103] See texts 59–66 in Stork et al. (2000).

[104] See Pfeiffer (1968), 152.

Athens; its real intellectual legacy, however, may have been in Alexandria on an altogether grander scale.[105]

Among the various intellectuals associated with Alexandria during this period, a number stand out. Perhaps the most important is Callimachus, a poet and a literary scholar who described himself as a grammarian (*grammatikos*).[106] Callimachus is important in the present context for his role in organizing the books in the library. His *Tables of Men Distinguished in Every Branch of Learning, and their Works*, filling 120 books, attempted to catalogue by subject the tens or hundreds of thousands of papyrus scrolls that had already been accumulated.[107] He arranged the books in sections, possibly as many as ten, including rhetoric, law, epic, tragedy, comedy, philosophy, history, and medicine.[108] This inevitably involved making decisions about where particular works belonged within the classification, and these decisions could sometimes be controversial. It is reported that while Callimachus placed Prodicus with the orators, others complained that he ought to be with the philosophers.[109] These efforts at organizing an ever-increasing body of written works no doubt played their role in the development of disciplinary specialization. There was now an official list of distinct intellectual subjects into which any particular work would have to be placed.

Another key figure associated with Alexandria is Eratosthenes, a pupil of Callimachus who had also studied philosophy in Athens with the Stoic Aristo and the Academic Arcesilaus. Under Ptolemy III, he became the librarian at Alexandria.[110] He has been described as a philosopher, geographer, astronomer, mathematician, and grammarian, and was no

---

[105] For the narrative of decline see Lynch (1972), 135–62. Cicero's judgement is in *Fin.* 5.9–14. For some doubts about the impact of the Lyceum on the library at Alexandria see Lynch (1972), 121–3, although he is more concerned with organizational arrangements than intellectual impact.

[106] The first person to describe themselves as a *grammatikos* in this new sense to mean a student of literature, as opposed to someone merely literate, was a Hellenistic Peripatetic, Praxiphanes (*DPhA* Vb 1509–13; texts in Wehrli (1969c)), who was a pupil of Theophrastus and who wrote literary criticism. See Sandys (1903), 7.

[107] See *Suda* s.v. *Kallimachos* (K 227) with Pfeiffer (1968), 127–34. How many scrolls there were in the library is unknown. Texts 58A, 58B, and 59 in Stork et al. (2000) all quote figures in the hundreds of thousands but modern scholars doubt it ever reached that scale (e.g. Thonemann (2016), 70).

[108] See Pfeiffer (1968), 128–9.

[109] See fr. 431 in Pfeiffer (1949), with Pfeiffer (1968), 131.

[110] See *Suda* s.v. *Eratosthenês* (E 2898), with Pfeiffer (1968), 152–70.

doubt all of these things.[111] He is perhaps best remembered for calculating the circumference of the earth to a surprising degree of accuracy.[112] His encyclopaedic range of interests led him to describe himself in a new way: he was not a philosopher (*philosophos*) or a grammarian (*grammatikos*), but rather a philologist (*philologos*),[113] the first in a new category of intellectual.

It may be instructive to compare Eratosthenes with another figure who had strong interests in both philosophy and geography, namely the Stoic Posidonius. While Eratosthenes adopted the label of philologist, suggesting a broad love of learning, Posidonius self-identified as a philosopher and, in particular, as a Stoic.[114] As such, he was committed to the Stoic division of philosophy into the three parts of logic, physics, and ethics. In debates about how this division ought to be understood Posidonius insisted on their organic unity.[115] While physics was an essential part of this unified conception of philosophy, what we would now call the special sciences were not. According to Seneca, Posidonius distinguished between philosophy and these other intellectual disciplines, which Seneca refers to as the liberal arts.[116] These other subjects, such as mathematics and astronomy, are mere instruments of philosophy and dependent on philosophy for their foundations. The philosopher is concerned to know the causes of and reasons for things, while the mathematician calculates and the astronomer observes.[117] Seneca adds that the philosopher is the only one who pursues knowledge of good and evil, and this is the only thing that can perfect the mind. It is unclear whether this final comment is Seneca's own, or part of his account of Posidonius's view, but either way it is interesting to note that here philosophy is described as an art. We have all the various liberal arts and we also have the art of

---

[111] He is not usually classified as a philosopher today, although he does receive a substantial entry in *DPhA* III, 188–236, where his philosophical activity is discussed at 204–8.

[112] See Irby-Massie and Keyser (2002), 120–1.

[113] See Suetonius, *Gramm.* 10.

[114] The ancient sources regularly describe him as a philosopher, and sometimes also a historian. He also had interests in mathematics, geography, hydrology, geology, and botany. All the evidence is in EK.

[115] See Sextus Empiricus, *Math.* 7.19 (EK F88, **LS 26D**).

[116] See Seneca, *Ep.* 88.21–8 (EK F90, part **LS 26F**), with discussion in Kidd (1978).

[117] This distinction is also drawn in Simplicius, *in Phys.* 291,21–292,31 (EK F18), who is reporting Geminus's summary of Posidonius.

philosophy, which, as we have already seen, Stoics in particular described as the art of living. Philosophy is the master art, explanatory rather than descriptive, distinct from the natural sciences, and concerned with matters both physical and ethical.[118] This might be seen as an example of a philosopher reasserting the importance of philosophy in response to the increasing autonomy of other disciplines. The encyclopaedic Posidonius engaged in a variety of these lesser arts alongside his work in the master art of philosophy.

The slowly emerging divisions of intellectual labour between philosophy, scientific arts, and literary arts were far from secure, and we could point to numerous exceptions. One example might be the work of Aratus, a Stoic who wrote an astronomical poem, the *Phaenomena*.[119] As one commentator has put it, 'a scientific subject was here treated with Stoic religious and philosophic feeling in a style derived from Hesiod'.[120] His use of poetry to convey scientific ideas was nothing new, and the tradition would continue after him with Lucretius. The fact that this still seemed a perfectly reasonable way to proceed, and was admired by later writers,[121] reminds us not to overstate the divisions between the newly emerging disciplines. But it also raises a further question: what was Aratus doing? Was it part of philosophy, as his Stoic commitments might suggest? Was it simply astronomy, albeit with philosophical overtones? Or was it poetry that just happened to have astronomical and philosophical subject matter? Had Aratus been a Presocratic, we might be less inclined to ask such questions, but in the Hellenistic period these sorts of distinctions now seem relevant. Today Aratus is more likely to appear in histories of science than in histories of philosophy or poetry, even though it has been said he made no original contribution to astronomy.[122]

---

[118] See Kidd (1978), 14, and, for further discussion, Veillard (2015), 189–97.

[119] For an edition with translation and commentary see Kidd (1997), and esp. 10–12 on its Stoic aspects. There is also a LCL edition.

[120] Pfeiffer (1968), 121.

[121] Aratus is cited regularly by Geminus in his *Introduction to the Phenomena*, an astronomical work probably written around 70 BC. Geminus may have also been a Stoic and some have suggested that he was a pupil of Posidonius (see Evans and Berggren (2006), 23). The Stoic Boethus of Sidon wrote a commentary on Aratus. Later, Cicero translated the *Phaenomena* into Latin. See further Kidd (1997), 44–8. It was also praised by Callimachus (see Pfeiffer (1968), 121).

[122] See Lloyd (1973), 63.

The final response to the classification of a work like Aratus's *Phae-nomena*, and by extension Aratus's classification as an intellectual, may in part come down to where the book ought to be filed within a library such as the one at Alexandria. A philosopher is someone who writes books that get put in the 'philosophy' section of the library. A polymath is someone who writes books that get put in a number of different sections in the library. Aratus's book was presumably filed under astronomy, not poetry, and it could not be in both places at once. Perhaps we ought not to underestimate the role of Callimachus and his successors in deciding what counts as an example of one discipline rather than another.

There are potentially two ways in which these developments might impact on the way in which people thought about philosophy. The first would be along the lines just suggested, namely that the new ways in which knowledge was classified in the libraries helped to define the subject matter of philosophy more precisely. Empirical investigations of the sort carried out by Milesian Presocratics or Aristotle were no longer thought by default to be part of philosophy; they now had their own disciplinary status. Philosophy was no longer a catch-all heading for the pursuit of knowledge, for now there were a number of new discip-lines, or at least categories in the library catalogue, that were also devoted to knowledge but no longer part of philosophy. The domain of philoso-phy was beginning to shrink.[123]

A second way in which these changes might have impacted on phi-losophy brings us back to the main concerns of this chapter. In response to the development of these new scientific and literary disciplines, some may have paused to reflect on the nature and role of philosophy, which could no longer be characterized simply as the pursuit of knowledge. What did philosophy offer that was truly distinctive? The Stoics and Epicureans had a ready answer to this question: it offered a way of life motivated by a desire for tranquillity and shaped by a range of thera-peutic practices designed to remove mistaken beliefs that stand in the way. Although these Stoic and Epicurean ideas about philosophy were formed well before the gradual development of intellectual specialization

[123] According to this sort of narrative, philosophy has continued to shrink ever since, losing physics and psychology in more recent centuries. What we call philosophy today, on this view, is simply the leftovers that cannot be refined into an exact science.

could have had much impact, these later developments might account for the subsequent popularity of this way of thinking about philosophy towards the end of the Hellenistic period and into the first two centuries AD. As other disciplines gained an identity of their own, and philosophy could no longer be thought of as the universal pursuit of knowledge, the therapeutic model of philosophy familiar since Socrates offered a ready answer to the question, 'what is the distinctive role of philosophy?'.

It is of course difficult to know the extent to which the rise of new disciplines impacted upon how philosophers understood their own subject. The two possibilities I have just sketched are no more than that. But the wider point is, I hope, worth taking more seriously, namely that during the Hellenistic period divisions between different intellectual pursuits were gradually taking shape and that these developments were bound to have some sort of impact on philosophy as a subject and how it was conceived.

* * *

In this chapter we have focused on ways in which philosophers of the Hellenistic period presented what they were doing as an intensively practical enterprise, focused on therapeutic self-transformation that would, in turn, transform one's way of life. This was without doubt a central theme running through much of Hellenistic philosophy. It is tempting to present this as an alternative to the image of philosophy as a disinterested pursuit of knowledge closely aligned to the natural sciences. If one were to do that, then we would have to say that many of the Peripatetics of the period were somewhat out of step with this wider trend. One way to present this, as I hinted at earlier, would be to draw a contrast between a practical Socratic approach to philosophy and a more scientific Aristotelian approach.

Tempting as that is, we should perhaps pause to consider some other points first. As we saw in a previous chapter, the Peripatetic Hieronymus of Rhodes defined the goal of human life as freedom from disturbance.[124] He also wrote about anger and how to control it[125] and, while doing so, made use of medical analogies, just like so many of his Hellenistic

---

[124] See e.g. Cicero, *Acad.* 2.131 (fr. 13A in White (2004a)); Clement of Alexandria, *Strom.* 2.21.127 (fr. 12 in White (2004a)).
[125] See Plutarch, *De cohib. ira* 454e–f, 460b–d; Seneca, *De ira* 1.19.1–4 (fr. 25–7 in White (2004a)).

contemporaries.[126] Some Peripatetics of the period focused their attention on physics while others, following Aristotle's own encyclopaedic range of interests, engaged in a wide variety of burgeoning disciplines alongside philosophy. Yet the same could be said of some Stoics, not least Posidonius. The Peripatetic Praxiphanes seems to have had a special interest in literary criticism, prefiguring developments in Alexandria, but the same could also be said for the Stoic Crates of Mallos who was librarian at Pergamum, the great ancient rival of the Alexandrian library.[127] In short, the distance between the Stoics and Peripatetics of the period, in terms of their activities and range of interests, was perhaps not as great as the foregoing account might imply.

With the Epicureans, we have a clear case where the therapeutic goal was centre stage. Yet, as we have seen, the way to reach that goal, and to overcome fear and anxiety, is through a proper understanding of Nature. The two go hand in hand. In the case of Pyrrho and the later Pyrrhonians, tranquillity might be the goal, but the only way to reach it is to have a proper grasp of what we can and cannot know. Even the intensely practical Cynics of the period based their life of cosmopolitan simplicity on a series of knowledge claims about human nature and the contingency of social customs. None of these schools of thought advocated philosophy as a therapeutic enterprise *in contrast* to the pursuit of knowledge; on the contrary, in each case the pursuit of the appropriate sort of knowledge was fundamental. That's what made them philosophers.

---

[126] See Plutarch, *De cohib. ira* 460c (fr. 26 in White (2004a)).
[127] On Crates' literary criticism see Janko (2000), 120–34. He also had interests in grammatical theory, on which see Janko (1995).

APPENDIX

Looking East

When people first come into contact with one or more of the Hellenistic schools of philosophy it is not uncommon for them to comment that they are reminded of some aspects of Buddhism. At the most general level, one might point to a shared therapeutic project, but there are more specific parallels that have been pointed to as well.[1] We might note the Stoic claim that our unhappiness is ultimately the product of making mistaken judgements, the Epicurean claim that our fear of death is unfounded, and the Pyrrhonian claim that the best way of life is one without beliefs.[2] Many of the Hellenistic schools share with Buddhism an attitude of non-attachment towards external material things, along with the thought that this will contribute to achieving a state of tranquillity.

These parallels naturally lead some to wonder whether there might have been any Indian influence on the development of these Hellenistic schools of thought. In the cases of Stoicism and Epicureanism we have fairly clear accounts of the ways in which these philosophies drew on the work of earlier Greek philosophers—Heraclitus and Socrates for the Stoics; Democritus for the Epicureans—and so scholars have tended not to feel the need to look for other, more exotic, sources of influence.[3] In the case of Pyrrhonism, or at least Pyrrho himself, we do have some intriguing information that might well suggest an Indian influence on the development of his thought. According to ancient accounts, Pyrrho, along with a couple of other Greek philosophers, travelled with Alexander the Great to India where he encountered a number of ascetic Indian sages, the gymnosophists (naked wise men).[4] Diogenes Laertius claims

---

[1] For a brief account, from the perspective of Buddhism, see Gowans (2003), 42–6, and, on shared use of medical analogies, Gowans (2010). For a more substantial survey of parallels between Greek and Indian philosophy see McEvilley (2002).

[2] On Pyrrhonism and Buddhism see e.g. Bett (2000), 169–78; Kuzminski (2008); Halkias (2014), 73–8; Beckwith (2015). Conze (1963) notes the similarities between Pyrrho and Buddhism but also draws attention to parallels with Cicero's *Academica*.

[3] Hadot (2002), 96–7, denies both an Indian influence and any need to posit such an influence on the Hellenistic schools. See in response Beckwith (2015), 222–4.

[4] For ancient accounts see Plutarch, *Alex.* 64–5, Strabo 15.1.58–70, and Diog. Laert. 9.61 (IG III-22, LS 1A), with discussions in Flintoff (1980) and Bett (2000), 169–78. On the gymnosophists see Stoneman (1995), who suggests that they may have been Brahmans or

that Pyrrho's own philosophy developed as a result of his encounter with them.[5] The form that this influence took is perhaps harder to determine. Strabo reports that in order to talk with these Indian sages Pyrrho's travelling companion Onesicritus the Cynic had to make use of three intermediary translators.[6] As some commentators have noted, this language barrier makes it seem unlikely that any complex philosophical ideas could have been transmitted at this moment of 'first contact'.[7] But it is certainly possible that both Pyrrho and Onesicritus (and their other companion, Anaxarchus) were influenced by the example of the way of life of these Indian sages. Indeed, Diogenes Laertius reports that the gymnosophists criticized Anaxarchus for his way of life, and that this criticism influenced Pyrrho's own choice of a life of withdrawal.[8] There has been much debate about whether these Indian sages were Buddhists; they may have been examples of the sorts of ascetics that the Buddha reacted against when developing his own 'middle way' between the extremes of asceticism and hedonism.[9] Others have argued that they probably were Buddhists and have also noted that the Greek label 'gymnosophist' may have been indiscriminately applied to members of quite different groups.[10]

These hints at possible Indian influences on Pyrrho raise wider questions about the extent of interaction between Greek and Indian thought during the Hellenistic period. As we have seen, Pyrrho's encounter with the gymnosophists happened during Alexander's expedition into India. Other Greek philosophers came along too, such as Onesicritus, and Strabo reports at length Onesicritus's account of his discussions with the Indian sages.[11] It seems that accounts of these encounters made it back to Athens quickly because one source reports that Zeno of Citium commented on the Indian practice of suicide by fire:

Jains but were unlikely to have been Buddhists, while adding that distinctions between different groups of Indian ascetics would have been far from clear cut in this period.

[5] See Diog. Laert. 9.61 (DC 1A, IG III-22, LS 1A), 9.63 (DC 10, IG III-22, LS 1B).

[6] See Strabo 15.1.64.

[7] See e.g. Bett (2000), 177. Beckwith (2015), 218–22, suggests that such problems were probably overcome very quickly.

[8] See Diog. Laert. 9.63 (IG III-22, LS 1B), but note also the doubts raised in Hadot (2002), 96–7.

[9] On the Buddha's period of asceticism and subsequent rejection of it see his *Middle Length Discourses*, briefly summarized in Gowans (2003), 20. See also Gowans (2003), 43, who (like Stoneman (1995)) doubts the existence of any connection with Buddhism but suggests that Pyrrho may have been influenced by 'skeptical *samaṇas* [i.e. ascetics] he encountered' in India.

[10] See e.g. Halkias (2014), 74, who suggests that they 'may be broadly identified by what we understand today as Buddhists', and Halkias (2015) where he identifies the gymnosophist Calanus described by Arrian (*Anab.* 7.3) as a Buddhist.

[11] See Strabo 15.1.63–5 (cf. *SSR* V C 3).

Zeno said well of the Indians, that he would rather have seen one Indian roasted, than have learned the whole of the arguments about bearing pain.[12]

This suggests that the founder of Stoicism both knew of these early encounters and was impressed by what he heard. But of course that is very different from suggesting that any Indian ideas influenced the development of Zeno's own philosophy. Instead, as with Pyrrho, we have an admiration for a certain way of life, not to mention seeing philosophy put into practice in the most extreme possible way. This suggests mutual recognition rather than influence. Indeed, Onesicritus reports a conversation with an Indian sage called Mandanis, in which they compare notes on similar ideas in the Greek and Indian traditions.[13] Pythagoras, Socrates, and Diogenes the Cynic are mentioned as examples of Greek philosophers who share something in common with Indian wisdom. The important point to note here is that although Onesicritus may have found some things to admire among the doctrines and practices of the Indian sages, his own Cynicism was already completely formed before the encounter. Once again, we can point to mutual recognition, even admiration perhaps, but not influence.

After Alexander's death, the eastern part of the vast territory he conquered became the Seleucid Empire, administered by Seleucus from Antioch. This extended right up to the border with India and included the province of Bactria (roughly, present-day Afghanistan).[14] The Indian territory invaded by Alexander did not form part of the Seleucid Empire and remained independent, but Greeks settled in the area and the Indian rulers were open to Greek culture and enjoyed cordial relations with Hellenistic Bactria. Most significant in the present context is the activity of the third of the rulers of this Indian territory, Asoka (ruled 268–232 BC).[15] Asoka's place in the history of Buddhism is well established. He was a lay practitioner of Buddhism and a key figure in its dissemination. A number of his edicts survive as inscriptions (including some written in Greek), and these give us information about his efforts to spread knowledge of Buddhism both within his own kingdom and further afield.[16] One of these inscriptions reports that Asoka sent Buddhist envoys to the lands of the

[12] Clement of Alexandria, *Strom.* 2.20 (*SVF* 1.241), and cited in Hadot (2002), 97. Compare with Strabo's report (15.1.64–5) of Onesicritus's account of witnessing an Indian suicide by fire.

[13] See Strabo 15.1.65 (*SSR* V C 3). For a further discussion of Onesicritus see Brown (1949).

[14] There is inevitably a vast literature on this; one classic study that touches on many of the topics mentioned here is Tarn (1938).

[15] For a full account see Thapar (1961).

[16] The edicts are edited and translated in Hultzsch (1925). They are also translated in Thapar (1961), 250–66. For discussions see Thapar (1961), 137–81, and Scott (1985). On the Greek inscriptions see Sick (2007).

'Yonas' (from 'Ionians', i.e. Greeks), and it goes on to name the Mediterranean rulers to whom they were sent.[17] Some of these envoys were themselves Greeks who had embraced Buddhism.[18] Indeed, the inscription not only says that these envoys were sent, but also claims that these areas were successfully conquered by Dharma, Buddhist teaching. In exchange, some of these Hellenistic kings, notably Ptolemy II of Egypt, sent envoys to India.[19] Some have claimed that Buddhist communities developed in the Mediterranean world, with a text by Philo describing an unusual and otherwise unknown monastic community cited as evidence.[20] Others have claimed to have found Buddhist gravestones in Alexandria.[21] Whether or not we accept these last claims, it seems clear that Pyrrho's encounter with the gymnosophists was not a single, exceptional point of contact, but rather simply the first of a series of such encounters, culminating just after the end of the Hellenistic period with an Indian sage called Zarmarus meeting the Roman Emperor Augustus in Athens.[22] There was probably more knowledge of and interaction with Indian philosophy during the Hellenistic period than one might initially suppose. Whether there was any direct philosophical influence is another matter.

Quite separate from questions of influence is the extent to which there was philosophical activity in the Hellenistic East. We do know that Hellenistic philosophers made it as far east as Bactria: the Peripatetic Clearchus of Soli is named in an inscription in the city of Aï Khanoum, and the remains of a philosophical work on papyrus have been found in the same place.[23] The text is a philosophical dialogue and it discusses the nature of Ideas, so in both form and content it appears to be Platonic. However, some have suggested that it might be a fragment of an Aristotelian criticism of Plato's theory of Ideas, perhaps from one of Aristotle's own lost dialogues.[24] Equally it might be from

---

[17]   See Rock Edict 13, in Hultzsch (1925), 22–5, 43–9, and Thapar (1961), 255–7.

[18]   See the account in the *Mahāvaṃsa*, in Geiger (1912), 82.

[19]   See Pliny, *Nat. hist.* 6.58.

[20]   See Thundy (1993), 244–5, referring to Philo's *On the Contemplative Life*. Philo calls these monks *therapeutai*, which Thundy suggests is an attempt to render *theravada*. He proposes that these monks were 'probably the successors of the missionaries whom Emperor Asoka sent to Egypt'.

[21]   See the critical discussion in Fraser (1972), ii, 312, n. 391.

[22]   See Dio Cassius 54.9.8–10. See also Strabo 15.1.73, who claims that after the meeting Zarmarus willingly committed suicide by burning.

[23]   For the inscription see Robert (1968). For the papyrus see the editions in Rapin, Hadot, and Cavallo (1987) and Lerner (2003), the second of which includes an English translation. The papyrus itself does not survive but the remains of a wall preserve its imprint, from which it has been possible to recover some text.

[24]   Aristotle's lost dialogues *Sophist* and *On Philosophy* have been proposed as possible sources. See Isnardi Parente (1992), 181–2, and Rapin, Hadot, and Cavallo (1987), 248, respectively.

a later Peripatetic. However, as one commentator has noted, it is also possible
that it might be a local product, written by a member of a philosophical school in
Aï Khanoum.[25] On the basis of the evidence it is impossible for us to say anything
for certain about its authorship, but its presence in Aï Khanoum does seem to
point to philosophical activity of some sort on the eastern edges of the Hellenistic
world.[26]

A quite different piece of evidence for Indo-Greek philosophical activity is a
Buddhist dialogue called *The Questions of Milinda* (*Milindapañha*).[27] This text,
in Pali, recounts a series of philosophical discussions set *c.* 155 BC between the
Graeco-Bactrian king Menander (i.e. Milinda) and a Buddhist monk called
Nāgasena, who was taught by a Greek Buddhist monk called Dharmarakṣita,
one of Asoka's many missionaries.[28] The text takes the form of a series of
questions from Menander asking Nāgasena to clarify a wide range of issues in
Buddhist thought. Nāgasena challenges Menander's belief in an essential self,
denying that any particular part of a person, or the form of the body, or
consciousness counts as the true person.[29] In response to another interlocutor,
who may also have been Greek, Nāgasena denies that the soul can be identified
with breath.[30] A little later, he insists on the importance of virtue and claims it is
the foundation for happiness.[31] There is nothing here to suggest any explicit link
with the philosophy of the Athenian schools, but we can at least see a shared set
of philosophical interests. Perhaps this work of philosophy, written on the far
eastern edge of the Hellenistic world, should also count as part of the story of
Hellenistic philosophy.

[25] See Lerner (2003), 50.
[26] Not quite so far east, we are also told that the Stoic Archedemus left Athens to set up a
Stoic school in Babylon; see Plutarch, *De exil.* 605b (*SVF* 3.Arch.2).
[27] The Pali text is in Trenckner (1880). It is translated in Rhys Davids (1890) and Horner
(1963–4). There is an extended discussion in Rhys Davids (1930). See also Sick (2007).
[28] Although the dialogue is set squarely within the Hellenistic period, it may be that the
text as we now have it was composed slightly later. Rhys Davids (1930), 5, dates it to the first
century BC. Dharmarakṣita is mentioned as one of Asoka's envoys in the *Mahāvaṃsa*
(Geiger (1912), 82).
[29] See Rhys Davids (1890), 40–5.
[30] See Rhys Davids (1890), 48–9. The interlocutor's name Anantakāya may derive from
Antiochus in Greek (see Rhys Davids (1890), xix).
[31] See Rhys Davids (1890), 53–4.

Chronology

All dates are BC. Inevitably many are only approximate, but for the sake of simplicity I have avoided adding 'c.' before or '?' after each one that is not completely secure.

399   Trial and execution of Socrates in Athens
387   Plato founds the Academy
384   Birth of Aristotle
347   Death of Plato
341   Birth of Epicurus
335   Aristotle founds the Lyceum
334   Alexander, Pyrrho, and others meet the gymnosophists in India
323   Death of Alexander the Great; the formal beginning of the 'Hellenistic' period
322   Death of Aristotle; Theophrastus becomes head of Lyceum
310   The Peripatetic Clearchus of Soli visits Aï Khanoum in Bactria
306   Epicurus buys plot of land just outside Athens, the site of the Epicurean Garden
305   Zeno of Citium founds the Stoic school in Athens
295   Ptolemy I establishes the Library of Alexandria
287   Death of Theophrastus; Strato becomes head of the Lyceum
270   Death of Epicurus
268   Arcesilaus becomes head of the Academy, initiates shift towards scepticism
261   Death of Zeno of Citium; Cleanthes becomes head of the Stoa
230   Death of Cleanthes; Chrysippus becomes head of the Stoa
167   Carneades becomes head of the Academy
155   Embassy of three Athenian philosophers (Diogenes of Babylon, Carneades, Critolaus) to Rome
144   The Stoic Panaetius goes to Rome
135   Birth of Posidonius
110   Philo of Larissa becomes head of the Academy; death of Panaetius; birth of Philodemus
106   Birth of Cicero
88–6 Sulla's siege of Athens, destroying the Academy and possibly the Epicurean Garden and the Lyceum; Philo flees to Rome, Antiochus to Alexandria, Posidonius to Rhodes

79   Cicero studies with Antiochus in Athens

74   Philodemus arrives in Italy

55   Lucretius's *On the Nature of Things* published

51   Death of Posidonius

45–4   Cicero writes the bulk of his philosophical works

43   Death of Cicero, on the order of Mark Anthony

40   Death of Philodemus

31   Octavian's defeat of Mark Anthony and Cleopatra at the Battle of Actium; the formal end of the 'Hellenistic' period

27   Octavian becomes 'Augustus', the first Roman Emperor

Guide to Hellenistic Philosophers

This list includes philosophers from the Hellenistic period mentioned in this book. Some have been discussed at length; others just named in passing. Dates generally follow those in the *OCD*, which provides fuller entries, as does the magisterial *DPhA* (in French). I also include references to selected texts and collections of fragmentary evidence. To put this list in context, the *DPhA* records some 600 philosophers from the fourth to the first century BC (see Goulet (2013), 23), although for many of these we know little more than their names.

Aenesidemus of Cnossos (1st cent. BC): Reviver of Pyrrhonism, probably after defecting from the Academy. Texts: Polito (2014), with translations.

Antiochus of Ascalon (*c.* 130–*c.* 68 BC): Academic, a pupil of Philo of Larissa, departed from scepticism to develop a dogmatic philosophy uniting Platonism, Aristotelianism, and Stoicism. Texts: Mette (1986–7); Sedley (2012), 334–46, with translations.

Antipater of Tarsus (*c.* 210–*c.* 130 BC): Stoic, succeeded Diogenes of Babylon as head of the Stoa; taught Panaetius. Texts: *SVF* 3.

Apollodorus of Athens (2nd cent. BC): Epicurean, head of the Garden in Athens, reported to have written some 400 books.

Aratus (*c.* 315–*c.* 240 BC): Astronomical poet influenced by Stoicism, studied in Athens with Zeno of Citium. Texts: *Phaenomena* in Kidd (1997), with a translation; also a LCL edition.

Arcesilaus (*c.* 318–242 BC): Academic, elected head of the Academy and responsible for its turn towards scepticism. Texts: Mette (1984).

Archedemus of Tarsus (*c.* 180–*c.* 110 BC): Stoic, a pupil of Diogenes of Babylon and Antipater, went to Babylon where he founded a Stoic school. Texts: *SVF* 3.

Aristo of Ceos (fl. *c.* 225 BC): Peripatetic, a pupil of Lyco and his successor as head of the Lyceum. Texts: Wehrli (1968c); Stork et al. (2006), with translations.

Aristo of Chios (*c.* 320–*c.* 240 BC): Stoic, a pupil of Zeno of Citium, usually considered heterodox in ethics. Texts: *SVF* 1.

Athenodorus of Tarsus (1st cent. BC): Stoic, librarian at Pergamum, later moved to Rome where he knew Cato the Younger, nicknamed 'Cordylion' to distinguish him from another Stoic of the same name nicknamed 'Calvus'.

Atticus, Titus Pomponius (110–32 BC): Epicurean, a friend and correspondent of Cicero, settled in Athens.

Bion of Borysthenes (*c.* 335–*c.* 245 BC): Cynic, at least in temperament, who valued only ethics. Texts: Kindstrand (1976); translations in Sayre (1948), Dobbin (2012).

Boethus of Sidon (2nd cent. BC): Stoic, a pupil of Diogenes of Babylon, heterodox in physics. Texts: *SVF* 3.

Carneades (214–129 BC): Academic, head of the Academy and a sceptical critic of the Stoa. Texts: Mette (1985).

Cato 'the Younger', Marcus Porcius (95–46 BC): Roman Stoic, associate of Cicero, committed suicide rather than submit to Julius Caesar; appears as a spokesman in Cicero's philosophical works and was the subject of one of Plutarch's *Lives*.

Chrysippus of Soli (*c.* 280–*c.* 205 BC): Stoic, third head of the Stoa, succeeding Cleanthes; wrote 705 books and is generally held to be the most important of the Athenian Stoics. Texts: *SVF* 2 and 3.

Cicero, Marcus Tullius (106–43 BC): Statesman and philosopher whose outlook owes much to the moderate scepticism of the Academic Philo of Larissa. Texts: Pohlenz (1918), Plasberg (1922), Plasberg and Ax (1933), Winterbottom (1994), Reynolds (1998), Powell (2006); translations in Griffin and Atkins (1991), Walsh (1997), Rudd (1998), Walsh (2000), Sharples (1991), Annas and Woolf (2001), Brittain (2006). All also available in LCL.

Cleanthes of Assos (331–232 BC): Stoic, second head of the Stoa after Zeno of Citium, noted for his interests in physics and theology. Texts: *SVF* 1; for his *Hymn to Zeus*, Thom (2005), with translation.

Clearchus of Soli (fl. *c.* 340–*c.* 290 BC): Peripatetic, a pupil of Aristotle, travelled to Bactria in the wake of Alexander of Great. Texts: Wehrli (1968a).

Clitomachus (187–110 BC): Academic, pupil of Carneades and teacher of Philo of Larissa, reported to have written over 400 books. Texts: Mette (1985).

Colotes of Lampsacus (*c.* 325–*c.* 260 BC): Epicurean, studied with Epicurus in Lampsacus before Epicurus moved to Athens; wrote works against Plato, attracting the polemic *Against Colotes* by the later Platonist Plutarch. Texts: Crönert (1906).

Crates of Mallos (fl. *c.* 160 BC): Stoic; a philosopher, grammarian, and librarian at Pergamum, remembered for his allegorical interpretations of Homer.

Crates of Thebes (*c.* 368–*c.* 288 BC): Cynic, follower of Diogenes of Sinope and teacher of Zeno of Citium. Texts: *SSR* V H.

Critolaus of Phaselis (2nd cent. BC): Peripatetic, head of the Lyceum and member of the embassy to Rome in 155 BC alongside Carneades and Diogenes of Babylon, noted for his criticisms of Stoicism. Texts: Wehrli (1969c); selection translated in Sharples (2010).

Dardanus (2nd–1st cent. BC): Stoic, joint head of the Stoa in Athens with Mnesarchus; together they were the last heads of the Athenian Stoa.

Demetrius of Laconia (fl. *c*. 100 BC): Epicurean, a contemporary of Zeno of Sidon; fragments of his works have been recovered from Herculaneum.

Demetrius of Phaleron (b. *c*. 350 BC): Peripatetic, a pupil of Theophrastus, governor of Athens and later librarian at Alexandria. Texts: Wehrli (1968b); Stork et al. (2000), with translations.

Diodorus Cronus (d. *c*. 284 BC): Logician, associated with the Megarian school, his pupils included Philo of Megara and Zeno of Citium. Texts: *SSR* II F.

Diodotus (fl. *c*. 85 BC): Stoic, tutor to Cicero, in whose house he lived.

Diogenes of Babylon (*c*. 240–152 BC): Stoic, succeeded Zeno of Tarsus as head of the Stoa, a member of the embassy to Rome in 155, taught Panaetius. Texts: *SVF* 3.

Epicurus of Samos (341–270 BC): Founder of the school named after him, taught first in Mytilene and Lampsacus before relocating to Athens and establishing his Garden, a community of Epicureans. Texts: Usener (1887), now dated; Bailey (1926), the letters and sayings only, with translations; Arrighetti (1973), fuller collection including papyrus discoveries, with Italian translation.

Eratosthenes (*c*. 285–194 BC): Polymath, studied with Arcesilaus and Aristo of Chios in Athens, later became librarian in Alexandria, wrote works on philosophy, mathematics, literary criticism, and geography, all of which are lost.

Geminus (fl. *c*. 90–*c*. 35 BC): Stoic, possibly a pupil of Posidonius at Rhodes; his astronomical treatise *Phaenomena* survives. Texts: Evans and Berggren (2006), translation into English.

Hermarchus of Mytilene (fl. *c*. 310–*c*. 260 BC): Epicurean, a close associate of Epicurus and his successor as head of the school. Texts: Longo Auricchio (1988).

Hieronymous of Rhodes (fl. *c*. 290–*c*. 230 BC): Peripatetic, later left the Lyceum to found his own school. Texts: Wehrli (1969c); White (2004a), with translations.

Lacydes of Cyrene (fl. *c*. 240–*c*. 210 BC): Academic, Arcesilaus' successor as head of the Academy, credited in some sources as the founder of the 'New Academy'. Texts: Mette (1985), 39–51.

Lucretius Carus, Titus (*c*. 95–*c*. 55 BC): Epicurean, author of *On the Nature of Things* but otherwise little is known about him. Texts: Leonard and Smith (1942); Bailey (1947), with translation; LCL edition (revised by M. F. Smith), with translation; further translations in Latham (1951), Melville (1997), Stallings (2007).

Lyco of Troas (*c*. 300–*c*. 225 BC): Peripatetic, a pupil of Strato and his successor as head of the Lyceum, which he led for over forty years. Texts: Wehrli (1968c); Stork et al. (2004), with translations.

Menippus of Gadara (3rd cent. BC): Cynic, the author of satires addressing moral topics, now lost.

Metrocles (3rd cent. BC): Cynic, a follower of Crates, also attended the lectures of Theophrastus. Texts: *SSR* V L.

Metrodorus of Lampsacus (*c.* 330–*c.* 277 BC): Epicurean, a close associate of Epicurus. Texts: Körte (1890).

Metrodorus of Stratonicea (2nd cent. BC): Academic, a pupil of Carneades who defected from the Epicurean Garden.

Mnesarchus (2nd–1st cent. BC): Stoic, joint head of the Stoa in Athens with Dardanus; together they were the last heads of the Athenian Stoa.

Onesicritus (4th cent. BC): Cynic, travelled to India with Alexander and Pyrrho, met with the gymnosophists. Texts: *SSR* V C.

Panaetius of Rhodes (*c.* 185–109 BC): Stoic, studied in Pergamum and Athens, later moved to Rome; in 129 he succeeded Antipater as head of the Stoa in Athens. Texts: Straaten (1952) and Alesse (1997).

Patro (1st cent. BC): Epicurean, head of the Epicurean garden in Athens, succeeding Phaedrus in 70, corresponded with Cicero.

Phaedrus (*c.* 140–*c.* 70 BC): Epicurean, taught in Rome with Cicero among his audience, later became head of the Epicurean Garden in Athens.

Philodemus of Gadara (*c.* 110–*c.* 35 BC): Epicurean, a pupil of Zeno of Sidon in Athens but settled in Italy, possibly in Herculaneum, where many of his works were recovered from the Villa of the Papyri. Texts (a selection): De Lacy and De Lacy (1978), Obbink (1996), Janko (2000), Henry (2009), Janko (2011), all with translations.

Philo of Larissa (159–84 BC): Academic, the last sceptical head of the Academy, fled to Rome in 88 during the siege of Athens, taught Cicero. Texts: Mette (1986–7); Brittain (2001), with translations.

Philo of Megara (fl. *c.* 300 BC): Logician, a pupil of Diodorus Chronus, associated with the Megarian school, although perhaps erroneously connected with Megara the place. Texts: *SSR* II G.

Polemo (*c.* 350–*c.* 270 BC): Academic, head of the Academy before it turned sceptical, wrote mainly on ethics, taught and influenced Zeno of Citium.

Polyaenus of Lampsacus (d. *c.* 270 BC): Epicurean, a close associate of Epicurus. Texts: Guerra (1991).

Polybius (*c.* 200–*c.* 118 BC): Greek political leader who became an associate of Scipio Africanus and the Stoic Panaetius, chiefly remembered as a historian, but his *Histories* include contributions to political philosophy. Texts: LCL, with translation.

Posidonius of Apamea (*c.* 135–*c.* 50 BC): Stoic, with an encyclopaedic range of interests, studied in Athens under Panaetius before founding his own school in Rhodes. Texts: Edelstein and Kidd (1972), translated in Kidd (1999).

Praxiphanes (fl. *c.* 300–*c.* 250 BC): Peripatetic, active in Rhodes, remembered for his literary criticism. Texts: Wehrli (1969b).

Pyrrho of Ellis (*c.* 365–*c.* 275 BC): Sceptical philosopher, known mainly via the accounts of his pupil Timon, travelled to India with Alexander. Texts: Decleva Caizzi (1981).

Siro (1st cent. BC): Epicurean, active in Bay of Naples area, a friend of Cicero, counted Virgil among his pupils.

Strato of Lampsacus (d. 269 BC): Peripatetic, succeeded Theophrastus to become third head of the Lyceum, nicknamed 'the physicist'. Texts: Wehrli (1969a); Sharples (2011), with translations.

Teles (fl. *c.* 235 BC): Cynic, author of popular diatribes commending the Cynic way of life. Texts: Hense (1909); translated in Dobbin (2012).

Theophrastus of Eresus (*c.* 371–*c.* 287 BC): Peripatetic, pupil of Aristotle and his successor as head of the Lyceum. Texts (a selection): *Metaphysics* in Ross and Fobes (1929), Raalte (1993), and Gutas (2010), all with translations; biological works *Enquiry into Plants* and *On the Causes of Plants* in LCL; fragmentary evidence on a wide range of subjects in FHSG, with translations.

Timon of Phlius (*c.* 320–*c.* 230 BC): Pyrrhonian, a pupil of Pyrrho and our main source of information about him. Texts: Di Marco (1989).

Varro, Marcus Terentius (116–27 BC): Roman scholar and statesman, studied with Antiochus in Athens, said to have written over 600 books, appears as a spokesman in Cicero's philosophical works.

Zeno of Citium (335–263 BC): Founder of the Stoic school in Athens, having previously been a follower of Crates and a student of Polemo. Texts: *SVF* 1.

Zeno of Sidon (fl. *c.* 125–*c.* 75 BC): Epicurean, head of the Epicurean Garden in Athens; Philodemus and Cicero attended his lectures. Texts: Angeli and Colaizzo (1979).

Zeno of Tarsus (fl. *c.* 200 BC): Stoic, succeeded Chrysippus as head of the Stoa. Texts: *SVF* 3.

Guide to Further Reading

Ancient Texts

During the course of writing this book, I have come to the view that by far the best way into Hellenistic philosophy is via the philosophical works of Cicero. They are the most important collection of Hellenistic philosophical texts to survive. They are not only often our earliest or only source of information about philosophers from throughout the Hellenistic period, they are also carefully crafted and highly readable introductions to philosophy, written in the period itself by someone who had been taught by, or was in close contact with, some of the leading members of the principal schools.

There are a number of fairly recent critical editions of the Latin texts in the Oxford Classical Texts series (Winterbottom (1994), Reynolds (1998), Powell (2006)), but for some works it is necessary to rely on older Teubner editions (e.g. Pohlenz (1918), Plasberg (1922), Plasberg and Ax (1933)). For most readers, the LCL editions with facing translations are likely to be easier to locate and more convenient to use. However, the translations in these volumes have in most cases been superseded by more recent versions that often contain helpful notes. In particular, the following translations are recommended: *Academics*, Brittain (2006); *On Duties*, Griffin and Atkins (1991) or Walsh (2000); *On Fate*, Sharples (1991); *On Moral Ends*, Annas and Woolf (2001); *On the Nature of the Gods*, Walsh (1997); *Laws*, Rudd (1998); *Republic*, Rudd (1998).

Of the views he discusses, Cicero is least sympathetic towards Epicureanism, so in order to get a more balanced picture it will be important to hear from the Epicureans in their own voice. Thankfully we can through another Latin author, Lucretius. In many respects Lucretius's *On the Nature of Things* is the most important Epicurean text to survive, at least in terms of its subsequent influence. It is available in a wide variety of editions and translations. Among editions of the Latin text, Leonard and Smith (1942) and Bailey (1947) both contain detailed commentaries and the latter also includes a translation into prose. The LCL version, as revised by M. F. Smith, is recommended and includes a prose translation. Lucretius's text, though, is a poem and some translators have tried to reproduce his poetry rather than turn it into prose. Readers more interested in philosophy than poetry may feel that a prose version better suits their needs, and another prose version is Latham (1951). For those who would like something that is closer to the form of Lucretius's text, verse translations include Melville (1997), which is the translation quoted in this book, and Stallings (2007), in rhyming couplets.

Modern Studies

Introductions to the three main Hellenistic philosophical traditions can be found in Sellars (2006), Thorsrud (2009), and O'Keefe (2010). In the same series, note also Desmond (2008) and Baltussen (2017), on Cynics and Peripatetics respectively. Collections of essays offering fuller overviews can be found in Inwood (2003), Warren (2009), and Bett (2010). For a larger study of the period see Algra et al. (1999). For more technical commentary on many of the ancient texts discussed or mentioned in this book, readers should consult Long and Sedley (1987).

For advanced work on Hellenistic philosophy, a good place to begin is the series of volumes associated with the 'Symposium Hellenisticum' meetings. Taken in order, they also give a good picture of the rise and development of scholarly work over recent decades. In particular I note: Schofield, Burnyeat, and Barnes (1980); Schofield and Striker (1986); Barnes and Mignucci (1988); Brunschwig and Nussbaum (1993); Laks and Schofield (1995); Inwood and Mansfeld (1997); Frede and Laks (2002); Frede and Inwood (2005); Ioppolo and Sedley (2007); Annas and Betegh (2016).

Bibliography

Alesse, F. (1997), *Panezio di Rodi, Testimonianze* (Naples: Bibliopolis).

Algra, K. (2003), 'Stoic Theology', in Inwood, B. (ed.), *The Cambridge Companion to the Stoics* (Cambridge: Cambridge University Press), 153–78.

Algra, K., Barnes, J., Mansfeld, J., and Schofield, M. (eds.) (1999), *The Cambridge History of Hellenistic Philosophy* (Cambridge: Cambridge University Press).

Algra, K., Koenen, M., and Schrijvers, P. (eds.) (1997), *Lucretius and his Intellectual Background* (Amsterdam: North-Holland).

Angeli, A., and Colaizzo, M. (1979), 'I Frammenti di Zenone Sidonio', *Cronache Ercolanesi* 9, 47–133.

Annas, J. (1990), 'Stoic Epistemology', in Everson, S. (ed.), *Epistemology*, Companions to Ancient Thought 1 (Cambridge: Cambridge University Press), 184–203.

Annas, J. (1992), *Hellenistic Philosophy of Mind* (Berkeley, CA: University of California Press).

Annas, J. (1993a), *The Morality of Happiness* (New York: Oxford University Press).

Annas, J. (1993b), 'Virtue as the Use of Other Goods', *Apeiron* 24, 53–66.

Annas, J. (1994), 'Plato the Skeptic', in Vander Waerdt, P. A. (ed.), *The Socratic Movement* (Ithaca, NY: Cornell University Press), 309–40.

Annas, J., and Barnes, J. (1985), *The Modes of Scepticism: Ancient Texts and Modern Interpretations* (Cambridge: Cambridge University Press).

Annas, J., and Barnes, J. (1994), *Sextus Empiricus, Outlines of Scepticism* (Cambridge: Cambridge University Press).

Annas, J., and Betegh, G. (eds.) (2016), *Cicero's De Finibus: Philosophical Approaches* (Cambridge: Cambridge University Press).

Annas, J., and Woolf, R. (2001), *Cicero: On Moral Ends* (Cambridge: Cambridge University Press).

Armstrong, D., Fish, J., Johnston, P. A., and Skinner, M. B. (eds.) (2004), *Vergil, Philodemus, and the Augustans* (Austin, TX: University of Texas Press).

Arnim, H. von (1903–24), *Stoicorum Veterum Fragmenta*, 4 vols (Leipzig: Teubner).

Arrighetti, G. (1973), *Epicuro, Opere*, Second Edition (Turin: Giulio Einaudi Editore).

Asmis, E. (1991), 'Philodemus's Poetic Theory and *On the Good King According to Homer*', *Classical Antiquity* 10, 1–45.

Asmis, E. (1999), 'Epicurean Epistemology', in Algra, K., Barnes, J., Mansfeld, J., and Schofield, M. (eds.), *The Cambridge History of Hellenistic Philosophy* (Cambridge: Cambridge University Press), 260–94.

Asmis, E. (2009), 'Epicurean Empiricism', in Warren, J. (ed.), *The Cambridge Companion to Epicureanism* (Cambridge: Cambridge University Press), 84–104.

Atherton, C. (1993), *The Stoics on Ambiguity* (Cambridge: Cambridge University Press).

Ayres, L. (ed.) (1995), *The Passionate Intellect: Essays on the Transformation of Classical Traditions* (New Brunswick, NJ: Transaction Publishers).

Bailey, C. (1926), *Epicurus, The Extant Remains* (Oxford: Clarendon Press).

Bailey, C. (1928), *The Greek Atomists and Epicurus* (Oxford: Clarendon Press).

Bailey, C. (1947), *Titi Lucreti Cari De Rerum Natura Libri Sex*, 3 vols (Oxford: Clarendon Press).

Baltussen, H. (2008), *Philosophy and Exegesis in Simplicius* (London: Duckworth).

Baltussen, H. (2017), *The Peripatetics: Aristotle's Heirs, 322 BCE–200 CE* (Abingdon: Routledge).

Barnes, J. (1982), *Aristotle* (Oxford: Oxford University Press).

Barnes, J. (1989), 'Antiochus of Ascalon', in Griffin, M. T., and Barnes, J. (eds.), *Philosophia Togata* (Oxford: Clarendon Press), 51–96.

Barnes, J. (1997), 'Roman Aristotle', in Barnes, J., and Griffin, M. T. (eds.), *Philosophia Togata II: Plato and Aristotle at Rome* (Oxford: Clarendon Press), 1–70.

Barnes, J., and Griffin, M. T. (eds.) (1997), *Philosophia Togata II: Plato and Aristotle at Rome* (Oxford: Clarendon Press).

Barnes, J., and Mignucci, M. (eds.) (1988), *Matter and Metaphysics* (Naples: Bibliopolis).

Beckwith, C. I. (2015), *Greek Buddha: Pyrrho's Encounter with Early Buddhism in Central Asia* (Princeton, NJ: Princeton University Press).

Bentham, J. (1907), *An Introduction to the Principles of Morals and Legislation* (Oxford: Clarendon Press).

Berkowitz, L., and Squitier, K. A. (1990), *Thesaurus Linguae Graecae: Canon of Greek Authors and Works* (New York: Oxford University Press).

Bett, R. (2000), *Pyrrho, his Antecedents, and his Legacy* (Oxford: Oxford University Press).

Bett, R. (ed.) (2010), *The Cambridge Companion to Ancient Scepticism* (Cambridge: Cambridge University Press).

Blank, D., and Atherton, C. (2003), 'The Stoic Contribution to Traditional Grammar', in Inwood, B. (ed.), *The Cambridge Companion to the Stoics* (Cambridge: Cambridge University Press), 310–27.

Bobzien, S. (1993), 'Chrysippus' Modal Logic and its Relation to Philo and Diodorus', in Döring, K., and Ebert, T. (eds.), *Dialektiker und Stoiker* (Stuttgart: Franz Steiner Verlag), 63–84.

Bobzien, S. (1998a), *Determinism and Freedom in Stoic Philosophy* (Oxford: Clarendon Press).

Bobzien, S. (1998b), 'The Inadvertent Conception and Late Birth of the Free-Will Problem', *Phronesis* 43, 133–75.

Bobzien, S. (1999a), 'Logic: The "Megarics"', in Algra, K., Barnes, J., Mansfeld, J., and Schofield, M. (eds.), *The Cambridge History of Hellenistic Philosophy* (Cambridge: Cambridge University Press), 83–92.

Bobzien, S. (1999b), 'Logic: The Stoics', in Algra, K., Barnes, J., Mansfeld, J., and Schofield, M. (eds.), *The Cambridge History of Hellenistic Philosophy* (Cambridge: Cambridge University Press), 92–157.

Bobzien, S. (1999c), 'Chrysippus' Theory of Causes', in Ierodiakonou, K. (ed.) (1999), *Topics in Stoic Philosophy* (Oxford: Clarendon Press), 196–242.

Bobzien, S. (2000), 'Did Epicurus Discover the Free Will Problem?', *Oxford Studies in Ancient Philosophy* 19, 287–337.

Bobzien, S. (2003), 'Logic', in Inwood, B. (ed.), *The Cambridge Companion to the Stoics* (Cambridge: Cambridge University Press), 85–123.

Bocheński, I. M. (1951), *Ancient Formal Logic* (Amsterdam: North-Holland).

Boys-Stones, G. R. (2001), *Post-Hellenistic Philosophy: A Study of its Development from the Stoics to Origen* (Oxford: Oxford University Press).

Brain, P. (1986), *Galen on Bloodletting: A Study of the Origins, Development and Validity of his Opinions, with a Translation of the Three Works* (Cambridge: Cambridge University Press).

Branham, R. B., and Goulet-Cazé, M.-O. (eds.) (1996), *The Cynics: The Cynic Movement in Antiquity and its Legacy* (Berkeley, CA: University of California Press).

Brennan, T. (2005), *The Stoic Life: Emotions, Duties, and Fate* (Oxford: Clarendon Press).

Brittain, C. (2001), *Philo of Larissa: The Last of the Academic Sceptics* (Oxford: Oxford University Press).

Brittain, C. (2006), *Cicero: On Academic Scepticism* (Indianapolis, IN: Hackett).

Brittain, C. (2012), 'Antiochus' Epistemology', in Sedley, D. (ed.), *The Philosophy of Antiochus* (Cambridge: Cambridge University Press), 104–30.

Brown, T. S. (1949), *Onesicritus: A Study in Hellenistic Historiography* (Berkeley, CA: University of California Press).

Brunschwig, J. (1986), 'The Cradle Argument in Epicureanism and Stoicism', in Schofield, M., and Striker, G. (eds.), *The Norms of Nature: Studies in Hellenistic Ethics* (Cambridge: Cambridge University Press), 113–44.

Brunschwig, J. (1994), *Papers in Hellenistic Philosophy* (Cambridge: Cambridge University Press).

Brunschwig, J. (2003), 'Stoic Metaphysics', in Inwood, B. (ed.), *The Cambridge Companion to the Stoics* (Cambridge: Cambridge University Press), 206–32.

Brunschwig, J., and Nussbaum, M. C. (eds.) (1993), *Passions and Perceptions: Studies in Hellenistic Philosophy of Mind* (Cambridge: Cambridge University Press).

Burnyeat, M. (ed.) (1983), *The Skeptical Tradition* (Berkeley, CA: University of California Press).

Camp, J. M. (1986), *The Athenian Agora* (London: Thames and Hudson).

Carlini, A. (ed.) (1992), *Studi su codici e papiri filosofici: Platone, Aristotele, Ierocle* (Florence: Leo S. Olschki Editore).

Carlisle, C., and Ganeri, J. (eds.) (2010), *Philosophy as Therapeia*, Royal Institute of Philosophy Supplement 66 (Cambridge: Cambridge University Press).

Casson, L. (2001), *Libraries in the Ancient World* (New Haven, CT: Yale University Press).

Caston, V. (1999), 'Something and Nothing: The Stoics on Concepts and Universals', *Oxford Studies in Ancient Philosophy* 17, 145–213.

Chadwick, H. (1953), *Origen, Contra Celsum* (Cambridge: Cambridge University Press).

Chandler, C. (2006), *Philodemus, On Rhetoric Books 1 and 2: Translation and Exegetical Essays* (New York: Routledge).

Charlesworth, M. J. (1965), *St. Anselm's Proslogion* (Oxford: Clarendon Press).

Chase, M., Clark, S. R. L., and McGhee, M. (eds.) (2013), *Philosophy as a Way of Life: Ancients and Moderns* (Chichester: Wiley Blackwell).

Cherniss, H. (1976), *Plutarch, Moralia Volume XIII Part II* (Cambridge, MA: Harvard University Press).

Clark, G. (2000), *Porphyry, On Abstinence from Killing Animals* (London: Duckworth).

Clark, G., and Rajak, T. (eds.) (2002), *Philosophy and Power in the Graeco-Roman World* (Oxford: Oxford University Press).

Clay, D. (2009), 'The Athenian Garden', in Warren, J. (ed.), *The Cambridge Companion to Epicureanism* (Cambridge: Cambridge University Press), 9–28.

Clayman, D. L. (2009), *Timon of Phlius: Pyrrhonism into Poetry* (Berlin: Walter de Gruyter).

Conze, E. (1963), 'Buddhist Philosophy and its European Parallels', *Philosophy East and West* 13, 9–23; repr. in Conze, E. (1967), *Thirty Years of Buddhist Studies* (Oxford: Bruno Cassirer).

Cooper, J. (1998), 'Posidonius on Emotions', in Sihvola, J., and Engberg-Pedersen, T. (eds.), *The Emotions in Hellenistic Philosophy* (Dordrecht: Kluwer), 71–111.

Cooper, J. (1999), 'Pleasure and Desire in Epicurus', in his *Reason and Emotion: Essays on Ancient Moral Psychology and Ethical Theory* (Princeton, NJ: Princeton University Press), 485–514.

Cooper, J. (2012), *Pursuits of Wisdom: Six Ways of Life in Ancient Philosophy from Socrates to Plotinus* (Princeton, NJ: Princeton University Press).

Crönert, W. (1906), *Kolotes und Menedemos* (Leipzig: Avenarius).

Decleva Caizzi, F. (1981), *Pirrone Testimonianze* (Naples: Bibliopolis).

Decleva Caizzi, F. (1992), 'Aenesidemus and the Academy', *Classical Quarterly* 42, 176–89.

De Lacy, P. H. (1978–84), *Galen, On the Doctrines of Hippocrates and Plato*, 3 vols (Berlin: Akademie Verlag).

De Lacy, P. H., and De Lacy, E. A. (1978), *Philodemus, On Methods of Inference* (Naples: Bibliopolis).

Desclos, M.-L., and Fortenbaugh, W. W. (eds.) (2011), *Strato of Lampsacus: Text, Translation, and Discussion* (New Brunswick, NJ: Transaction Publishers).

Desmond, W. (2008), *Cynics* (Stocksfield: Acumen).

DeWitt, N. W. (1954), *Epicurus and his Philosophy* (Minneapolis, MN: University of Minnesota Press).

Diels, H. (1879), *Doxographi Graeci* (Berlin: Reimer).

Diels, H., and Kranz, W. (1952), *Die Fragmente der Vorsokratiker*, 3 vols (Berlin: Weidmann).

Dihle, A. (1982), *The Theory of the Will in Classical Antiquity* (Berkeley, CA: University of California Press).

Dihle, A. (1986), 'Philosophie – Fachwissenschaft – Allgemeinbildung', in Flashar, H., and Gigon, O. (eds.), *Aspects de la philosophie hellénistique*, Entretiens sur l'antiquité classique 32 (Geneva: Fondation Hardt), 185–223.

Dihle, A. (1990), *Philosophie als Lebenskunst* (Opladen: Westdeutscher Verlag).

Dillon, J. (1977), *The Middle Platonists: A Study of Platonism 80 BC to AD 220* (London: Duckworth).

Dillon, J. (2003), *The Heirs of Plato: A Study of the Old Academy (347–274 BC)* (Oxford: Clarendon Press).

Dillon, J., and Long, A. A. (eds.) (1988), *The Question of 'Eclecticism': Studies in Later Greek Philosophy* (Berkeley, CA: University of California Press).

Di Marco, M. (1989), *Timone di Fliunte, Silli* (Rome: Edizioni dell'Ateneo).

Dobbin, R. (2012), *The Cynic Philosophers from Diogenes to Julian* (London: Penguin).

Donini, P. L. (1995), 'Struttura delle passioni e del vizio e loro cura in Crisippo', *Elenchos* 16, 305–29.

Dorandi, T. (1982), *Filodemo, Il buon re secondo Omero* (Naples: Bibliopolis).

Dorandi, T. (1999a), 'Chronology', in Algra, K., Barnes, J., Mansfield, J., and Schofield, M. (eds.), *The Cambridge History of Hellenistic Philosophy* (Cambridge: Cambridge University Press), 31–54.

Dorandi, T. (1999b), 'Organization and Structure of the Philosophical Schools', in Algra, K., Barnes, J., Mansfeld, J., and Schofield, M. (eds.), *The Cambridge History of Hellenistic Philosophy* (Cambridge: Cambridge University Press), 55–62.

Dorandi, T. (2013), *Diogenes Laertius, Lives of Eminent Philosophers* (Cambridge: Cambridge University Press).

Döring, K., and Ebert, T. (eds.) (1993), *Dialektiker und Stoiker* (Stuttgart: Franz Steiner Verlag).

Dougan, T. W., and Henry, R. M. (1905–34), *M. Tulli Ciceronis Tusculanarum Disputationum Libri Quinque*, 2 vols (Cambridge: Cambridge University Press).

Douglas, A. E. (1995), 'Form and Content in the Tusculan Disputations', in Powell, J. G. F. (ed.), *Cicero the Philosopher* (Oxford: Clarendon Press), 197–218.

Dudley, D. R. (1937), *A History of Cynicism from Diogenes to the Sixth Century AD* (London: Methuen).

Dyck, A. R. (1996), *A Commentary on Cicero, De Officiis* (Ann Arbor, MI: The University of Michigan Press).

Edelstein, L., and Kidd, I. G. (1972), *Posidonius I: The Fragments* (Cambridge: Cambridge University Press).

Engberg-Pedersen, T. (1990), *The Stoic Theory of Oikeiosis* (Aarhus: Aarhus University Press).

Englert, W. G. (1987), *Epicurus on the Swerve and Voluntary Action* (Atlanta, GA: Scholars Press).

Erler, M. (1997), 'Physics and Therapy: Meditative Elements in Lucretius' *De rerum natura*', in Algra, K., Koenen, M., and Schrijvers, P. (eds.), *Lucretius and his Intellectual Background* (Amsterdam: North-Holland), 79–92.

Erskine, A. (1990), *The Hellenistic Stoa: Political Thought and Action* (London: Duckworth).

Evans, J., and Berggren, J. L. (2006), *Geminos's Introduction to the Phenomena: A Translation and Study of a Hellenistic Survey of Astronomy* (Princeton, NJ: Princeton University Press).

Everson, S. (ed.) (1990a), *Epistemology*, Companions to Ancient Thought 1 (Cambridge: Cambridge University Press).

Everson, S. (1990b), 'Epicurus on the Truth of the Senses', in his *Epistemology*, Companions to Ancient Thought 1 (Cambridge: Cambridge University Press), 161–83.

Everson, S. (1999), 'Epicurean Psychology', in Algra, K., Barnes, J., Mansfeld, J., and Schofield, M. (eds.), *The Cambridge History of Hellenistic Philosophy* (Cambridge: Cambridge University Press), 542–59.

Fish, J. (2011), 'Not all Politicians Are Sisyphus: What Roman Epicureans Were Taught about Politics', in Fish, J., and Sanders, K. R. (eds.), *Epicurus and the Epicurean Tradition* (Cambridge: Cambridge University Press), 72–104.

Fish, J., and Sanders, K. R. (eds.) (2011), *Epicurus and the Epicurean Tradition* (Cambridge: Cambridge University Press).

Flashar, H., and Gigon, O. (eds.) (1986), *Aspects de la philosophie hellénistique*, Entretiens sur l'antiquité classique 32 (Geneva: Fondation Hardt).

Flintoff, E. (1980), 'Pyrrho and India', *Phronesis* 25, 88–108.

Forman, D. (2016), 'Leibniz and the Stoics: Fate, Freedom, and Providence', in Sellars, J. (ed.), *The Routledge Handbook of the Stoic Tradition* (Abingdon: Routledge), 226–42.

Fortenbaugh, W. W., Huby, P. M., Sharples, R. W., and Gutas, D. (1992), *Theophrastus of Eresus: Sources for his Life, Writings, Thought, and Influence*, 2 vols (Leiden: Brill).

Fortenbaugh, W. W., and Schütrumpf, E. (eds.) (2000), *Demetrius of Phalerum: Text: Translation, and Discussion* (New Brunswick, NJ: Transaction Publishers).

Fortenbaugh, W. W., and White, S. A. (eds.) (2004), *Lyco of Troas and Hieronymus of Rhodes: Text, Translation, and Discussion* (New Brunswick, NJ: Transaction Publishers).

Fortenbaugh, W. W., and White, S. A. (eds.) (2006), *Aristo of Ceos: Text, Translation, and Discussion* (New Brunswick, NJ: Transaction Publishers).

Fowler, D. P. (1989), 'Lucretius and Politics', in Griffin, M. T., and Barnes, J. (eds.), *Philosophia Togata* (Oxford: Clarendon Press), 120–50.

Fraser, P. M. (1972), *Ptolemaic Alexandria*, 3 vols (Oxford: Clarendon Press).

Frede, D. (2003), 'Stoic Determinism', in Inwood, B. (ed.), *The Cambridge Companion to the Stoics* (Cambridge: Cambridge University Press), 179–205.

Frede, D., and Inwood, B. (eds.) (2005), *Language and Learning: Philosophy of Language in the Hellenistic Age* (Cambridge: Cambridge University Press).

Frede, D., and Laks, A. (eds.) (2002), *Traditions of Theology: Studies in Hellenistic Theology, its Background and Aftermath* (Leiden: Brill).

Frede, M. (1983), 'Stoics and Skeptics on Clear and Distinct Impressions', in Burnyeat, M. (ed.), *The Skeptical Tradition* (Berkeley, CA: University of California Press), 65–93.

Frede, M. (1986), 'The Stoic Doctrine of the Affections of the Soul', in Schofield, M., and Striker, G. (eds.), *The Norms of Nature: Studies in Hellenistic Ethics* (Cambridge: Cambridge University Press), 93–110.

Frede, M. (1999a), 'Stoic Epistemology', in Algra, K., Barnes, J., Mansfeld, J., and Schofield, M. (eds.), *The Cambridge History of Hellenistic Philosophy* (Cambridge: Cambridge University Press), 295–322.

Frede, M. (1999b), 'Epilogue', in Algra, K., Barnes, J., Mansfeld, J., and Schofield, M. (eds.), *The Cambridge History of Hellenistic Philosophy* (Cambridge: Cambridge University Press), 771–97.

Frede, M. (2011), *A Free Will: Origins of the Notion in Ancient Thought* (Berkeley, CA: University of California Press).

French, R. (1994), *Ancient Natural History* (London: Routledge).

Furley, D. (1967), *Two Studies in the Greek Atomists* (Princeton, NJ: Princeton University Press).

Furley, D. (1986), 'Nothing to Us?', in Schofield, M., and Striker, G. (eds.), *The Norms of Nature: Studies in Hellenistic Ethics* (Cambridge: Cambridge University Press), 75–91.

Furley, D. (ed.) (1999), *From Aristotle to Augustine*, Routledge History of Philosophy 2 (London: Routledge).

Gale, M. R. (ed.) (2007), *Lucretius* (Oxford: Oxford University Press).

Garofalo, I. (1988), *Erasistrati Fragmenta* (Pisa: Giardini Editori e Stampatori).

Geiger, W. (1912), *The Mahāvaṃsa or The Great Chronicle of Ceylon* (London: Oxford University Press for Pali Text Society).

Giannantoni, G. (1990), *Socratis et Socraticorum Reliquiae*, 4 vols (Naples: Bibliopolis).

Gigante, M. (1995), *Philodemus in Italy: The Books from Herculaneum*, trans. D. Obbink (Ann Arbor, MI: The University of Michigan Press).

Gill, C. (1988), 'Personhood and Personality: The Four-Personae Theory in Cicero, *De Officiis* I', *Oxford Studies in Ancient Philosophy* 6, 169–99.

Gill, C. (1998), 'Did Galen Understand Platonic and Stoic Thinking on Emotions?', in Sihvola, J., and Engberg-Pedersen, T. (eds.), *The Emotions in Hellenistic Philosophy* (Dordrecht: Kluwer), 113–48.

Gill, C. (2003), 'The School in the Roman Imperial Period', in Inwood, B. (ed.), *The Cambridge Companion to the Stoics* (Cambridge: Cambridge University Press), 33–58.

Gill, C. (2006), *The Structured Self in Hellenistic and Roman Thought* (Oxford: Oxford University Press).

Gillespie, S., and Hardie, P. (eds.) (2007), *The Cambridge Companion to Lucretius* (Cambridge: Cambridge University Press).

Glucker, J. (1978), *Antiochus and the Late Academy* (Göttingen: Vandenhoeck & Ruprecht).

Glucker, J. (1988), 'Cicero's Philosophical Affiliations', in Dillon, J., and Long, A. A. (eds.), *The Question of 'Eclecticism': Studies in Later Greek Philosophy* (Berkeley, CA: University of California Press), 34–69.

Görler, W. (1995), 'Silencing the Troublemaker: *De Legibus* 1.39 and the Continuity of Cicero's Scepticism', in Powell, J. G. F. (ed.), *Cicero the Philosopher* (Oxford: Clarendon Press), 85–113.

Gould, J. B. (1970), *The Philosophy of Chrysippus* (Leiden: Brill).

Goulet, R. (ed.) (1989–2018), *Dictionnaire des Philosophes Antiques,* 7 vols and supplement (Paris: CNRS).

Goulet, R. (2013), 'Ancient Philosophers: A First Statistical Survey', in Chase, M., Clark, S. R. L., and McGhee, M. (eds.), *Philosophy as a Way of Life: Ancients and Moderns* (Chichester: Wiley Blackwell), 10–39.

Goulet-Cazé, M.-O. (2003), *Les Kynica du stoïcisme*, Hermes Einzelschriften 89 (Stuttgart: Franz Steiner Verlag).

Gowans, C. W. (2003), *Philosophy of the Buddha* (London: Routledge).

Gowans, C. W. (2010), 'Medical Analogies in Buddhist and Hellenistic Thought: Tranquillity and Anger', in Carlisle, C., and Ganeri, J. (eds.), *Philosophy as Therapeia*, Royal Institute of Philosophy Supplement 66 (Cambridge: Cambridge University Press), 11–33.

Graver, M. (2002), *Cicero on the Emotions: Tusculan Disputations 3 and 4* (Chicago, IL: The University of Chicago Press).

Griffin, M. J. (2015), *Aristotle's Categories in the Early Roman Empire* (Oxford: Oxford University Press).

Griffin, M. T. (1996), 'Cynicism and the Romans: Attraction and Repulsion', in Branham, R. B., and Goulet-Cazé, M.-O. (eds.), *The Cynics: The Cynic Movement in Antiquity and its Legacy* (Berkeley, CA: University of California Press), 190–204.

Griffin, M. T., and Atkins, E. M. (1991), *Cicero: On Duties* (Cambridge: Cambridge University Press).

Griffin, M. T., and Barnes, J. (eds.) (1989), *Philosophia Togata* (Oxford: Clarendon Press).

Guerra, A. T. (1991), *Polieno, Frammenti* (Naples: Bibliopolis).

Gutas, D. (2010), *Theophrastus on First Principles (known as his Metaphysics)* (Leiden: Brill).

Hadot, P. (1995), *Philosophy as a Way of Life: Spiritual Exercises from Socrates to Foucault*, trans. M. Chase (Oxford: Blackwell).

Hadot, P. (2002), *What Is Ancient Philosophy?*, trans. M. Chase (Cambridge, MA: Harvard University Press).

Hahm, D. E. (1977), *The Origins of Stoic Cosmology* (Columbus, OH: Ohio State University Press).

Hahm, D. E. (1995), 'Polybius' Applied Political Theory', Laks, A., and Schofield, M. (eds.), *Justice and Generosity: Studies in Hellenistic Social and Political Philosophy* (Cambridge: Cambridge University Press), 7–47.

Hahm, D. E. (2007), 'Critolaus and Late Hellenistic Peripatetic Philosophy', in Ioppolo, A. M., and Sedley, D. N. (eds.), *Pyrrhonists, Patricians, Platonizers: Hellenistic Philosophy in the Period 155–86 BC* (Naples: Bibliopolis), 47–101.

Halkias, G. T. (2014), 'When the Greeks Converted the Buddha: Asymmetrical Transfers of Knowledge in Indo-Greek Cultures', in Wick, P., and Rabens, V. (eds.), *Religions and Trade: Religious Formation, Transformation and Cross-Cultural Exchange between East and West* (Leiden: Brill), 65–115.

Halkias, G. T. (2015), 'The Self-Immolation of Kalanos and other Luminous Encounters Among Greeks and Indian Buddhists in the Hellenistic World', *Journal of the Oxford Centre for Buddhist Studies* 8, 163–86.

Hankinson, R. J. (2003), 'Stoic Epistemology', in Inwood, B. (ed.), *The Cambridge Companion to the Stoics* (Cambridge: Cambridge University Press), 59–84.

Hankinson, R. J. (2010), 'Aenesidemus and the Rebirth of Pyrrhonism', in Bett, R. (ed.), *The Cambridge Companion to Ancient Scepticism* (Cambridge: Cambridge University Press), 105–19.

Hardie, P. (2007), 'Lucretius and Later Latin Literature in Antiquity', in Gillespie, S., and Hardie, P. (eds.), *The Cambridge Companion to Lucretius* (Cambridge: Cambridge University Press), 111–27.

Hatzimichali, M. (2012), 'Antiochus' Biography', in Sedley, D. (ed.), *The Philosophy of Antiochus* (Cambridge: Cambridge University Press), 9–30.

Hatzimichali, M. (2013), 'The Texts of Plato and Aristotle in the First Century BC', in Schofield, M. (ed.), *Aristotle, Plato and Pythagoreanism in the First Century BC* (Cambridge: Cambridge University Press), 1–27.

Heath, T. (1913), *Aristarchus of Samos: The Ancient Copernicus* (Oxford: Clarendon Press).

Henry, W. B. (2009), *Philodemus, On Death* (Atlanta, GA: Society of Biblical Literature).

Hense, O. (1909), *Teletis Reliquiae* (Tübingen: J. C. B. Mohr).

Horner, I. B. (1963–4), *Milinda's Questions*, 2 vols (London: Luzac & Company).

Huby, P. (1967), 'The First Discovery of the Freewill Problem', *Philosophy* 42, 353–62.

Hultzsch, E. (1925), *Corpus Inscriptionum Indicarum Vol. I: Inscriptions of Asoka* (Oxford: Clarendon Press for The Government of India).

Hume, D. (1779), *Dialogues Concerning Natural Religion* ([London]).

Ierodiakonou, K. (ed.) (1999), *Topics in Stoic Philosophy* (Oxford: Clarendon Press).

Inwood, B. (1985), *Ethics and Human Action in Early Stoicism* (Oxford: Clarendon Press).

Inwood, B. (ed.) (2003), *The Cambridge Companion to the Stoics* (Cambridge: Cambridge University Press).

Inwood, B. (2014), *Ethics After Aristotle* (Cambridge, MA: Harvard University Press).

Inwood, B., and Gerson, L. P. (1997), *Hellenistic Philosophy: Introductory Readings*, Second Edition (Indianapolis, IN: Hackett).

Inwood, B., and Mansfeld, J. (eds.) (1997), *Assent and Argument: Studies in Cicero's Academic Books* (Leiden: Brill).

Ioppolo, A. M. (1980), *Aristone di Chio e lo Stoicismo antico* (Naples: Bibliopolis).

Ioppolo, A. M., and Sedley, D. N. (eds.) (2007), *Pyrrhonists, Patricians, Platonizers: Hellenistic Philosophy in the Period 155–86 BC* (Naples: Bibliopolis).

Irby-Massie, G. L., and Keyser, P. T. (2002), *Greek Science of the Hellenistic Era: A Sourcebook* (London: Routledge).

Isnardi Parente, M. (1992), 'Il papiro filosofico di Aï Khanoum', in Carlini, A. (ed.), *Studi su codici e papiri filosofici: Platone, Aristotele, Ierocle* (Florence: Leo S. Olschki Editore), 169–88.

Janko, R. (1995), 'Crates of Mallos, Dionysius Thrax, and the Tradition of Stoic Grammatical Theory', in Ayres, L. (ed.), *The Passionate Intellect: Essays on the Transformation of Classical Traditions* (New Brunswick, NJ: Transaction Publishers), 213–33.

Janko, R. (2000), *Philodemus, On Poems Book 1* (Oxford: Oxford University Press).

Janko, R. (2011), *Philodemus, On Poems Books 3–4 with the Fragment of Aristotle, On Poets* (Oxford: Oxford University Press).

Kahn, C. H. (1976), 'Why Existence Does Not Emerge as a Distinct Concept in Greek Philosophy', *Archiv für Geschichte der Philosophie* 58, 323–34.

Kahn, C. H. (1988), 'Discovering the Will: From Aristotle to Augustine', in Dillon, J., and Long, A. A. (eds.), *The Question of 'Eclecticism': Studies in Later Greek Philosophy* (Berkeley, CA: University of California Press), 234–59.

Kahn, C. H. (2009), *Essays on Being* (Oxford: Oxford University Press).

Karamanolis, G. (2006), *Plato and Aristotle in Agreement? Platonists on Aristotle from Antiochus to Porphyry* (Oxford: Clarendon Press).

Kidd, D. (1997), *Aratus, Phaenomena* (Cambridge: Cambridge University Press).

Kidd, I. G. (1978), 'Philosophy and Science in Posidonius', *Antike und Abenland* 24, 7–15.

Kidd, I. G. (1999), *Posidonius III: The Translation of the Fragments* (Cambridge: Cambridge University Press).

Kindstrand, J. F. (1976), *Bion of Borysthenes: A Collection of the Fragments with Introduction and Commentary* (Uppsala: Acta Universitatis Upsaliensis).

Kleve, K. (1997), 'Lucretius and Philodemus', in Algra, K., Koenen, M., and Schrijvers, P. (eds.), *Lucretius and his Intellectual Background* (Amsterdam: North-Holland), 49–66.

Kneale, W., and Kneale, M. (1962), *The Development of Logic* (Oxford: Clarendon Press).

Konstan, D. (2008), *A Life Worthy of the Gods: The Materialist Psychology of Epicurus* (Las Vegas, NV: Parmenides Publishing).

Konstan, D. (2011), 'Epicurus on the Gods', in Fish, J., and Sanders, K. R. (eds.), *Epicurus and the Epicurean Tradition* (Cambridge: Cambridge University Press), 53–71.

Körte, A. (1890), *Metrodori Epicurei Fragmenta* (Leipzig: Teubner).

Kuzminski, A. (2008), *Pyrrhonism: How the Ancient Greeks Reinvented Buddhism* (Lanham, MD: Lexington Books).

Laks, A., and Schofield, M. (eds.) (1995), *Justice and Generosity: Studies in Hellenistic Social and Political Philosophy* (Cambridge: Cambridge University Press).

Lampe, K. (2015), *The Birth of Hedonism: The Cyrenaic Philosophers and Pleasure as a Way of Life* (Princeton, NJ: Princeton University Press).

Lapidge, M. (1978), 'Stoic Cosmology', in Rist, J. M. (ed.), *The Stoics* (Berkeley, CA: University of California Press), 161–85.

Latham, R. (1951), *Lucretius, On the Nature of the Universe* (Harmondsworth: Penguin).

Leibniz, G. W. (1710), *Essais de Théodicée sur la bonté de Dieu, la liberté de l'homme et l'origine du mal* (Amsterdam: Isaac Troyel).

Leibniz, G. W. (1951), *Theodicy*, trans. E. M. Huggard (London: Routledge & Kegan Paul).

Leonard, W. E., and Smith, S. B. (1942), *T. Lucreti Cari De Rerum Natura Libri Sex* (Madison, WI: The University of Wisconsin Press).

Leone, G. (2012), *Epicuro, Sulla Natura Libro II* (Naples: Bibliopolis).

Lerner, J. D. (2003), 'The Aï Khanoum Philosophical Papyrus', *Zeitschrift für Papyrologie und Epigraphik* 142, 45–51.

Lévy, C. (2010), 'The Sceptical Academy: Decline and Afterlife', in Bett, R. (ed.), *The Cambridge Companion to Ancient Scepticism* (Cambridge: Cambridge University Press), 81–104.

Lloyd, G. E. R. (1973), *Greek Science after Aristotle* (London: Chatto & Windus).

Long, A. A. (ed.) (1971), *Problems in Stoicism* (London: The Athlone Press).

Long, A. A. (1975), 'Heraclitus and Stoicism', *Philosophia* 5, 133–56; repr. in Long, A. A. (1996a), *Stoic Studies* (Cambridge: Cambridge University Press), 35–57.

Long, A. A. (1982), 'Soul and Body in Stoicism', *Phronesis* 27, 34–57; repr. in Long, A. A. (1996a), *Stoic Studies* (Cambridge: Cambridge University Press), 224–49.

Long, A. A. (1986), 'Diogenes Laertius, Life of Arcesilaus', *Elenchos* 7, 429–49.

Long, A. A. (1988), 'Socrates in Hellenistic Philosophy', *Classical Quarterly* 38, 150–71; repr. in Long, A. A. (1996a), *Stoic Studies* (Cambridge: Cambridge University Press), 1–34.

Long, A. A. (1996a), *Stoic Studies* (Cambridge: Cambridge University Press).

Long, A. A. (1996b), 'The Socratic Tradition: Diogenes, Crates, and Hellenistic Ethics', in Branham, R. B., and Goulet-Cazé, M.-O. (eds.), *The Cynics: The Cynic Movement in Antiquity and its Legacy* (Berkeley, CA: University of California Press), 28–46.

Long, A. A. (2003), 'Hellenistic Ethics as the Art of Life', *Lampas* 36, 27–41; repr. in Long, A. A. (2006), *From Epicurus to Epictetus: Studies in Hellenistic and Roman Philosophy* (Oxford: Clarendon Press), 23–39.

Long, A. A. (2006), *From Epicurus to Epictetus: Studies in Hellenistic and Roman Philosophy* (Oxford: Clarendon Press).

Long, A. A. (2015), *Greek Models of Mind and Self* (Cambridge, MA: Harvard University Press).

Long, A. A., and Sedley, D. N. (1987), *The Hellenistic Philosophers*, 2 vols (Cambridge: Cambridge University Press).

Longo Auricchio, F. (1988), *Ermarco, Frammenti* (Naples: Bibliopolis).

Lynch, J. P. (1972), *Aristotle's School: A Study of a Greek Educational Institution* (Berkeley, CA: University of California Press).

McEvilley, T. (2002), *The Shape of Ancient Thought: Comparative Studies in Greek and Indian Philosophies* (New York: Allworth Press).

Magee, J. (2016), *Calcidius, On Plato's Timaeus* (Cambridge, MA: Harvard University Press).

Mansfeld, J. (1995), 'Aenesidemus and the Academics', in Ayres, L. (ed.), *The Passionate Intellect: Essays on the Transformation of Classical Traditions* (New Brunswick, NJ: Transaction Publishers), 235–48.

Marrone, L. (1987), 'Testi Stoici Ercolanesi', *Cronache Ercolanesi* 17, 181–4.

Marrone, L. (1988), 'Testi Stoici Ercolanesi II', *Cronache Ercolanesi* 18, 223–5.

Marrone, L. (1997), 'Le *Questioni Logiche* di Crisippo (*PHerc*. 307)', *Cronache Ercolanesi* 27, 83–100.

Marshall, P. (1992), *Demanding the Impossible: A History of Anarchism* (London: HarperCollins).

Mates, B. (1961), *Stoic Logic* (Berkeley, CA: University of California Press).

Mayor, J. B. (1880–5), *M. Tullii Ciceronis De Natura Deorum Libri Tres*, 3 vols (Cambridge: Cambridge University Press).

Meijer, P. A. (2007), *Stoic Theology: Proofs for the Existence of the Cosmic God and of the Traditional Gods* (Delft: Eburon).

Melville, R. (1997), *Lucretius, On the Nature of the Universe* (Oxford: Oxford University Press).

Mette, H. J. (1984), 'Zwei Akademiker heute: Krantor von Soloi und Arkesilaos von Pitane', *Lustrum* 26, 7–94.

Mette, H. J. (1985), 'Weitere Akademiker heute: Von Lakydes bis zu Kleitomachos', *Lustrum* 27, 39–148.

Mette, H. J. (1986–7), 'Philon von Larisa und Antiochos von Askalon', *Lustrum* 28–9, 9–63.

Miller, J., and Inwood, B. (eds.) (2003), *Hellenistic and Early Modern Philosophy* (Cambridge: Cambridge University Press).

Mitsis, P. (1988), *Epicurus' Ethical Theory: The Pleasures of Invulnerability* (Ithaca, NY: Cornell University Press).

Modrak, D. K. W. (2011), 'Physicalism in Strato's Psychology', in Desclos, M.-L., and Fortenbaugh, W. W. (eds.), *Strato of Lampsacus: Text, Translation, and Discussion* (New Brunswick, NJ: Transaction Publishers), 383–97.

Morel, P.-M. (2009), 'Epicurean Atomism', in Warren, J. (ed.), *The Cambridge Companion to Epicureanism* (Cambridge: Cambridge University Press), 65–83.

Muehll, P. Von der (1922), *Epicuri Epistulae Tres et Ratae Sententiae* (Leipzig: Teubner).

Nagel, T. (1979), *Mortal Questions* (Cambridge: Cambridge University Press).

Németh, A. (2017), *Epicurus on the Self* (Abingdon: Routledge).

Nussbaum, M. C. (1994), *The Therapy of Desire: Theory and Practice in Hellenistic Ethics* (Princeton, NJ: Princeton University Press).

Nutton, V. (2013), *Ancient Medicine*, Second Edition (Abingdon: Routledge).

Obbink, D. (1996), *Philodemus, On Piety: Part 1* (Oxford: Clarendon Press).

Obbink, D. (1999), 'The Stoic Sage in the Cosmic City', in Ierodiakonou, K. (ed.), *Topics in Stoic Philosophy* (Oxford: Clarendon Press), 178–95.

Obbink, D., and Vander Waerdt, P. A. (1991), 'Diogenes of Babylon: The Stoic Sage in the City of Fools', *Greek, Roman, and Byzantine Studies* 32, 355–96.

O'Keefe, T. (2005), *Epicurus on Freedom* (Cambridge: Cambridge University Press).

O'Keefe, T. (2010), *Epicureanism* (Durham: Acumen).

O'Neil, E. N. (1977), *Teles: The Cynic Teacher* (Missoula, MT: Scholars Press).

Onians, R. B. (1951), *The Origins of European Thought* (Cambridge: Cambridge University Press).

Ophuijsen, J. M. van, and Raalte, M. van (eds.) (1998), *Theophrastus: Reappraising the Sources* (New Brunswick, NJ: Transaction Publishers).

Osler, M. J. (ed.) (1991), *Atoms, Pneuma, and Tranquillity: Epicurean and Stoic Themes in European Thought* (Cambridge: Cambridge University Press).

Papazian, M. (2007), 'The Ontological Argument of Diogenes of Babylon', *Phronesis* 52, 188–209.

Pease, A. S. (1955–8), *M. Tulli Ciceronis De Natura Deorum*, 2 vols (Cambridge, MA: Harvard University Press).

Pembroke, S. G. (1971), 'Oikeiôsis', in Long, A. A. (ed.), *Problems in Stoicism* (London: The Athlone Press), 114–49.

Pfeiffer, R. (1949), *Callimachus*, 2 vols (Oxford: Clarendon Press).

Pfeiffer, R. (1968), *History of Classical Scholarship from the Beginnings to the End of the Hellenistic Age* (Oxford: Clarendon Press).

Plasberg, O. (1922), *M. Tulli Ciceronis . . . Academicorum Reliquiae cum Lucullo* (Leipzig: Teubner).

Plasberg, O., and Ax, W. (1933), *M. Tulli Ciceronis . . . De Natura Deorum* (Leipzig: Teubner).

Pohlenz, M. (1918), *M. Tulli Ciceronis . . . Tusculanae Disputationes* (Leipzig: Teubner).

Polito, R. (2004), *The Sceptical Road: Aenesidemus' Appropriation of Heraclitus* (Leiden: Brill).

Polito, R. (2007), 'Was Skepticism a Philosophy? Reception, Self-Definition, Internal Conflicts', *Classical Philology* 102, 333–62.

Polito, R. (2012), 'Antiochus and the Academy', in Sedley, D. (ed.), *The Philosophy of Antiochus* (Cambridge: Cambridge University Press), 31–54.

Polito, R. (2014), *Aenesidemus of Cnossus: Testimonia* (Cambridge: Cambridge University Press).

Pomeroy, A. J. (1999), *Arius Didymus, Epitome of Stoic Ethics* (Atlanta, GA: Society of Biblical Literature).

Popkin, R. H. (2003), *The History of Scepticism from Savonarola to Bayle* (Oxford: Oxford University Press).

Porter, J. I. (1996), 'The Philosophy of Aristo of Chios', in Branham, R. B., and Goulet-Cazé, M.-O. (eds.), *The Cynics: The Cynic Movement in Antiquity and its Legacy* (Berkeley, CA: University of California Press), 156–89.

Powell, J. G. F. (ed.) (1995), *Cicero the Philosopher* (Oxford: Clarendon Press).

Powell, J. G. F. (2006), *M. Tulli Ciceronis De Re Publica, De Legibus, Cato Maior de Senectute, Laelius de Amicitia* (Oxford: Clarendon Press).

Raalte, M. van (1993), *Theophrastus, Metaphysics* (Leiden: Brill).

Ramelli, I. (2002), *Epicurea: Testi di Epicuro e Testimonianze Epicuree nella raccolta di Hermann Usener* (Milan: Bompiani).

Rapin, C., Hadot, P., and Cavallo, G. (1987), 'Les textes littéraires grecs de la Trésorerie d'Aï Khanoum', *Bulletin de correspondance hellénique* 111, 225–66.

Raubitschek, A. E. (1949), 'Phaidros and his Roman Pupils', *Hesperia* 18, 96–103.

Reynolds, L. D. (1998), *M. Tulli Ciceronis De Finibus Bonorum et Malorum Libri Quinque* (Oxford: Clarendon Press).

Rhys Davids, C. A. F. (1930), *The Milinda Questions* (London: G. Routledge & Sons).

Rhys Davids, T. W. (1890), *The Questions of King Milinda* (London: Oxford University Press).

Rist, J. M. (ed.) (1978), *The Stoics* (Berkeley, CA: University of California Press).

Robert, L. (1968), 'De Delphes à l'Oxus, inscriptions grecques nouvelles de la Bactriane', *Comptes rendus des séances de l'Académie des Inscriptions et Belles-Lettres* 112, 416–57.

Rohde, E. (1925), *Psyche: The Cult of Souls and Belief in Immortality among the Greeks*, trans. W. B. Hillis (London: Kegan Paul, Trench, Trubner & Co.).

Roskam, G. (2007), *Live Unnoticed (Lathe Biôsas): On the Vicissitudes of an Epicurean Doctrine* (Leiden: Brill).

Ross, W. D. (1955), *Aristotelis Fragmenta Selecta* (Oxford: Clarendon Press).

Ross, W. D., and Fobes, F. H. (1929), *Theophrastus, Metaphysics* (Oxford: Clarendon Press).

Rowe, C., and Schofield, M. (eds.) (2000), *The Cambridge History of Greek and Roman Political Thought* (Cambridge: Cambridge University Press).

Rudd, N. (1998), *Cicero, The Republic and The Laws* (Oxford: Oxford University Press).

Salles, R. (ed.) (2009), *God and Cosmos in Stoicism* (Oxford: Oxford University Press).

Sambursky, S. (1959), *Physics of the Stoics* (London: Routledge & Kegan Paul).

Sanders, K. R. (2011), 'Philodemus and the Fear of Premature Death', in Fish, J., and Sanders, K. R. (eds.), *Epicurus and the Epicurean Tradition* (Cambridge: Cambridge University Press), 211–34.

Sandys, J. E. (1903), *A History of Classical Scholarship: From the Sixth Century BC to the End of the Middle Ages* (Cambridge: Cambridge University Press).

Sayre, F. (1948), *The Greek Cynics* (Baltimore, MD: J. H. Furst Company).

Scaltsas, T., and Mason, A. S. (eds.) (2002), *Zeno of Citium and his Legacy: The Philosophy of Zeno* (Larnaca: The Municipality of Larnaca).

Schofield, M. (1991), *The Stoic Idea of the City* (Cambridge: Cambridge University Press).

Schofield, M. (1995), 'Cicero's Definition of *Res Publica*', in Powell, J. G. F. (ed.), *Cicero the Philosopher* (Oxford: Clarendon Press), 63–83.

Schofield, M. (2002), 'Academic Therapy: Philo of Larissa and Cicero's Project in the *Tusculans*', in Clark, G., and Rajak, T. (eds.), *Philosophy and Power in the Graeco-Roman World* (Oxford: Oxford University Press), 91–109.

Schofield, M. (2003), 'Stoic Ethics', in Inwood, B. (ed.), *The Cambridge Companion to the Stoics* (Cambridge: Cambridge University Press), 233–56.

Schofield, M. (2007), 'Aenesidemus: Pyrrhonist and "Heraclitean"', in Ioppolo, A. M., and Sedley, D. N. (eds.), *Pyrrhonists, Patricians, Platonizers: Hellenistic Philosophy in the Period 155–86 BC* (Naples: Bibliopolis), 269–338.

Schofield, M. (ed.) (2013), *Aristotle, Plato and Pythagoreanism in the First Century BC* (Cambridge: Cambridge University Press).

Schofield, M., Burnyeat, M., and Barnes, J. (eds.) (1980), *Doubt and Dogmatism: Studies in Hellenistic Epistemology* (Oxford: Clarendon Press).

Schofield, M., and Striker, G. (eds.) (1986), *The Norms of Nature: Studies in Hellenistic Ethics* (Cambridge: Cambridge University Press).

Scholz, P. (2004), 'Peripatetic Philosophers as Wandering Scholars: Some Remarks on the Socio-Political Conditions of Philosophizing in the Third Century BCE', in Fortenbaugh, W. W., and White, S. A. (eds.), *Lyco of Troas and Hieronymus of Rhodes: Text, Translation, and Discussion* (New Brunswick, NJ: Transaction Publishers), 315–53.

Scott, D. A. (1985), 'Ashokan Missionary Expansion of Buddhism among the Greeks (in N.W. India, Bactria and the Levant)', *Religion* 15, 131–41.

Sedley, D. (1977), 'Diodorus Cronus and Hellenistic Philosophy', *Proceedings of the Cambridge Philological Society* 203 (n.s. 23), 74–120.

Sedley, D. (1983), 'The Motivation of Greek Skepticism', in Burnyeat, M. (ed.), *The Skeptical Tradition* (Berkeley, CA: University of California Press), 9–29.

Sedley, D. (1988), 'Epicurean Anti-Reductionism', in Barnes, J., and Mignucci, M. (eds.), *Matter and Metaphysics* (Naples: Bibliopolis), 295–327.

Sedley, D. (1989), 'Philosophical Allegiance in the Greco-Roman World', in Griffin, M. T., and Barnes, J. (eds.), *Philosophia Togata* (Oxford: Clarendon Press), 97–119.

Sedley, D. (1998), *Lucretius and the Transformation of Greek Wisdom* (Cambridge: Cambridge University Press).

Sedley, D. (2002a), 'The Origins of Stoic God', in Frede, D., and Laks, A. (eds.), *Traditions of Theology: Studies in Hellenistic Theology, its Background and Aftermath* (Leiden: Brill), 41–83.

Sedley, D. (2002b), 'Zeno's Definition of *phantasia kataleptike*', in Scaltsas, T., and Mason, A. S. (eds.), *Zeno of Citium and his Legacy: The Philosophy of Zeno* (Larnaca: The Municipality of Larnaca), 135–54.

Sedley, D. (2003), 'Philodemus and the Decentralisation of Philosophy', *Cronache Ercolanesi* 33, 31–41.

Sedley, D. (2009), 'Epicureanism in the Roman Republic', in Warren, J. (ed.), *The Cambridge Companion to Epicureanism* (Cambridge: Cambridge University Press), 29–45.

Sedley, D. (2011), 'Epicurus' Theological Innatism', in Fish, J., and Sanders, K. R. (eds.), *Epicurus and the Epicurean Tradition* (Cambridge: Cambridge University Press), 29–52.

Sedley, D. (ed.) (2012), *The Philosophy of Antiochus* (Cambridge: Cambridge University Press).

Sellars, J. (2003), *The Art of Living: The Stoics on the Nature and Function of Philosophy* (Aldershot: Ashgate).

Sellars, J. (2006), *Stoicism* (Chesham: Acumen).

Sellars, J. (2007), 'Stoic Cosmopolitanism and Zeno's *Republic*', *History of Political Thought* 28, 1–29.

Sellars, J. (2012), 'Is God a Mindless Vegetable? Cudworth on Stoic Theology', *Intellectual History Review* 21, 121–33.

Sellars, J. (ed.) (2016), *The Routledge Handbook of the Stoic Tradition* (Abingdon: Routledge).

Sharples, R. W. (1991), *Cicero: On Fate (De Fato) and Boethius: The Consolation of Philosophy (Philosophiae Consolationis) IV.5–7, V* (Warminster: Aris & Phillips).

Sharples, R. W. (1999), 'The Peripatetic School', in Furley, D. (ed.), *From Aristotle to Augustine*, Routledge History of Philosophy 2 (London: Routledge), 147–87.

Sharples, R. W. (2007), 'Peripatetics on Happiness', Sorabji, R., and Sharples, R. W. (eds.), *Greek and Roman Philosophy, 100 BC–200 AD*, BICS Supplement 94, 2 vols (London: Institute of Classical Studies), 627–37.

Sharples, R. W. (2010), *Peripatetic Philosophy 200 BC to AD 200: An Introduction and Collection of Sources in Translation* (Cambridge: Cambridge University Press).

Sharples, R. W. (2011), 'Strato of Lampsacus: The Sources, Texts, and Translations', in Desclos, M.-L., and Fortenbaugh, W. W. (eds.), *Strato of Lampsacus: Text, Translation, and Discussion* (New Brunswick, NJ: Transaction Publishers), 5–229.

Shields, C. J. (1994), 'Socrates among the Skeptics', in Vander Waerdt, P. A. (ed.), *The Socratic Movement* (Ithaca, NY: Cornell University Press), 341–66.

Shipley, G. (2000), *The Greek World After Alexander, 323–30 BC* (London: Routledge).

Sick, D. H. (2007), 'When Socrates Met the Buddha: Greek and Indian Dialectic in Hellenistic Bactria and India', *Journal of the Royal Asiatic Society* 17, 253–78.

Sider, D. (1997), *The Epigrams of Philodemos* (New York: Oxford University Press).

Sihvola, J., and Engberg-Pedersen, T. (eds.) (1998), *The Emotions in Hellenistic Philosophy* (Dordrecht: Kluwer).

Snyder, H. G. (2000), *Teachers and Texts in the Ancient World* (London: Routledge).

Sorabji, R. (1988), *Matter, Space, and Motion: Theories in Antiquity and Their Sequel* (London: Duckworth).

Sorabji, R. (ed.) (1997a), *Aristotle and After*, BICS Supplement 68 (London: Institute of Classical Studies).

Sorabji, R. (1997b), 'Is Stoic Philosophy Helpful as Psychotherapy?', in Sorabji, R. (ed.), *Aristotle and After*, BICS Supplement 68 (London: Institute of Classical Studies), 197–209.

Sorabji, R. (1998), 'Chrysippus – Posidonius – Seneca: A High-Level Debate on Emotion', in Sihvola, J., and Engberg-Pedersen, T. (eds.), *The Emotions in Hellenistic Philosophy* (Dordrecht: Kluwer), 149–69.

Sorabji, R. (2000), *Emotion and Peace of Mind: From Stoic Agitation to Christian Temptation* (Oxford: Oxford University Press).

Sorabji, R., and Sharples, R. W. (eds.) (2007), *Greek and Roman Philosophy, 100 BC–200 AD*, BICS Supplement 94, 2 vols (London: Institute of Classical Studies).

Staden, H. von (1989), *Herophilus: The Art of Medicine in Early Alexandria* (Cambridge: Cambridge University Press).

Stallings, A. E. (2007), *Lucretius: The Nature of Things* (London: Penguin).

Steckerl, F. (1958), *The Fragments of Praxagoras of Cos and his School* (Leiden: Brill).

Stoneman, R. (1995), 'Naked Philosophers: The Brahmans in the Alexander Historians and the Alexander Romance', *The Journal of Hellenic Studies* 115, 99–114.

Stork, P., Dorandi, T., Fortenbaugh, W. W., and van Ophuijsen, J. M. (2006), 'Aristo of Ceos: The Sources, Text, and Translation', in Fortenbaugh, W. W., and White, S. A. (eds.), *Aristo of Ceos: Text, Translation, and Discussion* (New Brunswick, NJ: Transaction Publishers), 1–177.

Stork, P., Fortenbaugh, W. W., Dorandi, T., and van Ophuijsen, J. M. (2004), 'Lyco of Troas: The Sources, Text, and Translation', in Fortenbaugh, W. W., and

White, S. A. (eds.), *Lyco of Troas and Hieronymus of Rhodes: Text, Translation, and Discussion* (New Brunswick, NJ: Transaction Publishers), 1–78.

Stork, P., van Ophuijsen, J. M., and Dorandi, T. (2000), 'Demetrius of Phalerum: The Sources, Text, and Translation', in Fortenbaugh, W. W., and Schütrumpf, E. (eds.), *Demetrius of Phalerum: Text: Translation, and Discussion* (New Brunswick, NJ: Transaction Publishers), 1–310.

Straaten, M. van (1952), *Panaetii Rhodi Fragmenta* (Leiden: Brill).

Striker, G. (1977), 'Epicurus on the Truth of Sense Impressions', *Archiv für Geschichte der Philosophie* 59, 125–42; repr. in Striker, G. (1996), *Essays on Hellenistic Epistemology and Ethics* (Cambridge: Cambridge University Press), 77–91.

Striker, G. (1980), 'Sceptical Strategies', in Schofield, M., Burnyeat, M., and Barnes, J. (eds.), *Doubt and Dogmatism: Studies in Hellenistic Epistemology* (Oxford: Clarendon Press), 54–83; repr. in Striker, G. (1996), *Essays on Hellenistic Epistemology and Ethics* (Cambridge: Cambridge University Press), 92–115.

Striker, G. (1986), 'Antipater, or the Art of Living', in Schofield, M., and Striker, G. (eds.), *The Norms of Nature: Studies in Hellenistic Ethics* (Cambridge: Cambridge University Press), 185–204; repr. in Striker, G. (1996), *Essays on Hellenistic Epistemology and Ethics* (Cambridge: Cambridge University Press), 298–315.

Striker, G. (1991), 'Following Nature: A Study in Stoic Ethics', *Oxford Studies in Ancient Philosophy* 9, 1–73; repr. in Striker, G. (1996), *Essays on Hellenistic Epistemology and Ethics* (Cambridge: Cambridge University Press), 221–80.

Striker, G. (1993), 'Epicurean Hedonism', in Brunschwig, J., and Nussbaum, M. C. (eds.), *Passions and Perceptions: Studies in Hellenistic Philosophy of Mind* (Cambridge: Cambridge University Press), 3–17; repr. in Striker, G. (1996), *Essays on Hellenistic Epistemology and Ethics* (Cambridge: Cambridge University Press), 196–208.

Striker, G. (1994), 'Plato's Socrates and the Stoics', in Vander Waerdt, P. A. (ed.), *The Socratic Movement* (Ithaca, NY: Cornell University Press), 241–51; repr. in Striker, G. (1996), *Essays on Hellenistic Epistemology and Ethics* (Cambridge: Cambridge University Press), 316–24.

Striker, G. (1996), *Essays on Hellenistic Epistemology and Ethics* (Cambridge: Cambridge University Press).

Svavarsson, S. H. (2010), 'Pyrrho and Early Pyrrhonism', in Bett, R. (ed.), *The Cambridge Companion to Ancient Scepticism* (Cambridge: Cambridge University Press), 36–57.

Tarn, W. W. (1938), *The Greeks in Bactria and India* (Cambridge: Cambridge University Press).

Tarrant, H. (2007), 'Antiochus: A New Beginning?', in Sorabji, R., and Sharples, R. W. (eds.), *Greek and Roman Philosophy, 100 BC–200 AD*, BICS Supplement 94, 2 vols (London: Institute of Classical Studies), 317–32.

Taylor, C. C. W. (1980), 'All Perceptions are True', in Schofield, M., Burnyeat, M., and Barnes, J. (eds.), *Doubt and Dogmatism: Studies in Hellenistic Epistemology* (Oxford: Clarendon Press), 105–24.

Thapar, R. (1961), *Aśoka and the Decline of the Mauryas* (Oxford: Oxford University Press).

Thom, J. C. (2001), 'Cleanthes, Chrysippus and the Pythagorean Golden Verses', *Acta Classica* 44, 197–219.

Thom, J. C. (2005), *Cleanthes' Hymn to Zeus* (Tübingen: Mohr Siebeck).

Thonemann, P. (2016), *The Hellenistic Age* (Oxford: Oxford University Press).

Thorsrud, H. (2009), *Ancient Scepticism* (Stocksfield: Acumen).

Thorsrud, H. (2010), 'Arcesilaus and Carneades', in Bett, R. (ed.), *The Cambridge Companion to Ancient Scepticism* (Cambridge: Cambridge University Press), 58–80.

Thundy, Z. P. (1993), *Buddha and Christ: Nativity Stories and Indian Traditions* (Leiden: Brill).

Tieleman, T. (1996), *Galen and Chrysippus on the Soul: Argument and Refutation in the De Placitis Books II–III* (Leiden: Brill).

Tieleman, T. (2003), *Chrysippus' On Affections: Reconstruction and Interpretation* (Leiden: Brill).

Tieleman, T. (2007), 'Panaetius' Place in the History of Stoicism with Special Reference to his Moral Psychology', in Ioppolo, A. M., and Sedley, D. N. (eds.), *Pyrrhonists, Patricians, Platonizers: Hellenistic Philosophy in the Period 155–86 BC* (Naples: Bibliopolis), 103–42.

Todd, R. B. (1976), *Alexander of Aphrodisias on Stoic Physics* (Leiden: Brill).

Todd, R. B. (1978), 'Monism and Immanence: The Foundations of Stoic Physics', in Rist, J. M. (ed.), *The Stoics* (Berkeley, CA: University of California Press), 137–60.

Trenckner, V. (1880), *The Milindapañho, Being Dialogues Between King Milinda and the Buddhist Sage Nāgasena* (London: Williams and Norgate).

Tsouna, V. (1998), *The Epistemology of the Cyrenaic School* (Cambridge: Cambridge University Press).

Tsouna, V. (2007), *The Ethics of Philodemus* (Oxford: Oxford University Press).

Usener, H. (1887), *Epicurea* (Leipzig: Teubner); facs. repr. in Ramelli, I. (2002), *Epicurea: Testi di Epicuro e Testimonianze Epicuree nella raccolta di Hermann Usener* (Milan: Bompiani).

Vander Waerdt, P. A. (ed.) (1994), *The Socratic Movement* (Ithaca, NY: Cornell University Press).

Veillard, C. (2015), *Les Stoïciens II: Le stoïcisme intermédiaire* (Paris: Les Belles Lettres).

Vogt, K. M. (2008), *Law, Reason, and the Cosmic City* (New York: Oxford University Press).

Wachsmuth, C., and Hense, O. (1884–1912), *Ioannis Stobaei Anthologium*, 5 vols (Berlin: Weidmann).

Walsh, P. G. (1997), *Cicero: The Nature of the Gods* (Oxford: Oxford University Press).

Walsh, P. G. (2000), *Cicero: On Obligations* (Oxford: Oxford University Press).

Warren, J. (2002), *Epicurus and Democritean Ethics: An Archaeology of Ataraxia* (Cambridge: Cambridge University Press).

Warren, J. (2004a), *Facing Death: Epicurus and his Critics* (Oxford: Clarendon Press).

Warren, J. (2004b), 'Ancient Atomists on the Plurality of Worlds', *Classical Quarterly* 54, 354–65.

Warren, J. (ed.) (2009), *The Cambridge Companion to Epicureanism* (Cambridge: Cambridge University Press).

Waterfield, R. (2000), *The First Philosophers: The Presocratics and Sophists* (Oxford: Oxford University Press).

Wehrli, F. (1968a), *Die Schule des Aristoteles, Texte und Kommentar, IV: Demetrios von Phaleron* (Basel & Stuttgart: Schwabe & Co.).

Wehrli, F. (1968b), *Die Schule des Aristoteles, Texte und Kommentar, VI: Lykon und Ariston von Keos* (Basel & Stuttgart: Schwabe & Co.).

Wehrli, F. (1969a), *Die Schule des Aristoteles, Texte und Kommentar, III: Klearchos* (Basel & Stuttgart: Schwabe & Co.).

Wehrli, F. (1969b), *Die Schule des Aristoteles, Texte und Kommentar, V: Straton von Lampsakos* (Basel & Stuttgart: Schwabe & Co.).

Wehrli, F. (1969c), *Die Schule des Aristoteles, Texte und Kommentar, IX: Phainias von Eresos, Chamaileon, Praxiphanes* (Basel & Stuttgart: Schwabe & Co.).

Wehrli, F. (1969d), *Die Schule des Aristoteles, Texte und Kommentar, X: Hieronymos von Rhodos, Kritolaos und Seine Schüler* (Basel & Stuttgart: Schwabe & Co.).

Wendlandt, L., and Baltzly, D. (2004), 'Knowing Freedom: Epicurean Philosophy Beyond Atomism and the Swerve', *Phronesis* 49, 41–71.

White, M. J. (2003), 'Stoic Natural Philosophy (Physics and Cosmology)', in Inwood, B. (ed.), *The Cambridge Companion to the Stoics* (Cambridge: Cambridge University Press), 124–52.

White, S. A. (1995), 'Cicero and the Therapists', in Powell, J. G. F. (ed.), *Cicero the Philosopher* (Oxford: Clarendon Press), 219–46.

White, S. A. (2002), 'Happiness in the Hellenistic Lyceum', *Apeiron* 35, 69–93.

White, S. A. (2004a), 'Hieronymous of Rhodes: The Sources, Text, and Translation', in Fortenbaugh, W. W., and White, S. A. (eds.), *Lyco of Troas and Hieronymus of Rhodes: Text, Translation, and Discussion* (New Brunswick, NJ: Transaction Publishers), 79–276.

White, S. A. (2004b), 'Lyco and Hieronymous on the Good Life', in Fortenbaugh, W. W., and White, S. A. (eds.), *Lyco of Troas and Hieronymus of Rhodes: Text, Translation, and Discussion* (New Brunswick, NJ: Transaction Publishers), 389–409.

Wick, P., and Rabens, V. (eds.) (2014), *Religions and Trade: Religious Formation, Transformation and Cross-Cultural Exchange between East and West* (Leiden: Brill).

Williams, B. (1994), 'Do Not Disturb', *London Review of Books* 16 no. 20, 25–6.

Williams, B. (1997), 'Stoic Philosophy and the Emotions: Reply to Richard Sorabji', in Sorabji, R. (ed.), *Aristotle and After*, BICS Supplement 68 (London: Institute of Classical Studies), 211–13.

Wilson, C. (2008), *Epicureanism at the Origins of Modernity* (Oxford: Clarendon Press).

Winterbottom, M. (1994), *M. Tulli Ciceronis De Officiis* (Oxford: Clarendon Press).

Woodruff, P. (1988), 'Aporetic Pyrrhonism', *Oxford Studies in Ancient Philosophy* 6, 139–68.

Woolf, R. (2004), 'What Kind of Hedonist was Epicurus?', *Phronesis* 49, 303–22.

Woolf, R. (2009), 'Pleasure and Desire', in Warren, J. (ed.), *The Cambridge Companion to Epicureanism* (Cambridge: Cambridge University Press), 158–78.

Woolf, R. (2015), *Cicero: The Philosophy of a Roman Sceptic* (Abingdon: Routledge).

Zeller, E. (1870), *The Stoics, Epicureans, and Sceptics*, trans. O. J. Reichel (London: Longmans, Green, and Co.).

Index of Passages

This index lists ancient texts mentioned in the notes, with cross-references to IG and LS. References to other collections of texts are not included here, but can be found in the notes.

Epicurus (*cont.*)
    41–2 (IG I-2, LS 10A) 72
    42 (IG I-2, LS 12B) 72
    45 (IG I-2, LS 13A) 72
    46–8 (IG I-2, LS 15A) 38
    54 (IG I-2, LS 12D) 72
    57 (IG I-2, LS 9A) 72
    63 (IG I-2, LS 14A) 87
    63–5 (IG I-2, LS 14A) 88
    66 (IG I-2, LS 14A) 88
    67 (IG I-2, LS 14A) 88
    78 (IG I-2) 185
    82 (IG I-2) 185
Ep. Men.
    122 (IG I-4, LS 25A) 184
    123 (IG I-4, LS 23B) 78, 184
    124–7 (IG I-4, LS 24A) 151
    125 (IG I-4, LS 24A) 152
    127 (IG I-4, LS 21B) 122
    128 (IG I-4, LS 21B) 117, 119
    131 (IG I-4, LS 21B) 123
    131–2 (IG I-4, LS 21B) 118
    133 (IG I-4) 151
    133–4 (IG I-4, LS 20A) 134
Rat. Sent.
    4 (IG I-5, LS 21C) 151
    8 (IG I-5, LS 21D) 119, 120
    11 (IG I-5, LS 25B) 185
    14 (IG I-5) 165
    17 (IG I-5, LS 22B) 167
    18 (IG I-5, LS 21E) 120
    19 (IG I-5, LS 24C) 155
    31 (IG I-5, LS 22A) 166
    32 (IG I-5, LS 22A) 165
    33 (IG I-5, LS 22A) 165
    34 (IG I-5, LS 22A) 167
    35 (IG I-5, LS 22A) 167
    37 (IG I-5, LS 22B) 166
    38 (IG I-5) 166
Sent. Vat.
    7 (IG I-6) 167
    23 (IG I-6, LS 22F) 168
    33 (IG I-6, LS 21G) 122
    34 (IG I-6, LS 22F) 168
    39 (IG I-6, LS 22F) 169
    40 (IG I-6, LS 20D) 134
    70 (IG I-6, LS 22D) 167
Eusebius
Praep. evang.
    14.6.4–6 (LS 68F) 55, 197
    14.8.1–15 49
    14.18.2–3 (IG III-24, LS 1F) 26, 55

    14.18.4 (LS 1F) 54
    15.20.6 (LS 53W) 99
Galen
Hist. Phil.
    3 199
PHP
    1.6.12 94
    1.6.13–1.8.1 95
    1.7.1 97
    2.8.38 96
    3.1.9–25 95
    3.1.10 98
    3.1.25 (LS 65H) 97
    5.2.22 188, 191
    5.2.23 188
    5.7.52 191
    7.3.10 96
Ven. sect. Er.
    2 96
Hippolytus
Haer.
    1.21 (LS 62A) 148
    9.10.5 53
Lactantius
Div. inst.
    2.9.14 81
    5.14.3–5 (LS 68M) 19, 22, 175
    5.16–2–3 175
Lucian
Vit. auct.
    21–5 (part LS 37L) 40, 193
Lucretius
    1.62–148 75
    1.146–634 62
    1.146–58 185
    1.146–8 32, 186
    1.149–58 186
    1.150 61
    1.418–34 (LS 5B) 63
    1.599–634 (LS 9C) 72
    2.7–14 (LS 21W) 170, 190
    2.53–4 (LS 21W) 186
    2.59–61 (LS 21W) 32, 186
    2.80–111 (LS 11B) 73
    2.112–24 (LS 11B) 73
    2.167–83 76
    2.216–24 (IG I-28, LS 11H) 135
    2.225–50 (IG I-28, LS 11H) 135
    2.251–6 (IG I-28, LS 20F) 135
    2.257–62 (IG I-28, LS 20F) 136
    2.285 (IG I-28, LS 20F) 136

Index

The most important discussions are marked in bold.